APPOINTED *for* HIS GLORY

In *Appointed for His Glory*, Kay Gardner illuminates the ultimate pro-life message: that Christ's death on the Cross was a rescue mission to save as many lives as would receive Him. The Gospel is the most powerful tool we have to empower and strengthen those facing unplanned pregnancies, and as Kay shares story after story from her nineteen years serving in crisis pregnancy ministry, a common theme appears: it is the Gospel that makes the difference. This book is a powerful resource for anyone seeking to protect babies in the womb, rescue parents from the horrors of abortion, and ultimately, point people to the peace and freedom available through Jesus Christ.

—**GARY HAMRICK**, Sr. Pastor of Cornerstone Chapel Church

Appointed for His Glory is a timely and grace-filled call for pregnancy resource centers to boldly and compassionately share the hope of the Gospel. With theological depth and practical wisdom, Kay Gardner equips advocates to recognize sacred moments where eternal lives are changed. This book reflects a deep commitment not only to protecting life, but to seeing the women and men we serve living life in Christ, impacting families and changing generations. An essential resource for anyone serving on the front lines of life and faith.

—**NIKI MATTSON**, CEO, Mosaic Virginia

Appointed for His Glory is an amazing book that could only be written by someone who has experienced the highs and lows of working for decades in a pregnancy resource center. Kay Gardner not only addresses the great impact that can be made while serving women in need, but the life change that can happen when someone makes a decision to accept Christ as Savior and Lord. The emphasis and importance of evangelism comes through in the pages, but more significantly, it shows that true change comes only from a saving knowledge of Jesus Christ. This is a must-read for anyone in the pro-life movement.

—**JIM DEMPSEY**, Chief Development Officer, Cru, Former Board Chair, Sanctity of Life Ministries, VA

I was raised in a Muslim family but had never heard the Gospel of Jesus Christ. When my husband abandoned our three daughters and me, I visited a pregnancy center to confirm I wasn't pregnant. I wasn't looking for God; I was simply looking for help. God had me meet a lady who welcomed me with love, listened to my pain, and shared the Gospel with me for the very first time. Through her gentle guidance, I prayed to surrender my life to the Lord. That moment began my journey with Christ, which changed my life forever.

—**FATIMA**, former client

Kay's heart for the Gospel and years of experience counseling clients and training PRC advocates have equipped her to create outstanding evangelical training materials. Whether you are in PRC leadership, a new team member, or someone looking for an inspiring and practical evangelism and discipleship tool, I encourage you to pore over this handbook and prayerfully apply its Christ-centered principles within your ministry.

—**KELLEY WESLEY**, Advisor to PRCs and Ministries, former CEO of Sanctity of Life Ministries, VA

Appointed for His Glory has had a profound impact on me personally. It has equipped me to talk about faith in a natural and meaningful way and has been a valuable training tool for advocates caring for clients in traumatic situations. Kay shows practical and real examples of how to share one's faith in a winsome and sincere way. From the beginning, I've known THIS is so very needed in the pregnancy center world.

—**LANIE JAMES**, Client Services Director, Mosaic Virginia

Kay Gardner has provided a much-needed, practical guide for PRC advocates who are dealing with the root problem of unwanted pregnancies—lives that are not surrendered to the Lord Jesus Christ.

—**DR. RONALD M. REESE**, PhD, former Board Chair, longtime advisor of Sanctity of Life Ministries, VA, now Mosaic Virginia, Lansdowne

Serving as a pastor for over thirty-five years, I've had the privilege to come alongside many people who have been impacted by crisis pregnancies. I've seen how the broad range of services offered by PRC groups has not only saved the lives of unborn children, but also provided for necessary and meaningful care of women and newborn children. But when it comes to sharing Christ with those who visit PRC locations, Kay Gardner offers a most helpful resource in *Appointed for His Glory.* Her passion for evangelism and her wealth of experience in seeing people receive Christ place her in a unique and valuable place to offer help. I found Kay's spiritual insights to be deep and profound, and her practical applications useful and transferable in any PRC at any location. I wholeheartedly endorse what she has written and pray her efforts will round out all that PRC groups can offer.

—**REV. STEVE DAWSON**, Executive Director, Keystone Christian Ministries

As a Knights of Columbus member, my work has facilitated and overseen the planning and strategy of five New York pregnancy centers—four out of five nonsectarian. With twenty-five local councils, we provided ultrasound equipment that saved many lives. I am impressed that *Appointed for His Glory* places emphasis on *both* the client, to prevent abortion, and the spiritual needs of the mother. The content of this book offers much to the reader, with the need for faith being stronger than ever.

—**DEAN HAMINGSON**, Advisor to five New York pregnancy centers

I came to the pregnancy center because I was driving my friend for a pregnancy test. I had no idea God had a plan that would free me from the shame of a past abortion. I met one of their advocates, and I began to meet regularly with a kind lady who shared Jesus's forgiveness with me. This led to giving my life to Jesus. Today, like every day, I feel free because of Jesus!

—**MERAWIT**, a former client

Appointed for His Glory reinforces what is most essential in pregnancy center ministry: pointing people to the saving love of Christ. With biblical depth, practical wisdom, and a strong evangelistic heartbeat, Kay trains advocates to share the Gospel intentionally and confidently. I recommend it to any center longing to see both physical and spiritual life flourish.

—**VINCE HINDERS**, Pastor Redeeming Grace Church, Board Director, Mosaic Virginia

If there were ever a time for a training handbook to be published on sharing the Gospel, it is now! Kay Gardner uses her vast experience guiding client advocates to turn hearts back to the Father. I pray this handbook will be utilized to bring God glory and to save more souls and preborn lives. Considering the dramatic changes in our culture, *Appointed for His Glory* is an essential training tool for years to come.

—**KAREN SNUFFER**, Executive Director of Care Net Pregnancy Resource Centers, NOVA

As this training handbook reinforces, when the heart changes, choices change! Sharing Christ's love and principles is the foundation on which counseling is based. Kay has extensive experience, scriptural knowledge, compassion, and insight, bringing Christ to women and families facing unexpected, life-changing events. Her expertise and writing acumen shape *Appointed for His Glory* into a vital handbook for anyone working with women and families.

—**DON MOORE**, former Board Director and volunteer of Sanctity of Life Ministries, VA, now Mosaic Virginia, Lansdowne

APPOINTED *for* HIS GLORY

Sharing the Good News of Christ at the Pregnancy Resource Center

KAY R. GARDNER

Appointed for His Glory: Sharing the Good News of Christ at the Pregnancy Resource Center

Published by KK Christian Press
ISBN: 979-8-9907060-2-6

Pregnancy crisis intervention is conducted by those staff and volunteers who have undergone specific training, yet are not (necessarily) licensed professional advocates. Rigorous, formal preparation and one-on-one mentoring followed by a practicum of observation assures readiness to serve in this specialized area—as "peer advocates" (or simply "advocates") or "client advocates." This practice is commonly accepted, following formal training comparable to other venues involving peer counseling, regarding alcohol/drug addiction, mental health, family support, etc.

Unless otherwise noted, the names of people used in illustrations have been changed to protect anonymity.

First Printing 2026

Dedicated to:

The Lord Jesus Christ, whose gift of salvation is available to all.
Kelley Wesley, dear friend and former CEO of Sanctity of Life
Ministries, whose passion for spreading the Gospel is contagious.
To our beloved clients whose transformative stories bring glory to God.
To those yet to know Him through the testimonies of His children.

We will rejoice in your salvation,
And in the name of our God, we will set up our banners!
May the LORD fulfill all your petitions.
(Psalm 20:5 NKJV)

"Neither the life of a preborn
nor the life of faith is disposable."

Kay R. Gardner

Contents

CHAPTER TWO

INTENTIONAL GOSPEL SHARING - 29

CHAPTER THREE

LIFTING THE VEIL OF UNBELIEF - 57

CHAPTER FOUR
THE TESTIMONY - 83

CHAPTER FIVE

PREPARING YOUR THREE-MINUTE TESTIMONY - 113

CHAPTER SIX

GOSPEL CONVERSATIONS - 123

CHAPTER SEVEN

COMPASSION IN ACTION: HOW-TOS OF GOSPEL SHARING - 141

CHAPTER EIGHT

PRACTICUM: CLIENT AND ADVOCATE CONVERSATIONS - 173

CHAPTER NINE

OVERVIEW: HOW IT ALL WORKS - 205

CHAPTER TEN

PRAYER: SEEKING TRUTH, RECEIVING GUIDANCE - 213

Foreword

For over a twenty-five-year period, it has been a privilege to collaborate with my colleague Kay, training advocates at pregnancy resource centers (PRCs) in the US and internationally. When Kay told me she was writing a handbook on effective evangelism for clients, I was thrilled and could not wait to read and share it with others! This excellently written, in-depth, and experiential guide, *Appointed for His Glory: Sharing Christ at the Pregnancy Resource Center*, is a much-needed tool for the PRC movement.

While PRCs in the US have grown in programs, outreach, and budget, new challenges have also arisen. Effective marketing and program strategies designed to reach abortion-vulnerable clients can often result in the message of Jesus Christ being "crowded out." Message of life priorities during a one-hour appointment can leave little time for Gospel sharing.

Yet, as followers of Jesus Christ, Scripture exhorts us that we are all called to evangelism. Jesus commands His disciples, "Go therefore and make disciples of all nations" (Matthew 28:19 ESV). The apostle Paul writes, "For I am not ashamed of the gospel, for it is the power of God for salvation to everyone who believes, to the Jew first and also to the Greek" (Romans 1:16 ESV).

Kay's handbook helps advocates prayerfully and skillfully approach unplanned pregnancy as a symptom of their client's need for God. She provides real examples of how to help a client view even their most difficult problems as opportunities for hope and change. Kay's book includes examples of effective intake transitions that flow naturally into spiritual conversations.

This handbook reinforces the belief that "when the heart changes, choices change." Additional testimonies shared contain stories of clients who learn about the love of Jesus, how He can make a way where there seems to be no way, and about clients who submit their lives to Jesus and choose life for their babies. It also includes testimonies of clients who come back to the PRC for mentoring sessions that help them grow in their faith, benefit from healthy resources, pursue church relationships, and become thriving mothers.

How does the PRC advocate combine the message of life with the message of Jesus Christ proficiently? Kay's gift of evangelism and years of experience counseling clients and training PRC advocates have equipped her to create outstanding evangelical training materials.

Whether you are in PRC leadership, a new team member, or someone looking for an inspiring and practical evangelism and discipleship tool, I encourage you to pore over this handbook and prayerfully apply its Christ-centered principles within your ministry.

Kelley Wesley
Advisor to PRCs and Ministries

Preface

A bolder vision is emerging at the pregnancy resource center. It is attended by an ancient question that invites participation. "Whom shall I send, And who will go for Us?" As His children, we have the honor of responding, "Here am I! Send me" (Isaiah 6:8 NKJV).

God's expanded vision for our centers is dressed in a unique spiritual opportunity—one that reaches into eternity but unfolds in a center's everyday life. Not a drift of mission but a *delicate shift* fosters the transformation of a client's life through Jesus Christ.

Bold is a word that presses deeply into the call of the Great Commission. Believing boldly entails compassion in action—that of *delivering* His message. In its original form, bold (Greek: *tharreo*) is connected to a Greek word (*thero*), which means "to be warm," that is, "warmth of temperament associated with confidence."[1]

Warmly conversational is the simple virtue of faith-sharing. It is prompted by a heart of *caring* about another's salvation. Because spiritual outreach is impoverished by fear, we invite Jesus to heat up our passion to share the life-changing message that impacted our own lives. Steps of grace will surely follow. "But you shall receive power when the Holy Spirit has come upon you" (Acts 1:8 NKJV).

When pregnancy centers embrace *intentional* evangelism, they discover their clients responding to the Gospel message! The pregnancy issues remain, yet we see the advent of *living* hope emerge—the sort that curls into the soul and settles into peace.

Appointed for His Glory honors God's call to the soul-winning opportunity that greets every advocate who serves with a pregnancy resource center. As a visible expression of Jesus, the advocate ministers to her client's greatest need—knowing Jesus personally. She welcomes the action of His Spirit with confidence, for she is tenderly known by name and *appointed* for His glory.

Note to the Reader

Appointed for His Glory has been written in the context of the pregnancy resource center, yet a wide application is possible within other venues of Christian ministry. Its preparation for Gospel sharing is intentional and practical and dependent on God's guidance through the Spirit. Its contents are useful in serving churches, Christian counseling/mentoring programs, and a variety of other outreaches seeking the heart of God that "none should perish" (2 Peter 3:9 NKJV).

NOTE: Pregnancy centers use various terms for those who meet with their clients. Although options exist, such as "advocate," "client advocate," or "peer advocate," the *Appointed for His Glory* handbook uses the title of "advocate." At the center, this person has been carefully selected as a godly person who undergoes training to share sound, biblical wisdom while promoting hope and support for the client.

In the Beginning

The year was 1875. An early, pro-life advocate quoted the words of a post-abortive woman: "Said one of these victims . . . 'I was almost insane with unavailing sorrow.'"[1]

"Insane with unavailing sorrow." These words slip through the centuries to speak the despair of a post-abortive woman. We have met her, loved her, and, sometimes, led her to healing. Yet, day after day, crisis arrives at centers around the world. In the shadows of the womb, a heartbeat sounds while a young mother's options weave darkly through the pain of a crisis. Where is hope to be found?

Softly, in the form of a gift, comes our offering. It is Jesus we will bring to her. It is He who mingles in the crucible of her suffering to speak in a voice that sounds like yours or mine.

Who Are You, O Believer?

I am the light of His countenance (Psalm 4:6), His lamplighter, who shines His light through the darkness.

Our Center: Like a "City on a Hilltop"

> "Your lives light up the world. For how can you hide a city that stands on a hilltop? And who would light a lamp and then hide it in an obscure place? Instead, it's placed where everyone in the house can benefit from its light. So don't hide your light!" (Matthew 5:14–16 TPT)

The pregnancy resource center, like His "city that stands on a hilltop," is God's beacon of hope. The more we share Jesus's new life, the more He is received.

Joy visits often when God's pleasure spills freely within our walls. Indeed, those who share His Good News rejoice when we "call [our] walls Salvation and [our] gates Praise" (Isaiah 60:18 NIV).

"Awake, you who sleep, Arise from the dead, And Christ will give you light."

Ephesians 5:14 NKJV

Jesus, Our Client's Greatest Need

Meeting daily with clients in crisis clearly reveals that a client's greatest need is knowing Christ. An unplanned pregnancy is the perfect storm to plumb spiritual depth and expose the need for something more.

Jesus Serves with Us

"Just as the Son of Man did not come to be served, but to serve." (Matthew 20:28)

Advocates enjoy a sense of adventure when approaching clients with faith-based expectations.

As we bring His light to the city on a hill, God brings His bouquets of blessings to disperse the darkness. We recognize the tender preparation that has gone before us when a client's voice grows animated. "How strange we're discussing this! My mother (or boyfriend or sister or friend) was just talking to me about God the other day, and now I'm in a conversation about Him!"

It's not "something strange" at all. Every detail blends with His will in this journey to the Gospel. Each day we discover anew that the amazing God we serve is forever serving us.

Divine Expectations

Expectation in the New Testament sense comes from a Greek word (*apokaradokia*) that means "the eager, intense look, which turns away from everything else to fix on the one object of desire; to watch with head outstretched."[2]

Advocates enjoy a sense of adventure when approaching clients with faith-based expectations. To perceive each client as God's divine appointment enlivens daring expectation: "I wonder what God is up to here!" Those responding to God's call to share their faith find excitement and deep contentment as they interface with the heart of God. We're consumed by desiring His best for others and giving voice to the Good News of Jesus Christ that no one "should perish" (2 Peter 3:9 ESV).

Birthing Christ at Your Center

Approaching God's mission with expectancy, we become His spiritual *midwives* at the ministry—*birthers* of God through the Holy Spirit. He is our capable source of power, the *birthing agent.* Scripture assures us of a growing passion that comes from deeply believing. "Rivers of living water will burst out from within you, flowing from your *innermost being*" (John 7:38 TPT, emphasis added).

Did you know that *innermost being* (*koilia*) means "womb" in Greek?[3] As we "carry" His Spirit within the womb of our innermost being, witnessing becomes the laboring, with the ultimate hope of *delivering* Him into the life of the seeker.

The Gospel Opportunity

What is at stake here? Opportunity! As centers advance their spiritual outreach, there's gleeful participation in knowing that the message of salvation at the ministry is wrapped in God's heart. As His appointed ones, we are summoned to a divinely tailored plan to share the Good News of salvation. How blessed to be involved in the destinies God has ordained!

A Bolder Vision

A bolder vision at our pregnancy resource centers exceeds the privilege of counting baby births at the end of the year. As we explore a client's spiritual interest, we know *happy beginnings* of a relationship with Christ can lead to *happy endings* by a client birthing her baby.

At every pregnancy resource center comes an opportunity to *deliver* the spoken Gospel. God's unrelenting grace is poised to bring new life to an expectant mother and sustained life to her preborn baby. Stories of transformation are waiting to meet us. Let us serve Jesus!

Chapter One

Seizing the *Kairos* Moment

Father, we receive your words of truth: "'In an acceptable time [kairos] I have heard you, And in the day of salvation, I have helped you.' Behold, now is the accepted time [kairos]; behold, now is the day of salvation."

(Prayer based on 2 Corinthians 6:2 NKJV)

As God's divine timing led to our own day of salvation, He prompts us again to the *kairos* moment. This time, on behalf of our client. With Jesus, we navigate the turbulence of crisis and nourish hope on its journey to redemption.

What Is a *Kairos* Moment?

The Greek word *kairos* can be described as "a time when conditions are right for the accomplishment of a crucial action: the opportune and decisive moment."[1] Tailored to connect timing with need, kairos brings precision to bear through moments drenched with grace. When Jesus spoke of new life, He spoke freely of its availability. "It is time [kairos] for God's Kingdom to be experienced in its fullness! Turn your lives back to God and put your trust in the hope-filled Gospel" (Mark 1:15 TPT).

Our fervent desire for the client who's open to hear is to receive the living hope of Jesus Christ. The kairos intervention seizes the opportune time imbued with His favor. "Remember me, O LORD, with the favor You have toward Your people" (Psalm 106:4 NKJV). Related to the Greek word *kara* (meaning "head"), kairos suggests "coming to a head" is fostered by exactness, readiness, and action.[2]

The advocate's personal testimony is the icebreaker for the Gospel.

Overview: Kairos and the Intake

Kairos arrives suddenly within the cadence of an intake. "My boyfriend left," the client sobs. "I'm by myself in this." Her pain is a kairos opportunity for God's divine appointment. By the horror of an unplanned pregnancy, God works. Soon she will hear of the Savior who loves her. As advocates, we "above all, constantly seek *God's kingdom* and his righteousness" (Matthew 6:33 TPT, emphasis added).

In the counseling room, *God's kingdom* is poised to grow when the advocate shares her story of meeting the Savior. The advocate's personal testimony is the icebreaker for the Gospel. The client's interest is stirring. The chase of His Spirit grows bold.

Kairos: The Pivotal Moment

With the advocate alert to the kairos opportunity, she waits for the pivotal moment that curves the conversation to spiritual discussion. Sometimes kairos asserts itself when the positive pregnancy test is disclosed and the client is recoiling. We barely hear her frantic whispers, "I don't know if I can do this." Her fear invites exploration.

"Tell me more," the advocate prods.

The client responds, wide-eyed, "I mean—everything in my life would change!"

"Are you saying that life's changes always have a negative impact?"

"Well, this change would! I don't know what to do!"

"In the past, what have you relied upon as a personal compass for direction when life gets crazy chaotic?"

"Myself."

"Has self-reliance worked well for you?" (This could be followed by the advocate sharing a trial from life, a topical testimony, and how God guided.) For the client, life has reached radical instability. She needs an anchor for her soul.

> We have this hope as an anchor for the soul,
> firm and secure. (Hebrews 6:19 NIV)

At this juncture, the divine opportunity of kairos "does not emphasize a point of time but rather a time-space filled with all kinds of possibilities."[3] The "time-space" invites a story by the advocate of God's intervention on her behalf.

A Client's Kairos Moment

During the intake, Claire, a thirty-year-old client, expressed that soon after immigrating to the United States, she discovered she was pregnant. Because she was estranged from the father of the baby, she reasoned that an abortion was the best solution. Now, months later, a pregnancy fathered by another man was confirmed. Visibly shaken, she was horrified. Sobbing, she shared, "God's punishing me for the abortion. Please tell me this isn't my life." When Claire spoke of her emptiness, she was describing a fragile and insecure life. She also said she was a Christian but had wandered from the faith. Unknown to her at the time, she was describing her need for the Savior pursuing her. The kairos moment had arrived.

Alert to the timing of God's intervention, the advocate shared a personal story (testimony) with Claire. She described how God met her needs during a time of personal upheaval. "Claire, the God who faithfully met my needs will be faithful to meet your needs if you will let Him."

A Gospel discussion refreshes the client's perspective about a loving God who is still pursuing her despite her wanderings—a God of forgiveness.

The advocate smiled and reassured Claire. "It's no coincidence you came to the center! God brought you. He personally knows you, and He's aware of your pregnancy and desires to walk this with you."

The advocate continued with sharing her testimony—the part about God's faithfulness through a crisis in her own life. When the Gospel was ultimately presented, Claire responded to the message that God loved her, died for her sins, and was seeking a relationship with her. The rededication of her life to Christ strengthens her for the challenging days ahead. A terrifying situation was being transformed into the glorious victory of choosing life.

The rededication of her life to Christ strengthens her for the challenging days ahead.

An Advocate's Kairos Moment

For several years, the pregnancy center held post-abortion Bible studies and one-on-one weekly meetings with female inmates at the nearby county jail. Lauren was a married inmate who had recently decided to follow Christ. The prison chaplain scheduled a mentor to help Lauren grow in her new faith. A catchy enthusiasm exudes the unmistakable joy of knowing Christ. Her advocate recalled, "Shortly after I met with Lauren, she exclaimed how God had saved her from her addiction to prescription drugs. She said, 'I was carrying so much guilt until Jesus came into my life!'"

As Lauren spoke about her conversion, she mentioned John 3:16. "Have you ever read it?"

The advocate replied, "Yes."

Lauren's second question followed. "What is *your* favorite word in John 3:16?"

Ironically, Lauren's question led to a kairos moment in the advocate's life. "That's a good question! I have never thought about a favorite word in John 3:16." The advocate quietly recited the familiar passage.

"For God so loved the world that He gave His only begotten Son that whoever believes in Him should not perish but have everlasting life" (NKJV). Then she said, "I think my favorite word is *loved*. Yes, *loved* is my favorite word!"

Lauren's eyes were shining now. "Do you know what *my* favorite word is?" Not waiting for a reply, she added. "It's a tiny word. A two-letter word." She proceeded to spell the letters. "S – o. So!" With a look of heaven on her face, she continued. "God so loved the world. He *so* loved, *so* loved, *so* loved." Clearly, the love of a Savior had already won her heart.

As for the advocate, she *tasted* John 3:16 for the first time. Her mindless familiarity with the verse had obscured the sensitive passion of a two-letter word. But this day was different. Despite years of believing Jesus was a God of love who loved the whole world, this day, God's kingdom opened wider.

During the long drive home, God's Spirit stirred warmly within, weaving through thoughts, deepening her love. His words settled into her soul and spirit. *God not only loves me, but He so loves, so loves, so loves me!*

The most basic commonality shared by each client is the need for a personal Savior in her life.

Kairos and Client Commonalities

It's amusing to think that two eyes, a nose, and a mouth are featured on every face, yet each person looks uniquely different. By the same token, every client presents commonalities to address, such as pregnant, not pregnant, support system, no support system, plus the basic consideration of three available options: adoption, parenting, or abortion. In addition, there are complexities challenging our advocates every day, such as a client's background textured with the complexities of ethnic, religious, and worldview diversity. Add personal and colorful life experiences to the mix, and we see the most basic commonality shared by each client is the need for a personal Savior in her life. In keeping with the common need, advocates stay alert to the session's kairos moments.

Despite pregnancy options or support system status, the following real-life clients capture the diverse sampling of clientele who visit a pregnancy resource center.

Who Is Our Client?

She is twenty-two years old; she is seventeen; she is thirty; she is turning forty-one.

She is a server at a restaurant; she is a pharmacist; she is a college freshman about to move on campus; she is a high school dropout; she is entering graduate school; she is jobless; she was just promoted; she is single; she is married; she is living with her boyfriend. She is in love; she is deserted by her boyfriend; she questions the baby's paternity; she is her siblings' role model; she's the black sheep of the family; she is churched; she seems disinterested in spiritual things. She is estranged from parents; she is living at home; she is needy of parental approval; she is a winsome, free spirit; she is the same age as her mother when she aborted.

She is a cultural Muslim; she is a practicing Buddhist; she is Christian; she is Hindu, she is agnostic; she says she is "nothing." She is Asian, Caucasian, African American, Middle Eastern, etc.

She has biases, beliefs, strengths, weaknesses, and, in her humanity, shares an emptiness designed to find contentment in a living Savior. *She* is our client.

The Client: Created to Know Him

As a unique person, believer or non-believer, our client was created in the image of God. She has a supernatural bearing but one of incompletion, that is, until her heart opens to the Savior who loves her. Whoever she is, the message remains. She was created as a "worshiper." Yet, in the absence of a relationship with Jesus, she will worship idols of her own making—a career, a relationship, materialism, or whatever else to fill the emptiness by squeezing these impostors into her spiritual void.

As our client arrives at the pregnancy center, unknown to her, she has walked into a divinely appointed window of time. The advocate approaches her with expectancy and the knowledge that God has entrusted this new client to her. His promise resonates: "I will heal their waywardness and love them freely." (Hosea 14:4 NIV).

"I will heal their waywardness and love them freely."

Hosea 14:4 NIV

Birthright in God's Family: Why It Matters

A definable, sacred encounter is in play as we stay attuned for the kairos moment. It releases God's plan and brings her to a spiritual crossroad. If our client is responsive to salvation, entrance into His spiritual family will begin a brand-new history as His child.

Whose family one belongs to is one of the most defining characteristics in the life of every individual. Whenever we meet someone new, introductions are made: "Hello, I'm glad to meet you. My name is Sally Smith." This basic information, so typically given—the surname—indicates the family she belongs to. In this case, the Smith family.

There's an application within a spiritual context as well. A commitment to Christ brings a new, spiritual heritage based on a divine birthright. When she has entered God's family as a new creation in Him, her life's purpose begins to masterfully unfold.

Liberated from reliance on the failing resource of her flesh—the *self-life*—she has now been equipped to live the sacred potential God has in store. After personally accepting Jesus into her life, the traits that once defined *who* she is are secondary to *whose* she is. This is a new experience. Before trusting Christ as Savior, she had no genuine, spiritual identity.

Entrance into Father God's family simultaneously equips her with new "spiritual DNA." God's nature is joined to her human spirit (1 Corinthians 6:17), thus, she becomes a "partaker of the divine nature" (2 Peter 1:4 NKJV). After she received the gift of Jesus's sacrifice on the Cross as paying the penalty for her sins, her old fleshly identity has been crucified with Him. She can now live as one who is dead to the old ways of the flesh (Romans 8:13). Housed in her human spirit is the life of Christ's resurrected Spirit. She can now choose to function *from* God's indwelling Spirit, who has given her a *new creation* identity.

> I have been crucified with Christ, it is no longer I who live, but Christ lives in me; and the life which I now live in the flesh I live by faith in the Son of God, who loved me and gave Himself for me. (Galatians 2:20 NKJV)

Receiving His Spirit has settled a person's most significant reality—who I am and whose I am.

Receiving His Spirit has settled a person's most significant reality—who I am and whose I am. One's primary identity is identified spiritually. In the most authentic sense, believers are first and foremost spirit beings who are housed in a body and have a soul (personality, mind, will, emotions). Based on Scripture, God's indwelling spirit has joined the human spirit to grant an identity of righteousness.

The new righteousness becomes increasingly manifested as we lean into Him. Like developing physical muscles, we bulk up the "faith muscle" when we exercise it.

Kairos and the Topic Testimony

Sometimes when a client is asked, "Do you have a faith background?" she replies, "Yes, I'm a Christian." When the topic is further pursued, she might express how distant she feels from God. Often this is stoked by self-sufficient living with little attention paid to God. Her unplanned pregnancy accentuates her need for God.

From a mentoring aspect, it doesn't matter whether a kairos moment leads to a dedication to Christ or a rededication to Him. (In actuality, we sometimes suspect that the rededications are first-time commitments.) Either way, a single client pursuing confirmation of pregnancy displays her need of God in her life.

How much the client is interested in spiritual things is not difficult to learn. When the advocate relates a spiritual turning point in her own life, doors of spiritual opportunity swing open. When the advocate shares a "topic testimony," she discusses a specific need in her life and how God came through. (By a "salvation testimony," the advocate discusses the void in her life and the longing to feel peace and have control over fear. She explains to her client, "I found my needs were met by drawing closer to God and experiencing Him in my life.)

The mentor asks her client, "In your life, how do you handle things when life becomes stressful?" (Managing stress with God's help would be a topic testimony.) When the client answers, we share how our compassionate God longs to have her invite Him into her challenging situation.

We may also ask the simple question, "Do you ever pray when things get really tough in your life?" Since many unbelievers pray when facing a predicament, the question is not offensive. On the contrary, it initiates spiritual discussion.

Only God can exchange falling in love with the world for falling in love with a Savior.

Learning to Hear the Kairos Moment

As one session progressed, a client named Alison spoke of attending a private school—her last year of high school before hightailing it to college. When the results of the pregnancy test returned positive, her panic was visible. Pregnancy and college plans are a dissonant mix.

As the advocate looked into the eyes of the young woman, she saw the familiar fear so prevalent in crisis. The teen's risky lifestyle kept her in turmoil, and now her worst fear was upon her. Would she be ready to exchange values that hadn't worked with something, or Someone, that could work? The pull of the world is strong. Only God can exchange falling in love with the world for falling in love with a Savior.

When Allison learned the center was Christian based, her initial reserve changed. She blurted, "I'm really a good girl. It's not what it seems! Lately, I feel God has been drawing me closer." Though sexually involved with her boyfriend, she said she had already initiated several talks with him about ending their physical relationship. "I feel so guilty," Alison confessed. "For some time, I've wanted to live the way God wants me to."

"I understand." The advocate nodded, quietly pleased to hear her awareness of God.

Alison said she had been praying about it. She said her pastor had asked from the pulpit, "What are you putting on the throne of your life? A boyfriend, a career, anything else other than the Savior?"

"His words made me feel so bad about what I was doing!" Alison said mournfully. "Yet, even then, I didn't take a stand!"

(Note the kairos moment approaching.)

"It sounds like you're still feeling sad about not taking a stand," the advocate said.

The teen's eyes suddenly glistened with tears.

The advocate spoke of how dearly God loved Alison, and there was nothing she could do or not do to change His great love for her, even if she wandered away from Him.

The advocate began to share her testimony of finding God at her own point of need. A discussion followed, and she asked Alison, "Do you think you would be ready to take a stand right now?"

(The kairos moment had arrived.)

Alison's eyes again filled with tears. "Yes. Yes, I am!"

The advocate reviewed the Gospel message with Alison to make certain she understood. Before Alison left, Jesus had taken His rightful place on the throne of her life. With the "stand" for Him now taken, a new confidence replaced her prior shame. Life had entered the safety of God's provision.

Though Alison's pregnancy was confirmed as positive, her new dedication to Christ was undeterred. Before leaving the center, she said, "I am going to be abstinent before I marry—like a real follower of Christ!"

When a client is happy about her pregnancy, the kairos moment enters the client session with an ease of its own—in the context of motherhood.

Creating a Kairos Moment

Linda, barely out of her teens, was happily pregnant. She had the support of a boyfriend with whom a future had already been planned. When a client is happy about her pregnancy, the kairos moment enters the client session with an ease of its own—in the context of motherhood.

Conversations go something like this:

> The advocate prepares a kairos moment by a question to the client. "What do you think is one of the greatest gifts a mother could possibly give to her child?"
>
> The client leans forward. "I don't know! What is it?"
>
> "Encouraging her child in the faith. Wouldn't you agree the world we're living in is quite troubled?"
>
> (The client readily agrees.)
>
> "That's why helping a child develop faith is such a gift."
>
> "Yes, I get that," she agrees. "My boyfriend is in the field of military intelligence, and he says there's always an ongoing threat to national security."

Because security is a basic human need, discussion with a client about her fears can easily shuttle into the kairos moment. The short dialogue with Linda created this opportunity. It led to the chance to expand and transition to the foundational security a Savior offers.

As the spiritual discussion got underway, Linda suddenly smiled. "This is so strange! My mother, just recently, was talking to me about the spiritual aspect of life."

The advocate had heard this before. Not infrequently, when we talk about God, we discover the client has recently experienced a rekindling of spiritual interest. God hears the prayers of staff and volunteers and responds by preparing clients for spiritual discussions during the session. In Linda's case, the prayers materialized into her prayer to receive Christ.

Banish the Negative Self-Talk

We can hinder the power of the Gospel by negative thinking, sometimes called negative self-talk. Scripture tells us:

> When your self-life craves the things that offend the Holy Spirit you hinder Him from living free within you! And the Holy Spirit's intense cravings hinder your self-life from dominating you! So then, the two incompatible and conflicting forces within you are your self-life of the flesh and the new creation life of the Spirit. (Galatians 5:17 TPT)

Some have said that the Gospel needs to be heard an average of seven times before a decision for Christ is made. When first meeting a client, we have no idea how many times she has been "watered with the Word." But Jesus knows. He knows those who are *not* ready to respond to Him yet need to hear His message of the Gospel, and He knows those who *are* ready to respond to Him. The advocate, like a divinely appointed "magi," brings a precious God-honoring gift to the Lord—sharing the eternal beauty of the Gospel message.

The following are Gospel-hindering thoughts that advocates can experience. The hindrances are countered by faith that prevails. At times, a client's flat demeanor camouflages her interest in the Gospel. In truth, her overwhelming fear of pregnancy magnifies vulnerability, and numbing down is her defense.

Because our flesh tends to judge by appearance, the client's appearance may hinder us from offering what she needs most—a personal Savior. Additional time and interaction with the client enable discerning where her heart is. God "does not see as man sees; for man looks at the outward appearance, but the LORD looks at the heart" (1 Samuel 16:7 NKJV).

When overcoming negative thoughts that hinder Gospel sharing, replace the negative thought with preaching to the choir—you. As you guide the client to the counseling room, focus on God's presence as you fill your mind with the truth of His Word: "I can do all things through Christ who strengthens me" (Philippians 4:13 NKJV).

Perseverance: Seven Client Examples

The seven client examples below typify how negative thoughts impede our sharing the Gospel with our clients. To persevere by faith brings

God pleasure. "But without faith it is impossible to please Him" (Hebrews 11:6 NKJV).

1. "My client is too sophisticated to be interested in the Gospel." (Persevere anyway.)

Laura, a tall, slender young woman in her late twenties, came to the center for a pregnancy test. Her long, dark hair was an appealing contrast to her cream-colored suit. It was easy to imagine this stately woman walking through the marbled corridors of the lavish hotel that employed her.

The advocate was tempted to forego a Gospel presentation with this lovely, statuesque client. *She's never going to be interested in talking about God—she's obviously much too sophisticated and worldly for an interest in spiritual things.* But this was not the case.

When the pregnancy test came back positive, the young woman spoke of how unexpected a pregnancy was. She had been in a long-term relationship, yet they had not yet seriously discussed marriage. As the intake proceeded, the discussion deepened. The client mentioned God. The advocate inserted, "Did you know we are a Christian center?"

The client replied, "I didn't know that! I'm also a Christian!" Then she added, "That's why I am going to carry this pregnancy to term."

Although this was positive for the advocate to hear, the woman needed restoration of her relationship with God. She proceeded to speak of feeling far away from God and lamented the past closeness she had enjoyed with Him. The kairos moment had arrived.

Discuss the meaning of being a cultural Christian versus being a true follower of Christ. The latter brings the contentment of following His guidelines for our lives.

It was perfect timing for the advocate to intervene with a testimony. At one time, she also had been seeking God on her terms. "I admit I wanted to be in the driver's seat."

The advocate continued, "Ultimately, I found peace with God by surrendering my life to Him." As the conversation continued, the discussion expanded to talking about biblical sexual integrity—that is, following God's will in her private, dating life.

It's often helpful to a client to discuss the meaning of being a *cultural Christian* versus being a true *follower of Christ.* The latter brings the contentment of following His guidelines for our lives. The advocate said, "Following Christ includes following His guidelines for abstinence. His heart is to help us avoid the pitfalls of the world's ways. His purpose isn't to break or bend us to obedience but to touch our hearts with the delight of following Him.

The advocate looked directly at Laura when she said, "Laura, it's apparent you have wandered off track spiritually."

"Yes, I know," Laura responded quietly.

"Are you in agreement with the basics of the Christian faith, such as we are all sinners?"

"Yes," Laura responded.

"That Jesus came to pay the penalty for our sins?"

"Yes."

"And that our God of love wants you to draw close to Him again?"

"Yes," she acknowledged.

"Would you like to pray a rededication prayer as a *defining point* to reset your walk with the Lord? It often helps to formalize your return to Him—a recommitment helps you get back on track."

The client readily agreed.

The advocate led a prayer for rededication. Afterward, before leaving, the young woman expressed thankfulness for helping her return to the Lord. As she stood up, she asked, "Can I give you a hug?"

NOTE: Rededication and dedication are discussed in the Gospel section of this book. The commitment prayer is located near the back of the spiritual tract titled *Would You Like to Know God Personally?* (See "Resources," appendix B.)

---

2. "My client is Hindu. She won't be interested in the Gospel." (Persevere anyway.)

Our divine appointment entered the counseling room. A lovely, twenty-seven-year-old client from India. As the intake questioning proceeded, the advocate mentioned to Sara that the center was a Christian organization, and the client amiably responded that she was Hindu. Doubtful thoughts about sharing the Gospel rushed into the advocate's mind, but, ignoring her feelings, she continued the spiritual discussion. She asked Sara, "Have you ever had a Christian friend?" (A good entry question for spiritual discussion with a person of another faith.)

"Yes. My sister is a Christian."

"And the two of you were brought up in the same household?"

The young lady giggled and vigorously answered, "Yes."

"I'll bet that's an interesting story."

"It is!" The client laughed.

"Tell me about it," the advocate urged.

"It's quite a story," Sara began. "My sister was born with something terribly wrong with her foot. In fact, it was so deformed she could barely walk. She was always praying to our gods about it, but nothing happened. Many times, she walked past a little Christian church down the hill in the village where we lived. One day my sister was feeling desperate, and, with great effort, she managed to walk to the church. People whispered about healings taking place there, and my sister wanted to pray to Jesus for her healing. Once at the church, people were kind, and soon prayers began for the healing of her foot. Miraculously, before their eyes, Jesus healed her! After that, my sister said she was a Christian."

> *"You can shut Him up for a fool, you can spit at Him and kill Him as a demon; or you can fall at His feet and call Him Lord and God."*
>
> C.S. Lewis

The advocate replied, "That's quite a story. I've never experienced a dramatic, physical miracle, but I have experienced the life-changing miracle of finding Christ and the peace He offers. Do you ever think about Jesus?"

The client answered, "Yes, because of my sister, I am very curious about Christianity. She and I have talked about it a lot." The kairos moment had arrived.

The advocate went on to share that for years she had examined other religions. "For a while I had given up searching because all the world religions think they're right! How can anyone know what to believe?"

The advocate said she finally settled on believing Christ was an enlightened person, a prophet. However, the belief was shattered when reading the thoughts of C.S. Lewis (1898–1963).

Lewis was a brilliant professor who had taught at both Oxford and Cambridge. In his book, *Mere Christianity,* page after page asserts reasonable answers to many of Christianity's most puzzling questions.

One of Lewis's famous apologetics is still useful in the counseling room when we hear the client say, "I'm not sure Jesus is God," or "I believe Jesus was an enlightened being (or a prophet or a moral teacher)." Many religions in the world regard Jesus as special but outlaw the declaration of Jesus as God. Lewis's apologetic confronts this thinking. He dubbed his rebuttal, "Liar, lunatic, or God." Lewis's rationale concludes that Jesus was and is who He said He was.

When some have said, "I'm ready to accept Jesus as a great moral teacher, but I don't accept His claim to be God," Lewis refutes this thinking.

"That is the one thing we must not say. A man who was merely a man and said the sort of things Jesus said would not be a great moral teacher. He would either be a lunatic—on a level with the man who says he is a poached egg—or else he would be the Devil of Hell. You can shut Him up for a fool, you can spit at Him and kill Him as a demon; or you can fall at His feet and call Him Lord and God," Lewis said.[4]

After a spiritual discussion took place, Sara's defenses had lowered. She desired to hear the Gospel message of the Christian faith. Her knowledge was largely confined to knowing about the power of Jesus because He had healed her sister. The advocate reached for a Gospel tract entitled *Would You Like to Know God Personally?*[5] She proceeded through each page in a conversational manner to name each of the four principles and read one of the correlating Scriptures that adds validity to its meaning.

Her client was already smiling. When only a prayer of surrender was left, the client's eagerness was clear. She reached for the tract, and she said, "I'll pray that prayer!"

As simple as that, Sara was "all in" for a personal and growing relationship with Jesus Christ. After she prayed to surrender her life to Christ, Sara expressed excitement. "I can hardly wait to tell my sister I've also become a Christian!"

A few weeks later, she told the advocate she had contacted her sister to tell her she had given her life to Christ. The sister, who lived in the Middle East, was excited about Sara's decision. Before they hung up, she asked Sara to mail her a Bible.

3. "My client is older. She already knows what she does and doesn't believe. She won't be interested in the Gospel." (Persevere anyway.)

Several years ago, a widowed lady in her early sixties, sweet and grandmotherly, arrived at the center. Francine had made an appointment for a pregnancy test. Once in the counseling room, she grinned sheepishly when she said, "I know I shouldn't be pregnant at my age, but I just need to make sure." After testing, the results clearly registered in her look of relief. The client spoke openly. "I'm a Christian," she began. As she elaborated, her tone became apologetic as she mentioned her sexually active lifestyle. A kairos moment for intervention.

In the discussion that followed, Francine heard the God-honoring message of abstinence. The advocate, having established a friendly rapport with her client, offered the thought, "At sixty-one years old, you likely have entered menopause. [Client affirmed.] The nurse, as our medical person, will be glad to talk about specifics if you have questions."

The advocate continued. "Francine, do you think the fear of being pregnant was related to guilt from not living your values as a Christian? That is, does the sexual lifestyle rob you of your peace?"

The woman vigorously nodded to both questions.

The advocate spoke of the need for Francine to get her life back on track with the Lord and enjoy the peace of following Him again. Near the end of the session, this dear lady prayed to rededicate her life to Christ. She looked visibly lifted when she left the center. A fresh beginning with Christ had brought a renewal of joy.

A fresh beginning with Christ had brought a renewal of joy.

4. "My client is too far gone. She won't be interested in the Gospel." (Persevere anyway.)

"I've done some awful things in my life . . ." Jackie's head dropped in shame, and her voice lowered. "Like prostitution." The kairos opportunity was disguised in the client's words of shame.

"Thank you for sharing so openly. Do you still feel burdened by your past?"

The client nodded.

"I want to share with you a wonderful way of permanently removing the burden of sin you're carrying. It's so comforting to know Jesus has already paid the penalty for any sin we have ever committed. Let's look at Romans 8:1."

"There is therefore now no condemnation to those who are in Christ Jesus."

Romans 8:1

The advocate had the client read from the ESV. "There is therefore now no condemnation to those who are in Christ Jesus."

The advocate continued. "This verse is directed to persons who have chosen to follow Christ. God doesn't condemn them because Jesus has paid their lifetime debt of sin. Our part is accepting His sacrifice for us."

It was time for the advocate to move into the more personal realm to witness the freedom she experienced in her own life. "I had committed a lot of sin, but I found peace by inviting Christ to take control of my life. I asked Him to make me the person He wanted me to be." As the advocate continued, she acknowledged the new sense of freedom she found from knowing sins are forgiven and removed. "This has given me a great love for Jesus, who paid the price for me."

She continued, "When someone pays a great debt on our behalf, we experience release and joy! Imagine if you owe someone lots of money, and then a person steps in on your behalf and pays it off for you." They had a brief discussion. "Would you like to receive the gift of Jesus personally paying for the sin in your life?"

"Yes."

"Jackie, you are very special and greatly humble in recognizing your need for a Savior."

The client managed to smile as she tearfully nodded.

That was the day Jackie prayed to entrust her life to God. She was homeless, but a maternity home was found. She felt discouraged but discovered newfound hope for her life. With her burden visibly lifted, God's plan was unfolding. "We will rejoice in your salvation" (Psalm 20:5 NKJV).

5. "My client already considers herself a Christian. She won't be interested in the Gospel." (Persevere anyway.)

Beth, an abortion-vulnerable client in her early twenties, came to the center for a pregnancy test. To her dismay, the outcome was positive.

"My boyfriend and I have already talked, and in the case of pregnancy, we're still undecided." When Beth learned the pregnancy center was Christian, she promptly asserted, "I consider myself a Christian." She also said that she wanted to start going to church again. (Keep in mind that some clients could be people pleasers who "play to the audience." Others confuse church attendance with knowing God personally.)

"That's always good to return to church, but I'm really talking about something deeper," the advocate said.

At this point, the Holy Spirit intervened. To the advocate's surprise, He was nudging her to explore the client considering herself a Christian. The advocate complied by asking an odd question. "Beth, do you feel that you know anything about Christianity?" This wasn't the advocate's usual manner of questioning, so it surprised her to hear the client's candid reply.

"No, I don't know anything."

God had prompted the kairos moment leading up to another question. The advocate asked, "Would you like to know more?"

Beth nodded, and the conversation entered the path to salvation. The advocate reached for the brochure *Would You Like to Know God Personally?* It covered points such as sin being something humankind does, but Jesus's love for us paid the penalty for our sins on the Cross. The message ended with an opportunity to pray a prayer of surrender.[6]

"Every gift of salvation has a giver and a receiver," the advocate explained. "Christ is the Giver and we, the receivers."

As Beth and her advocate read through the booklet, they arrived at the prayer of surrender.[7] It is first read aloud before the client is asked if she would like to pray. (State to the client that you are now going to read the prayer so she will know what she will be praying.)

Suddenly, Beth's eyes filled with tears. She said, "I know that I've been very emotional during this session, but probably not for the reason you think. It's because I have been wanting more of God in my life for some time." When this abortion-vulnerable client learned her pregnancy test results were positive, she had totally changed her perspective. She exclaimed, "I am so excited about the baby!"

Every gift of salvation has a giver and a receiver. Christ is the Giver and we, the receivers.

6. My client said she is already a Christian. "And my boyfriend in the waiting room isn't interested in religion." (Persevere anyway.)

Sierra and Jay came to the center together, but the session began with Sierra and her advocate. Going through the intake, Sierra mentioned she had recommitted her life to the Lord a few days before. She added, "My boyfriend isn't at all interested in spiritual things." Because of this input, when Jay was invited to join the session, the advocate did not attempt any spiritual discussion. (In hindsight, the advocate thought it would have been better to touch on the subject before discarding it altogether.)

Because Sierra and Jay came to the center an hour before closing, the advocate gauged it was time enough to perform a pregnancy test and send them on their way. Although pregnancy had been highly suspected, the couple appeared stunned by the positive confirmation.

Jay admitted that he preferred Sierra to get an abortion since "I have my whole life ahead of me."

As a couple, Sierra and Jay had strengths that could be helpful. For example, Sierra had a college degree and was employed. Jay, who worked part-time while in school, would be completing a bachelor's degree in engineering in two weeks. Their completed college degrees likely brought greater job options. Unlike many of the couples seen, their year-long relationship appeared somewhat stable. In addition, they openly said that they loved each other.

The advocate encouraged them not to rush decision-making. "Let's slow down and go through the process," she advised. (This statement often sets a couple at ease.) "We'll arrange an ultrasound, which is free of any charge."

Before leaving the center, the couple had scheduled the ultrasound for later that week. Though still looking dazed about the pregnancy, they left with the encouragement of new thoughts to consider.

Two hours later, the advocate left her office carrying a cardboard box with items to take home. In the parking lot, after placing the box in the back seat of her car, she was startled when she turned around and saw Jay standing nearby. "Oh, hello Jay!"

He nervously replied, "Can we talk for a few minutes?"

"Of course."

"My girlfriend and I have been talking, and we've decided to go back to church." (An indication of spiritual interest—but not yet the pivotal moment.)

"That's a good decision, Jay. I know God is in this situation with you."

God is the starting place.

They continued to talk as the young man began sharing more about his life. He said his biological father had abandoned the home when he was growing up, and he had spent his lifetime trying to prove to himself he wasn't like his father. He also said he was close to his stepdad but didn't want to disappoint him by the pregnancy. He went on to speak of career decisions and not being sure about what he wanted to do. On and on he spoke, citing his different career options, interests, concerns, and worries.

Finally, the advocate interrupted Jay's stream of consciousness. "Jay, I don't have all the ready answers to your questions, but I can tell you a good place to start. God tells us in Scripture that He has a plan for your life, and it is a plan for good and not for evil. This means God is the starting place."

Jay appeared open. He was listening intently.

The advocate continued. "Can I ask you some questions?"

"Yes," he replied.

"Do you believe in God?"

"Yes."

"Do you believe that Jesus died for your sins?"

"Yes."

"Do you want God to be a part of your life?"

"Yes."

"Would you be willing to invite Him personally into your life today so He can guide you?"

"Yes."

"Then right now, you can begin a new life with Him. Your relationship with Him will give you guidance and peace with the decisions in your life."

There, at a cement parking lot, a young man, a millennial, bowed his head to pray the heartfelt prayer that yielded his life to Christ. Before departing that day, Jay gladly received the names of two individual men who were available to meet with him and "walk through" the situation by offering spiritual support. Jay was growing up and, in the process, becoming more like his Father. The One in whose image he was made.

There, at a cement parking lot, a young man yielded his life to Christ.

7. "My client is a practicing Buddhist. She won't be interested in the Gospel!" (Persevere anyway.)

The advocate felt intimidated when she learned Kim was a practicing Buddhist rather than a cultural Buddhist. She knew a practicing Buddhist is more invested in her religion—perhaps dismissive of a discussion about Christianity. "Why bother?" thought the advocate.

But she was wrong.

Kim said she had been married for over ten years. She and her husband were rearing two young children. Early during the intake process she shared, "Our household finances are very tight, and supporting another child won't be easy. In fact, having this baby will really be a sacrifice." Her voice caught, and she glanced away. "To tell you the truth, my husband and I were planning to abort this pregnancy until late last night—then we talked again and decided to keep it. But I still don't feel peace."

(*Abortion-vulnerable*, thought the advocate.) The advocate dismissed the opportunity of spiritual sharing as she reminded herself, "She's a practicing Buddhist—she won't be interested in Christianity."

The pregnancy test was administered, and the results disclosed a positive test. The session with the client was at closure. Unexpectedly,

All life is sacred. The child you are carrying is a gift from God.

Kim asked, "What does your religion think about abortion?" (Once again, the Lord introduced the kairos moment, but this time through the client.)

The advocate replied, "As Christians, we don't believe abortion is God's best for us. In fact, we believe much like Buddhists—that all life is sacred. The child you are carrying is a gift from God."

The client grew silent—her head nodding slowly, pensively.

The advocate began to share a brief testimony based on her own life. "Kim, there was a time when I was searching for peace just as you are. Isn't that so? Isn't it God's peace you're desiring for your life?"

"Oh yes, I want to have peace!" Kim exclaimed.

The advocate spoke of how her own life had been filled with sinful choices, and prior to knowing Jesus, she had experienced a great deal of turmoil because of poor choices. She also spoke of the prayer she had said aloud on that pre-dawn morning of surrendering her life. "Kim, I didn't even know it was called a prayer of surrender, but God knew I was yielding my heart to Him, and, after praying, I felt His peace."

Kim was listening attentively.

Her advocate continued. "I didn't expect to feel peace. I didn't expect to feel anything! At the time, I had never done Bible studies. I was completely ignorant that Jesus is called the Prince of Peace. But knowing that now, it makes perfect sense after inviting Him into my life, I'd find peace. The peace comes from Him. Kim, may I share a little booklet with you that has meant a lot to me?"

Kim readily engaged, and the advocate shared the Gospel message with her. It included four essentials: (1) God loves us, and He wants a personal relationship with us. (2) We are sinners—estranged from Him. (3) Jesus paid the penalty for our sins and died on a cross. (4) We can receive His gift of salvation."

After discussing the Gospel message, the advocate asked, "Would you like to invite Jesus into your life and receive His peace?"

"Yes!" Kim replied.

In the sacred moment that followed, a practicing Buddhist asked Jesus to come into her life. After the prayer ended, the advocate asked, "Are you feeling any different?"

"Yes," Kim whispered. "I feel peace."

Questions to Glide into Kairos

Through our advertising, clients usually know our pregnancy resource centers are faith-based, but some arrive unaware. We need not be timid about who we are and who we represent. The intakes from most Christian centers ask about religious backgrounds. The lead-in question is often generalized such as, "Do you attend a church in the area?" From this simple question, spiritual conversation is sometimes initiated. Clients have great and various needs. They will not be prone to walking out when told, "We are a Christian-based ministry but love talking with people with many different backgrounds." They soon learn staff and volunteers treat all clients with love and respect amid diverse backgrounds.

1. Advocate: "Did you know we are a Christian center?"

"Oh, no!" the client says.

Advocate: (amused, smiling) "It's okay; we're 'Christian' in the best sense of the word! We're not judgmental here. Have you had some sort of previous experience with Christianity?"

(The client's initial response may allude to an earlier negative experience, which could be explored to initiate a spiritual conversation.) The advocate's question embodies a kairos moment filled with opportunity.

Listen well. Pray silently for the Lord to guide you into the right timing to share your testimony.

2. Advocate: "Did you know we are a Christian center?"

"No, I didn't know," replies the client, "but I would *never* get an abortion!"

Advocate: "You sound very much assured about that! Is that because of your personal faith background?"

A kairos moment. (Listen well. Pray silently for the Lord to guide you into the right timing to share your testimony.)

3. Advocate: "Did you know we are a Christian center?"

Because many clients link the words *Christian* and *church* interchangeably, a client may reply, "Yes, I'm a Christian too." (This statement needs to be explored.)

Client: "In fact, I've thought about getting back to church lately." (A kairos moment.)

(The advocate knows the importance of affirming client statements when she can.)

Advocate: "Yes, church is important. Actually, I am not talking about church as much as something even more essential than church attendance. It's something I didn't understand for a long time." (The client's interest was visibly piquing.) "Being a Christian is centered on a personal relationship with God. Do you know what I mean by that?"

Advocate (in discussing the personal relationship): "I always thought I had a personal relationship with God because I'd toss up a prayer whenever I needed something. But I had never committed myself to God. I treated Him more like a genie in a bottle."

The advocate proceeds to share her personal salvation testimony.

4. Advocate: "Did you know that we are a Christian center?"

The client: "No, I didn't know. I'm Catholic."

(There is an intake question directly asking the client about her faith background. If she references her personal faith such as Catholicism, Orthodox Christian, Methodist, or Episcopalian, all offer the sacrament of confirmation.)

Advocate: "Did you ever participate in confirmation as a child?" (This question leads to an understanding of where the client is spiritually.)

Client: "Yes, I was raised Catholic, and I went through confirmation when I was twelve years old."

Advocate: "Confirmation is meant to be a meaningful spiritual turning point of deepening faith. However, I've met many who tell me they went through their confirmation process for one of two reasons. The first was that friends were being confirmed at that time, so they didn't give much thought to its genuine meaning. Or they've said, "My parents completely expected me to be confirmed, so I never thought of it as a choice. It's a big church event planned when you become a certain age.'" (This may present a kairos moment when the client revisits an opportunity to go deeper *now* in her faith.) "Since you're now an adult, would you like to go deeper with God now?"

When we surrender ourselves and our situation to God, we are giving Him the freedom to work in our lives.

NOTE: Sometimes asking, "Did you know that we are a Christian center?" does not readily spark discussion. In that case, you can add, "Though we're a Christian center, we love serving women from all different faith backgrounds. Do you have a faith background?"

---

5. Advocate: "Do you ever think about God?

Client: "Yes," or "No," or "Sometimes."

Advocate: "When we surrender ourselves and our situation to God, we are giving Him the freedom to work in our lives." ("I remember . . ." Share your testimony.) "The Bible, in Psalm 139, tells us God has thousands and thousands of thoughts about us. Did you know that?" (Wait for her answer.) "Isn't it amazing the God of the universe thinks about you and me? The psalm reveals He has more thoughts about you than the grains of sand. Think of all the grains of sand on every beach in the world! This means He knows you, loves you, and is seeking you. Do you have any interest in going deeper with Him?"

6. Advocate: "Do you ever think about God?"

Client: "Yes," or "No," or "Sometimes."

Advocate: "He can make a way for you to walk through your situation. We're not talking elusively as if God is 'someplace out there in space,' but that He personally knows you and knows your situation intimately (Psalm 119:1–24). At one point in my life, I felt a great need to have something more in my life, a greater sense of purpose." (Share testimony) "Do you ever feel that you would like to go deeper with Him?" (A kairos moment.)

We're not talking elusively as if God is "someplace out there in space," but that He personally knows you.

7. Advocate: "Do you ever pray?"

Client: "Yes," or "No," or "Sometimes."

Advocate: "In my own life, I had always thought praying to be a matter of God doing the listening, not *me* doing the listening. As with any conversation, good communication goes two ways. He listens to our prayers, but we need to hear from Him as well. Scripture says, 'My sheep hear my voice,' which means God must be talking to us!" (Share your testimony and how to enter into deeper fellowship with Him.) "Our prayers are empowered through a personal relationship with God. James 5:16 says, 'for tremendous power is released through the passionate, heartfelt prayer of a godly believer!'" (TPT).

8. Advocate: "Did you know God has a plan for your situation?

Advocate continues: "Even though your situation is difficult, God knows all about it and has a perfect plan if we just lean on His wisdom. I remember in my own life when I was having a hard time . . ." (Share topic testimony.)

9. Advocate: "Did you know God is with you in this situation?"

Advocate continues: "He will sometimes let us go through hard circumstances to draw us closer to Him. It's likely God will have you use this experience to comfort someone else one day." (Turn to 2 Corinthians 1:4 TPT.) Have the client read:

> He always comes alongside us to comfort us in every suffering so that we can come alongside those who are in any painful trial. We can bring them this same comfort that God has poured out upon us. (2 Corinthians 1:4 TPT)

Kairos: Client/Advocate Exchange

Client: "I'm not very religious."

Advocate: "What do you mean by *religious*?" (Gleaning the client's perspective is a must.)

We are created with a mind, emotions, physical body, and a spiritual component, as well.

Client: "I think that religious means attending church or talking about God a lot."

Advocate: "So *religious* for you seems to involve more than just church attendance—it would include relating to God also?" (It is helpful to clarify.)

Client: "Yes."

Advocate: "That makes sense because as human beings, we're made up of four components. We are created with a mind, emotions, physical body, and a spiritual component, as well. If we leave one part out, you might say we're not running on all four cylinders! The spiritual part of us longs for something beyond ourselves; it's the part that brings thoughts about God's existence."

Client: "I never thought about it like that. I see your point. Quite frankly, I don't see why anyone would want to believe in God. Look at all the suffering in the world!" (The client is becoming increasingly genuine about questioning thoughts. Unanswered questions can hinder the client from responding to God.)

Advocate: "You're right. There is a lot of suffering going on in our world." (Always verbally agree when you can do so authentically.) "If you were God, what kind of a world do you imagine *you* would create?"

Client: "A world where people aren't fighting all the time, hating and hurting each other. One where people don't die from cancer or even die at all, for that matter!"

Advocate: "Yes, I can agree with you. That's an ideal world."

Client: (Nods in agreement.)

NOTE: A kairos opportunity has presented itself—a natural transition from the secular to the spiritual realm.

Advocate: "Have you ever thought about the fact that God *did* create a world exactly like the one you described? The world He created was perfectly at peace—no hatred, pain, sin, or disease."

NOTE: From here, proceed to describing the perfect garden of Eden, personal sin, and share your personal testimony that revealed the need for God's restoration in your life. You can add that there does exist a perfect place that God has reserved for those who have invited Him into their lives. It's called heaven. As His follower, heaven is our planned destiny with Him.

Advocate (homing in): "Have you ever had a close friend die?" (Wait for her answer, then comment and continue.) "Often when someone close to us dies, it causes us to think about our own eternal destination. Would that be true for you?" (If she shows interest, discuss the Gospel and God's plan of redemption for her personally.)

Relax. God Is in Control!

As the Spirit leads, God reveals opportunities for spiritual discussion. This could be by using common leading questions or even "situational" entries that come about in the context of the discussion. Sharing God's love is sharing God's heart for her. Our praying silent prayers during client sessions alert us to the kairos moment that leads to sharing the Gospel with her. By faith, we anticipate God will "show up" in perfect timing.

An advocate candidly recalls, "There have been times when I'm near the end of the client session, then realize I haven't shared the Gospel. I silently pray, 'Lord, please provide an entry to your Gospel so that I can share You.'" Be ready to watch God lead! Once again, He'll guide the advocate "back to the neighborhood" of the kairos moment—a timely, Spirit-infused moment that leads our client to the Savior of the world.

Seizing the Kairos Moment: Dr. Pasteur's Story

Intervention is the advocate's contribution at the pregnancy resource center. Life versus death is at the crossroads of choice. A new legacy readies with potential to thrive or die by one's spiritual choice. Though legacies reach into future years and bring impact, they begin with kairos moments. Whether at a pregnancy resource center or even a faraway laboratory in France over a century ago, we see life in the balance and a powerful legacy waiting to be fulfilled.

A new legacy readies with potential to thrive or die by one's spiritual choice.

Dr. Louie Pasteur, the famed scientist and immunologist, encountered a critical kairos moment during the development of the rabies vaccine. The little-known story shouts a potent message to those willing to overcome their fears to make a difference.

Before the 1880s, year after year, thousands of people died from rabies. Dr. Pasteur had been working on a vaccine for quite some time, and the progression of his work had become well-known. With the completion of the vaccine's successful clinical trials with animals, the next step was looming. It was time for a human trial. Who would his first human subject be? He already knew. Himself.

In the meantime, a desperate mother of a nine-year-old had heard press releases about the famous doctor's experimental vaccine. Locating Dr. Pasteur, she readily shared the story of her son, whose life was imperiled. Little Joseph Meister had been the victim of a savage attack by a rabid dog. It was common knowledge that rabies meant certain death—a terrible death, at that. Flu-like symptoms progressing to delirium, then coma, and ultimately death.

The distraught mother begged the doctor to give the experimental vaccine to her son. Dr. Pasteur was reluctant. He was not a medical doctor but a microbiologist who had earned a doctorate in chemistry and physics. Recognizing the life-and-death situation, he consulted with two medical doctors. Urgency was driving the situation on a fast track, and a decision was made to address the situation quickly. Dr. Pasteur yielded to the mother's pleas, and an experimental protocol was readily arranged. Over a span of three weeks, the child was injected with thirteen inoculations. After the treatment was completed, young Joseph Meister survived.[9]

Stepping outside of comfort zones, we bring the Gospel to brandish the ill-fated choice of abortion with the might of a living God.

Decades later, the elderly Dr. Pasteur was nearing death. He was asked a question. "With all your life-long accomplishments, if you had just three words to place on your headstone, what words would they be?"

The doctor's reply came quickly. "Joseph Meister lived."[10]

Just as Pasteur chose to bypass his personal timidity to seize a kairos moment to ensure life, client advocates also deal with life-and-death situations with clients—not only with the preborn but the client's decision about new life with Christ. The advocates are also confined by small windows of time. To a client open to hearing, we extend Jesus's love by seizing the opportunity. Stepping outside of comfort zones, we bring the Gospel to brandish the ill-fated choice of abortion with the might of a living God. A transformative decision to welcome Christ into one's life often results in the choice of life for the client's baby.

Advocates: Instruments of God's Grace

Advocates are on the frontlines, and God will meet us with a spirit-filled fortitude. Just as God anointed the apostle Paul with "spiritual stamina" to carry out God's will, He will do so for us. The Spirit ignited Paul's passion as he ministered from "morning till evening, explaining about the kingdom of God . . . to persuade them about Jesus." We learn that "some were convinced by what he said, but others would not believe" (Acts 28:23–24 NIV).

God divinely places His advocates at the respective centers. As His instruments of grace, we give credence to Jesus's authenticity through our personal testimonies. Just as in the past, readiness to respond varies. Despite our participation in the salvation process, the outcome belongs to Him.

Chapter Two

Intentional Gospel Sharing

Father, your Word says, "I believed, therefore I have spoken." As Your children, it is through your power that we believe and, therefore, will we speak faith into the lives of others. Tender their hearts, Lord.

(Prayer based on 2 Corinthians 4:13 NIV)

Typically, two different mindsets exist at every pregnancy resource center. Consider the following two centers.

Two Ministry Approaches: Unspoken Versus Spoken Gospel

One of the centers consists of a devoted Christian staff who compassionately focus on issues of pregnancy *without an intentional* Gospel presentation.

The other center consists of a devoted Christian staff who compassionately focus on issues of pregnancy and prayerfully provide an *intentional Gospel presentation.* When appropriate, it extends an invitation to receive Christ.

When the Gospel is included as part of a center's mission, every component of our services finds greater significance.

When the Gospel is included as part of a center's mission, every component of our services finds greater significance. An *intentional* offering of new life to the client (in addition to the focus on life for her baby) enlarges a mission's sole focus on babies to a spiritual outreach to the expectant mother. It brings God honor, and we celebrate His intervention by featuring client testimonies in newsletters, highlighting them in our fundraising events, and lauding them in our trainings. Tangible stories of clients receiving Christ touch hearts and inspire board members, staff, volunteers, churches, and donors with the thrill of participation in God's expanding kingdom through the Gospel.

> Now thanks be to God who always leads us in triumph in Christ, and through us diffuses the fragrance of His knowledge in every place. For we are to God the fragrance of Christ among those who are being saved and among those who are perishing. (2 Corinthians 2:14–15 NKJV)

The "unspoken Gospel" *silently* dwells within the hearts of godly staff and volunteers. Personified by Jesus, His presiding Spirit exudes a compelling fragrance to the clients. "There's peace here," marveled a young Muslim client who arrived at the center. Not infrequently, the exit surveys filled out by a departing client make note of "the kindness" extended by her Christian advocate. With nary a thought to the Savior who loves her, died for her sins, and longs to lift her burden, she displaces the honor to conclude *people are nice here.*

> For we are to God the fragrance of Christ among those who are being saved and among those who are perishing. To the one we are the aroma of death leading to death, and to the other the aroma of life leading to life. (2 Corinthians 2:15–16 NKJV)

This day, instead of a Shepherd, she longs for a Warrior God on her behalf.

The "*spoken* Gospel" also diffuses a lovely fragrance—one filled with the power of words flowing in sync with the center's peaceful ambience—the aroma of Jesus, the "Rose of Sharon." During the intake, the client who's spiritually open will hear the Gospel message. Perhaps it will prompt a childhood memory of a Sunday school classroom—that room with the picture she was drawn to: Jesus carrying a baby lamb upon His shoulders. But *this* day, instead of a Shepherd, she longs for a Warrior God on her behalf, a Savior of strength who will carry her burden of an unplanned pregnancy. Braced for the scorn of her family, she can't imagine herself the mother of a squirming baby. "Surreal," she manages to whisper.

Today, the young woman sits with her advocate, a woman who is gentle with her words but straightforward. Something about her inspires trust. "Therefore, since we have such hope, we use great boldness of speech" (2 Corinthians 3:12 NKJV). The advocate mentions God while speaking. The wooing has begun.

Toward the end of the session, after the advocate's salvation story is shared, the path to spiritual discussion becomes tangible. "When we have no relationship with the Savior, we are 'dead in [our] transgressions and sins'" (Ephesians 2:1 NIV). We can also feel deadened by numbness when we deal with difficult news. What does deadness need? Life! God's Spirit offers renewed life.

Gospel Intervention: "I Would Give Anything to Believe!"

The young woman's face tightens when the nurse announces the pregnancy test results. "Your test is positive," she says gently.

Once confirmed, the client's inability to cope is suddenly exposed. Nearly shouting, she says, "I would literally cut off my right arm if I could have the peace I see in people who believe—I would give *anything* to believe!" (Clearly, a kairos moment) Our client is about to learn that God grants to us a "measure of faith" to anyone who believes (Romans 12:3 NKJV).

A deeper discussion begins. The advocate addresses the client's impassioned statement directly. "Because you have such a great *desire* to believe, shows a measure of faith because you haven't dismissed Him altogether!"

The words appear strangely comforting to the client. Already, her need for a Savior is being tended to.

"You may be doing the seeking," continues the advocate, "but God is doing the pursuing." The peace you see in other people who believe is available for you too. Scripture tells us that if you seek God with all your heart, you will surely find Him (Jeremiah 29:13, paraphrased).

> *"Therefore, since we have such hope, we use great boldness of speech."*
>
> 2 Corinthians 3:12 NKJV

NOTE: To make this personally applicable, the advocate introduces her salvation testimony.

Advocate: "In my own life, I experienced God's persistence. I know, without a doubt, it was God's love pursuing me, and, without a doubt, His love is pursuing you!" The advocate shares her testimony, followed by the Gospel message. She uses a spiritual tract that's entitled *Have You Heard of the Four Spiritual Laws?*[1] Before leaving the center, the client prays the salvation prayer to commit her life to Christ.

The Gospel: God's Answer to Emptiness, Stress, and Crisis

The late evangelist Billy Graham once posed a question to Derek Bok, a friend and contemporary, who also happened to be the president of Harvard. After a lengthy visit with his longtime friend, it was time to depart, but not before Reverend Graham asked a final question about the students:

> "What is the number one struggle that the students of Harvard have to contend with?"
>
> President Bok "did not have to give it much thought for he quickly shot back: 'Living with emptiness.'"[2]

Undoubtedly, Mr. Bok's response is a timeless reflection of a world that still acclaims success in terms of education and wealth. Yet when God is omitted from the equation, little meaning or lasting purpose comforts the soul's thirst for Him.

In 2018, Harvard Medical School studied 67,000 college students and 100 institutions across the nation regarding college stress. It was found that one in five students surveyed reported thoughts of suicide in the past year. "Three out of four students reported having experienced at least one stressful life event in the last year." Additionally, "more than 20 percent of students reported experiencing six or more stressful life events in the last year."

The study showed that "one in four students reported being diagnosed with or treated for a mental health disorder in the prior year." And "one-fifth of all students surveyed had thoughts about suicide, with 9 percent reporting having attempted suicide and nearly 20 percent reporting self-injury."[3]

A report from the National Center for Education Statistics showed that

> the overall college enrollment rate for 18- to 24-year-olds (the age range representing the majority of students who are enrolled in college) was 39 percent in 2022. In this indicator, *college enrollment rate* is defined as the percentage of 18- to 24-year-olds enrolled as undergraduate or graduate students in 2- or 4-year institutions.[4]

Our hope for the woman is to be open to hearing God's transformative and comforting message. He loves her and seeks a relationship with her to enable His peace.

For pregnancy centers located near colleges and universities, there's a high correlation between location and the number of student clients seen. Because of the demanding educational environment and the *unexpected* stress of an unplanned pregnancy, abortion feels like a viable solution to quickly "normalize" the situation, supporting her desire "to go on with my life." As advocates, our hope for the woman struggling with an unplanned pregnancy is to be open to hearing God's transformative and comforting message. He loves her and seeks a relationship with her to enable His peace.

When asked, "Do you ever feel an emptiness in your life?" many clients will readily admit experiencing emptiness in their lives. Those who receive Christ at the center are often asked, "How are you feeling right now?" Moments after their prayer of commitment, the vast majority say, "I feel lighter," or "I feel better," or "I feel lifted." They are discovering that God is a tangible comforter—the One who meets them at their point of need. "God will continually revitalize you, implanting within you the passion to do what pleases Him" (Philippians 2:13 TPT).

As believers, advocates are God's divine instruments equipped with His Spirit to share the Gospel message. He looks for the willing heart to step out in faith and express the new life available to the penitent.

There is a "Gospel mathematics" involved as we reach out to others by faith. Just as the biblical story about the loaves and fishes (Matthew 14:13–21) tells of Jesus multiplying food to feed the multitude, we prayerfully ask God to multiply persons coming to the center so that they can be fed the food of the Gospel.

There is a "Gospel mathematics" involved as we reach out to others by faith.

Are We Meeting Our Center's Spiritual Potential?

> Stand at the crossroad and look; ask for the ancient paths, ask where the good way is . . . walk in it, and you will find rest for your souls. (Jeremiah 6:16 NIV)

Offering the opportunity to know Christ personally may not be a center's original mission, but God provides mobility toward His plan to reach vagrant hearts.

At the least, we must consider the words, "Stand at the crossroad and look; ask for the ancient paths." The prophet is saying to weigh and consider God-honoring possibilities. Is He calling your ministry to expand its current vision of prayerfully, *intentionally* introducing the God who loves your client?

A compassionate endeavor stems first from the heart, not merely assessing clients as "salvation prospects." In Him, our hearts meld with the Savior's to meet the mortal longing for peace—the peace Jesus offers to all.

Client decisions to trust Christ as one's Lord and Savior meet with great rejoicing. What a delight it brings to know our client's life is cupped in God's hands. By inviting Jesus to take control of her life, she is a part of His growing family, a reminder to the message bearer: "Let us not grow weary while doing good" (Galatians 6:9 NKJV). The salvation stories of clients yield heart-warming pleasure to all who believe in the sanctity of human life, whether an expectant mother or her baby.

Tracking Spiritual Decisions at the Center

If someone were to ask, "Why do you keep an account of numbers for spiritual decisions at your center?" (perhaps implying a "notch in the belt" mentality), we answer, "God keeps records. And we keep records. They are a reminder of what God is doing at the ministry."

Scripture specifically recorded the outcome of God's spiritual outreach through others.

- "About three thousand souls were added to them" (Acts 2:41 NKJV). We know that this happened in a single day, and it is thought that the number included men, women, and children.
- "Many of those who heard the word believed; and the number of the men came to be about five thousand" (Acts 4:4 NKJV).

Salvation: Ministry Mathematics

We know there's potential for powerful impact when believers step out in faith to share the Gospel.

Sharing our faith with a receptive client can lead to a harvest of additional souls for God's kingdom. After leading a client to Christ, we often encourage her to tell someone. "If you confess with your mouth the Lord Jesus and believe in your heart that God has raised Him from the dead, you will be saved" (Romans 10:9 NKJV). As she chooses to go deeper in her relationship with Christ, her faith is reinforced, and opportunity widens to impact her life and the life of her child.

We know there's potential for powerful impact when believers step out in faith to share the Gospel. The following illustration is based on a five-year window.

Let's imagine that your center has ten peer advocates. Each of these ten advocates leads one person to Christ in a single six-month period. At the end of this first six-month period, we now have twenty believers—the ten advocates and their ten new converts. If each were to continue the pattern by leading one person to Christ every six months, the twenty original people, plus their new converts, would bring the total to forty believers.

Again, in the next six-month period, each of these forty believers brings just one person to Christ, which brings the total to eighty believers. Now, each of the eighty bears witness to their faith—each bringing one person to Christ in the six-month period that follows. Counting the original ten advocates, we now have a total of 160 believers. As we *continue* this six-month cycle in which everyone brings a new person to faith every six months, we will double the number of believers every six months.

In summary, each six-month period, we have increased: From 20 to 40 to 80 to 160 to 320 to 640 to 1280 to 2560 to 5120. In the final six months, we will double to 10,540 believers as we reach the five-year mark. This illustrates the remarkable potential available when we intentionally share the Gospel!

Who Is God Bringing Today?

For the center willing to share the Gospel, every day is a day of adventure. A new mindset has become, "Who is God bringing us today?" Blessings are poised to meet our client. Perhaps a boyfriend, a husband, a child, girlfriend, or even the translator she brought to the center with her.

On two occasions, a translator came in with our English learner (EL) client, and both translator and client entrusted their lives to Christ during the session. In both cases, the translator was a friend who spoke the client's native language in addition to having mastered English. The translator's language ability was indispensable for the process of intake questioning.

In the first instance, when the spiritual topic was introduced, a tract was given to the client in her language. It was a verbatim match to the tract written in English, the one held by the advocate. Through the translator, the contents could be ably discussed. When the time came to ask the client if she wanted "to go deeper with God" and invite Christ into her life, the client replied, "Yes." The translator immediately chimed in to ask if she, too, could pray the prayer. Together, the client and her friend prayed for salvation.

In the second instance, the client had just prayed a prayer firming her commitment to Christ. Seconds later, the translator announced with a bright smile, "When my friend was praying that prayer, I was silently praying it too!"

Anomalies: Our Spiritual Perks

"Spiritual anomalies" seem to occur like a "spiritual perk" when centers have the heart to introduce God to clients. A center tells the story of an ad placed in the local college newsletter announcing their vacancy for an administrative position. A college student, graduating in two weeks, responded to the ad.

"Spiritual anomalies" seem to occur like a "spiritual perk" when centers have the heart to introduce God to clients.

As her interview got underway, the director mentioned that it was a Christian organization. The young woman responded, "As a child, I attended church." Soon she divulged that she had never actually invited Christ to be a part of her life. The interview continued its detour to include the director's personal testimony. Because of the woman's interest, the Gospel message soon followed.

A few minutes later, the young woman entrusted her life to Christ, and two weeks later, she began working at the center. In the years that followed, the young woman became a beloved staff member, an exceptional employee who continued to grow in her faith.

Every appointment brightens our awareness of reliance on the Holy Spirit. Yielded to Him, we have assurance He will lead us to discern truth. "When the truth-giving Spirit comes, he will unveil the reality of every truth within you. He won't speak on his own, but only what he hears from the Father" (John 16:13 TPT).

Defining *Believe*

In the original Greek language, *pisteuo* means "believe," also "to be persuaded of," and hence, "to place confidence in, to trust, signifies, in this sense of the word, reliance upon, not mere credence."[5] The client who is genuinely open to the Gospel message is already in the process of "being persuaded" by the wooing of God's Spirit. If this results in yielding her life to God, then she has entered a believing reliance on Him. This moves beyond doctrine and into a deeper relationship with Christ.

Believing is the movement of your will toward God and a decision to yield your life to Him.

In the counseling room, at times a young woman refers to her live-in boyfriend as her husband, though they haven't entered the commitment of marriage. She may have intellectually accepted the appearance of marriage, but cohabitation doesn't involve the depth of commitment of a marriage. By the same token, if the client states she intellectually accepts what Christ did on the Cross and believes a historical Jesus lived but is unwilling to receive His life and salvation personally, then she remains in darkness.

Illustration of *Believe*

How to present a visual illustration of what it means to *believe.*

Advocate: "The word *believe* is more than just intellectually agreeing that God is who He says He is, the Savior who died on a cross to pay for our sins. To believe is a movement toward God. Let me illustrate."

(Hold the two palms of your hands about a foot apart with palms vertical, facing one another.)

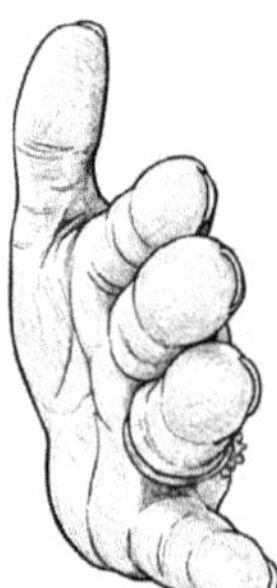

Advocate: "Let's say this is God (move your open-palmed right hand up and down, then stop) and this is you (move your open-palmed left hand up and down, then stop.)

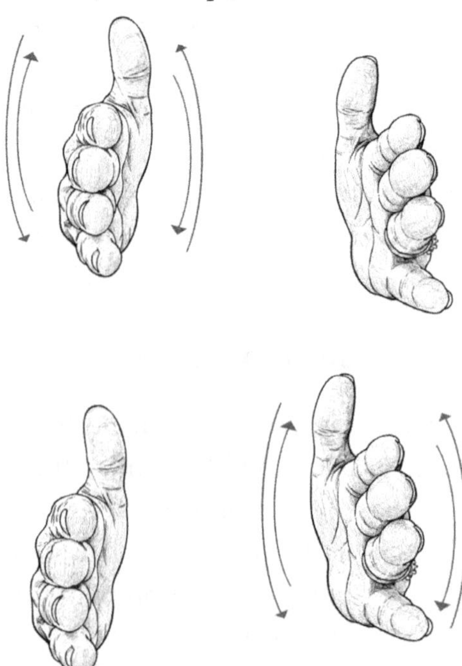

Advocate: (Point left index finger to the open palm of your right hand, which represents God as you speak.) "Belief is more than saying, 'I believe in a God who had a Son who died for my sins.'"

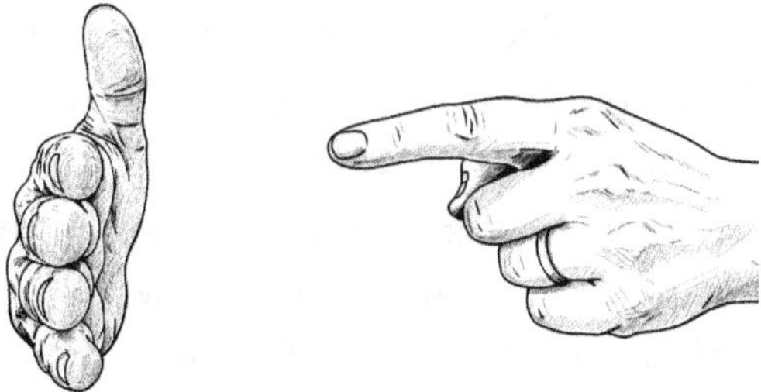

Advocate: "Instead, believing is like this." (Your two open palms face one another. Move the left palm, representing the client, slowly toward the right palm that represents God. Your palms meet, and fingers from each hand interlock.)

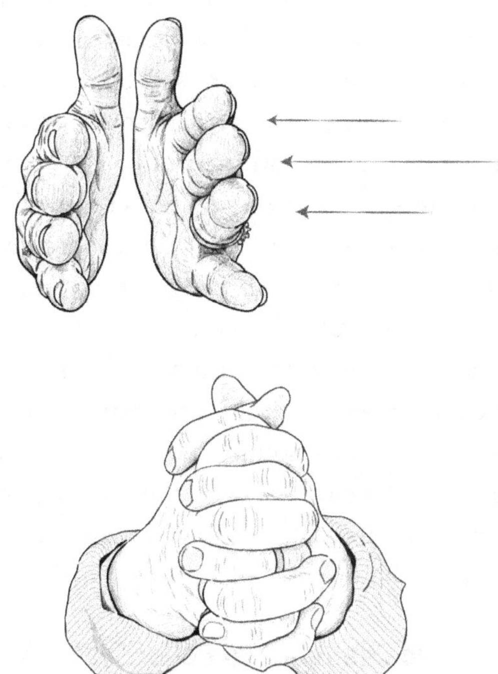

When you believe, you have entered a partnership with Him—a covenant.

"Believing is the movement of your will toward God and a decision to yield your life to Him, relying on Him through a personal, eternal relationship with Him. The spiritual word is *covenant.* When you believe, you have entered a partnership with Him—a *covenant* with Him."

Advocate (summarize the point): "As you walk in close partnership with Christ, this begins the process of knowing Him—*experiencing* His presence in your life. Do you have an interest in going deeper with Him?"

(If the client responds "yes," go through a spiritual tract with her to explain the Gospel further.)

A belief system starts with thoughts coming together and developing into a way of thinking that results in perspective.

Belief Systems

A belief system starts with thoughts coming together and developing into a way of thinking that results in *perspective.*

Think about it. Our decisions are based on the rationale we believe in. For example, before bedtime, I set my cell phone for a morning wake-up alarm. This reflects a belief system. That is, because I value punctuality (a belief), setting an alarm endorses the value of being punctual. It is important to me because I believe it is a responsible way to live. So alarm setting aligns with my belief system. In sum, a belief system consists of related thoughts that have developed into a perspective.

There's a belief system attached to reading this handbook. The belief could be, "It's good to expand my views." Or, as a Christian advocate, "I need to learn different ways to introduce a spiritual conversation."

Volunteers at the center contribute valuable time based on a belief system. Some may want to "give back" because, in an earlier crisis of their own, they had received support similar to what the pregnancy center offers. Or perhaps they *didn't* receive the support that could have prevented an abortion choice, and their hope is to prevent others from making the same mistake. Perspective drives motivation.

Clients also come to the center based on individual belief systems. A young woman may sincerely believe her pregnancy is the source of her problems, when instead, it's her *perspective,* her beliefs *about* the pregnancy, that are the source of causing a dilemma. Her intention for coming to the center may be varied. She may want a free confirming pregnancy test or a free ultrasound because her finances are limited. Or, she may have mistakenly believed the center performs abortions, or she's unsure what to do, and knowing we favor life for the child, she may have the hope of being dissuaded from abortion.

Two Clients—Two Belief Systems

Sharing the following story of two women with unplanned pregnancies enables the client to draw inferences and inspires her to choose life.

Advocate: "Our actions proceed from what we believe, and what we believe impacts our emotions. I recall two different women who came to the center several days apart. Both tested positive for pregnancy, but because they had radically different perspectives, they made two different choices.

"The first woman with an unplanned pregnancy came in and willingly engaged in a discussion about the crisis. However, toward the end of the session, she abruptly stood up and asserted, 'I hear everything you're saying, but, in my case, abortion is the best solution! I need to get on with my life.'" (Although abortion *removes* pregnancy, the client didn't grasp that abortion could negatively impact her life.)

"A few days later, another client entered the counseling room—this one with noticeable enthusiasm. Her confident stride into the room hollered the message, 'I've got my world under control!' Plopping into the couch cushions, she announced, 'I'm already sure I'm pregnant.' Then, with a flourish, she added, 'I can tell you this baby is really motivating me to do something with my life! I've enrolled in college!'"

The advocate sums up the experience: "These two real-life situations illustrate the way our beliefs drive our decision-making. Two unexpected pregnancies—both invading a comfortable status quo—but each met by two different attitudes based on two different belief systems. Predictably, there were two different outcomes. The first client was caught in despair of the unexpected, and by her perception of insurmountable obstacles, she chose an abortion. The second client, also initially stunned by the pregnancy, had been liberated by giving herself the freedom to explore the positive aspects of her situation. For her, this meant the strong motivation to enhance her life by pursuing higher education."

NOTE: The two examples are helpful to share with clients who need to hear that it isn't the pregnancy causing problems, but *what one believes about the pregnancy.* These examples can be shared at *any* pregnancy center. For instance, begin with, "There's a true story about two clients coming to a pregnancy center during the same week. They didn't know one another, but both dealt with unplanned pregnancies." After briefly telling the anonymous client stories, end with, "You see, it's not just the pregnancy situation, but the way we view it that leads to a choice we can be proud of." After telling the story, you can ask your client, "What are your thoughts?" (Don't miss the opportunity to get input from your client.)

Inference: A Client *Aha* Moment

When a client is considering abortion, in the most realistic sense, she is attempting to avoid suffering. It has been said that despair is suffering without meaning. This is why an advocate's topical testimony can deliver a powerful message to the client. For instance, the advocate says, "I understand how difficult this must be for you. I remember a time when I felt I had no plausible answers for a situation. (May include some details.) I had nowhere to turn, so I turned to God. He used my agonizing circumstance to bring me into a relationship with Him. I

It has been said that despair is suffering without meaning.

would never have believed it, but I never would have known God if that hadn't happened to me. He brings meaning and purpose into our circumstances." During most conversations, the client draws conclusions and make inferences. This leads to discussion.

An inference is "a conclusion or opinion that is formed because of known facts or evidence."[6] An inference made from hearing someone else's story will forge deeper understanding since inference is a "thought about a thought" that has already engaged a level of deeper thinking. When we hear someone else's thoughts, our own thoughts connect with what we're hearing, and we reach conclusions with a sounder impact.

The client in crisis views her pregnancy not as a temporary negative event but as something that will negatively impact her entire life.

When a client has heard her advocate's testimony, there is an opportunity to draw a positive inference for her life—having a thought about the advocate's thought. The client may think, "If God can make a difference in *her* life, maybe He could make a difference in mine."

Encourage your client's positive thinking by asking:

- Is there anything meaningful you can glean from your situation?
- Have you ever made a courageous decision in a difficult situation in the past that made you proud of yourself?
- Can you think of an experience that was extremely challenging in your past, but in the end, everything turned out better than you had thought it could?

Dr. Frankl, a psychiatrist, discovered firsthand how attitude can be a survival mode. During World War II, he witnessed inhumane conditions at Nazi concentration camps. He also witnessed the phenomenon of living nobly amid horrifying conditions.

> We who lived in concentration camps can remember the men who walked through the huts comforting others, giving away their last piece of bread. They may have been few, but they offer sufficient proof that everything can be taken from a man but one thing: the last of human freedoms—to choose one's own attitude in any given set of circumstances.[7]

Some would say a client contending with a crisis pregnancy is not enduring the suffering experienced by internment at an enemy camp. Yet pain is relative to the owner. Advocates who serve clients with unexpected pregnancies have witnessed the fear, sense of aloneness, and tangible agony. Part of the reason is that the client in crisis views her pregnancy not as a temporary negative event but as something that will negatively impact her entire life. "My life is over" is the pervasive thought. Fear colors her future darkly. She is craving closure, perhaps an abortion, to get on with her life. Validated by emotional pain, abortion becomes a feasible option.

God's intervention is needed. As we speak of His plan for her life, and how applicable His plan has been in our own lives, the client's interest is roused. Can there really be *something more?* At once we become participants and bystanders in the grandest of theatres led by His Spirit. Today the story of God's Son will be shared. Perhaps we shall witness the vaguest of beliefs reach for the Savior who loves her.

Clients Glean Insights Through Crisis

What a delight when an advocate finally hears her client's transformed perspective, such as, "I believe God meant this pregnancy for something good." Similar views have been heard, but usually *after* the baby is born, *after* the initial pregnancy shock, *after* the client adjusts to the new normal, *after* the validity of God's Word is experienced. Never mind. Hopefully, an abortion decision is not made before someone comes to her senses and rests on the hope of God's Word. "All things work together for good to those who love God, to those who are the called according to His purpose" (Romans 8:28 NKJV). In Christ, mercy draws us to the summit experience of our lives—a relationship with Christ.

Inspiring Courage in Your Client

One day, Audrie arrived at the center with her two-year-old in tow. The young mother began choking back tears when she shared with the advocate, "Yesterday, I left my husband. He has been physically abusive. This is not the first time either! I have driven nearly an entire day to escape him, and I will never go back." A pregnancy test confirmed her worst fears. Pregnant. "I have nothing," she said. "Ordinarily, I would never have an abortion. But in my situation, how can I provide for another baby?"

We worship a God of courage; look at the Cross!

Helping Audrie included providing her with tangible resources, which included information on housing and medical provision. In her case, it included a safe house an hour's drive away, located in a small town. Counseling would be important to help her recover from her past abuse and adapt to her new normal.

"Audrie, now that we've talked about how you could continue pragmatically with the pregnancy, I'd like to encourage you to take your time and not make a rash decision you may one day regret. It's been said that human potential, at its best, turns tragedy into triumph.[8] How do you see that applying to you?

"Audrie, what you may be viewing as a situation of tragedy could also become a triumph of your soundest values. It seems too little is said about courage these days. It's often spoken of as physical courage—like *doing* brave things on a battlefield. But courage can be just as brave in other situations too—like *your* situation."

The client nodded pensively.

"Be strong and of good courage, do not fear."

Deuteronomy 31:6

"God is so aware of your need for courage in this situation. In fact, we worship a God of courage; look at the Cross! Getting an abortion is a permanent decision that compromises your values. It's like you are continuing to set yourself up for abuse because it abuses your values! This causes regret, and even grief. Instead, it's time to make a courageous decision."

The advocate turned to Deuteronomy 31:6.

The client participated by reading the verse. "Be strong and of good courage, do not fear nor be afraid of them; for the LORD your God, He is the One who goes with you. He will not leave you nor forsake you" (NKJV).

The advocate asked, "Does this passage speak to you in any way?"

After a short discussion, the advocate shared the application of this verse during a challenging time in her own life.

NOTE: When attaching information to a story, like applying the Scripture verse to a real-life story, the recall is enhanced, and greater meaningfulness results. Research has shown that "when information is conveyed through a narrative," people "are 22 times more likely to remember that information."[9]

The Gospel followed, and Audrie received a new foundation for her life when she received Christ. She left the center knowing Jesus would walk through the situation with her. Eighteen months later, she visited the center to express her gratitude and update the center's staff.

"I have a job that provides for us, and the three of us are doing well," Audrie said.

Clients: International Students and Cultural Barriers

Depending upon where they are located, some centers see few international clients. Others see many. Whatever the case, an international student need not become an insurmountable challenge for sharing one's faith. Keep in mind that many international clients come from countries that restrict Christian evangelism to keep the population ignorant. Once studying in the United States, they are far from their homelands, and with barriers loosened, they are free to satisfy their curiosity, freely weigh considerations, and follow their hearts. Good discussions result from simple curiosity regarding America and the prevalent religious beliefs. Some international clients have come to the United States as children and were brought up with parents who maintain a distinct heritage. However, the twenty-something-year-old clients are often ready to make their own decisions about faith independent of their parents' beliefs.

Tips for Witnessing to International Clients

A salvation testimony bears witness to the significance of Jesus Christ in one's life. A witness to the faith has a testimony by which facts or events in one's life have brought a saving relationship with Jesus Christ.

When witnessing to a person with a different faith background from Christianity:

A real-life, personal story can spark interest.

1. Share your testimony: Glean the client's receptivity to gauge her interest in spiritual conversation. At first, the client may be motivated to listen only out of curiosity to find out what makes someone so impassioned by "religion." Yet a real-life, personal story can spark interest. Her reaction will be informative and provide cues for proceeding.

2. Explore Christian relationships: You might inquire if your client, particularly those who practice a non-Christian religion, has ever had a Christian friend. If yes, this may indicate openness and imply at least a baseline understanding of Christianity.

If she replies, "Yes, I know a girl who's a Christian, and we've become friends." Explore the comment. "Have you ever discussed your friend's faith with her?" Or, "Have you ever gone to church with her?"

If yes, "What were your thoughts about it?" You could also ask if her own beliefs about God have grown as she learned about her friend's faith.

3. Explore Christian experiences: Ask, "Did you attend local schools growing up, or did you attend a boarding school?" Many families abroad send their children to boarding schools, which are often Christian based. If a client has had any exposure to the faith by attending a Christian school, ask, "Did you ever make a personal commitment to becoming a follower of Christ?"

Depending upon her reply to the question about commitment, if she responds, "No, I've never made a commitment to Christ," gently ask additional questions. Share your testimony and the Gospel invitation with her.

Share your testimony and the Gospel invitation with her.

If her response is, "In my case, I did have lots of exposure to Christianity, but in my earlier years was not that interested," it's testimony time.

However, if she responds, "Yes, I have made a commitment to Christ in the past," ask, "Did the decision make a big change in your life?" (Explore where she is spiritually; find out if she has ever had the desire to study the Bible, etc.)

If she is single and is at the center for a pregnancy confirmation, then a rededication of her life to Jesus would help her get back on track.

Ask if she ever feels that she desires to have a deeper relationship with God. Add, "Following Him in our private lives can bring such joy to us. Greater intimacy with God brings us contentment."

Whether rededication is needed or a first-time dedication prayer is needed, both enable resetting their lives to follow Christ.

Because your testimony validates Gospel truth as applicable and genuine, be faithful to share.

4. Query her interest in being discipled: Share resources of churches, women's fellowship groups, online resources, etc., for growing in her faith. Many centers offer various topics with workbooks for their parenting classes. Many divergent topics are offered, and typically, the client herself chooses from this wide range of topics.

In the context of the parenting classes, discipleship classes could also be offered. Explain, "Being spiritually grounded enables us to prepare our child for life by strengthening his/her faith." Spiritually oriented teaching videos could be ordered (iPads provide convenience for this). Consider ordering parenting material with a strong biblical emphasis, or have qualified volunteers put together Bible lessons in the context of parenting.

It's an opportunity to be creative. If the client is attending a nearby college, perhaps one of the Christian ministry groups on campus could meet with her (Cru has a presence on many campuses) for discipleship purposes and/or spiritual support.

Be alert to ask good questions.

Resist the Enemy, and he will flee. Be aware that Satan, the Enemy of Your Soul (and your client's soul!), will attempt to dissuade you from sharing Christ. Your Gospel presentation may be the first time the client has heard this message. Because your testimony validates Gospel truth as applicable and genuine, be faithful to share.

Be prayerfully sensitive to the Spirit. Live in the freedom of this divine appointment; it has been *supernaturally* arranged by God. When meeting with a practicing Muslim or practicing________ (fill in the blank), remind yourself that the client is practicing the only religion she knows. By actively practicing her religion, this implies she values having spiritual beliefs for her life, something outside of herself to fill a need. (You could also ask how her religion fills basic human needs like security, purpose, how her faith defines her, etc. This can lead to a good discussion, groundwork for belief.)

Without Christ, there is no peace. As advocates, we know that since she doesn't worship the true, living God, our advantage in sharing is a recognition of what she lacks: the authenticity of peace. "I have told you these things so that in me you may have peace. In this world you will have trouble. But take heart! I have overcome the world" (John 16:33 NIV). Ask your client, "Do you ever struggle to have a sense of peace in your life?"

> "In this world you will have trouble. But take heart! I have overcome the world."
>
> John 16:33 NIV

Bringing Truth to the Client's Belief System

1. The Client with Body Piercings: ***Spiritually Hindered by Past***

The woman had visited the center, and arrangements were made for a maternity home. Because of the lab work required prior to entering the home, the center paid for a motel until the lab work results were in. Her advocate brought her lunch the next day. "Because it was summer, we sat in my car facing the client's motel room on the ground floor," the advocate recalls.

"Sitting next to me, she ate her sandwich, making no effort to talk. I silently wondered how to relate to this defiant young woman with an attitude. Her short brown hair was bleached in streaks of bright pink and yellow, and she had so many body piercings, it took a concerted effort not to gawk. Little silver studs formed a curvature around each rim of her ear. A midriff blouse exposed a five-month pregnant belly decorated with a naval ring. Nostrils, eyebrows, and tongue piercings added to the public display of chaos. Yet despite distractions, within her life of turmoil, the treasure of a preborn baby was housed. As the advocate pondered her approach to the client, she took a deep breath as she thought, *I'll just go for it!*

In her words: "Sitting behind the steering wheel, I repositioned myself so our eyes could connect. I smiled when I said, 'I see that you have quite a few piercings. I don't like needles myself! Did it hurt?'"

"No, not at all!" the twenty-something responded with a flip of her hair that, until then, had hidden her right eye.

With no earthly idea of where to head next, the advocate prayed silently. The answer came promptly, and she replied. "I know Someone else who had piercings, only His piercings hurt a lot. Six-inch iron nails were pounded through His wrists and His feet too."

The client replied dispassionately, "Yeah, I know all about that! I used to go to church as a little kid. Until stuff happened to me. Where was God when all that happened to me?"

"I'm so sorry for what you have been through, and right now, I'm unable to answer all your questions about it. [The client would soon be meeting with a counselor at the maternity home.] But I will tell you this. God does love you, and He desires to extend His comfort and healing in a flawed world that abuses free will."

The young woman stared at the dashboard, her thoughts confined as the advocate continued. "Jesus still is reaching out to you and cares

God is in the business of restoration.

for you. Right now, you're suffering a lot. You're homeless, abandoned by your boyfriend, pregnant, and have no job. Why not try God's way?"

Though the client seemed to be listening, this would not be the day of her salvation.

A few days later, lab work was now in order, and the client entered the maternity home as planned. After several weeks, the advocate contacted the home to ask if the young woman was adjusting. Speaking to one of the staff members, she was pleasantly surprised to hear, "Yes, she has adjusted. In fact, she is really doing well. She joined our Bible study and, just last week, she prayed to receive Christ."

The conversation with the girl with piercings brought an encounter with truth. It was the beginning of untangling the painful experiences that kept her captive to anger. The piercings had kept attention distracted to the *outside* while avoiding the pain she felt *inside*. Perhaps, in the days before committing to Christ, she had questioned herself, "What *do* I have to show for doing things my way?"

As a follower of Christ, God would guide her to a better way. A way of hope, protection, and provision for her and for her baby. God is in the business of restoration. "The One who began this gracious work in you will faithfully continue the process of maturing you until the unveiling of our Lord Jesus Christ" (Philippians 1:6 TPT).

"The One who began this gracious work in you will faithfully continue the process of maturing you."

Philippians 1:6 TPT

2. The Blonde Buddhist Client: ***Meeting Past Pain with Truth***

God's ways are transformative. He produces radical changes in the heart and leads to new directions. When one's heart experiences repentance (literally, thinking differently), life pivots to a healthier, new direction.

A tall blonde named Lexi walked into the counseling office and sat down. She was in her early forties, single, and soon it would be learned her relationship with the father of the baby was emotionally volatile. In addition, she was suffering from hyperemesis gravidarum (HG), a pregnancy complication typically characterized by nausea throughout the twentieth week, and at worst, day and night throughout the nine months. (In Lexi's case, symptoms lasted throughout the entire pregnancy.)

When the session got underway, Lexi learned it was a Christian center. "Oh, I didn't know you all were Christians. I'm a Buddhist." The woman didn't appear like a stereotypical Buddhist. The advocate asked if she had been a Buddhist all her life.

"No," she said. "I grew up in a home where both my parents were Christian pastors. Though I was always in church, being a PK, I always felt judged growing up." (By escaping from the pain she associated with Christianity, she felt protected from further judgment.)

The advocate segued into sharing her salvation testimony: "Although I wasn't a preacher's kid, I was raised in a church that didn't talk about a personal relationship with Christ, so it didn't adequately fill my spiritual hunger. I longed for something more, so I began studying different faiths. Frankly, it became confusing since the Hindus think they're right, the Buddhists think they're right, the Muslims think they're right, and the Christians think they're right. So, I reached the conclusion that no one can reach a conclusion! I settled on believing that Jesus and all the other key persons of the different world religions were simply enlightened and possibly in the category of a *prophet*. When I continued reading religious material, I discovered Jesus is the only prophet who claimed He was God. The question became: Do prophets lie? Many Buddhists consider Jesus an enlightened being. If true, would an enlightened being lie and say He was God?"

(This is an opportunity to discuss more with the client.)

The advocate continued, "God would use these mental musings to ultimately lead me to truth. When confronted with Jesus's unique claim to be God, the Holy Spirit empowered me to believe Him. This led to asking Him into my life, which instantly brought peace."

He produces radical changes in the heart and leads to new directions.

Lexi was a good listener, but she wasn't ready to make a major spiritual change. A follow-up visit offered additional opportunities for discussion.

Because a warm rapport had been established during the first session, her returning visit for an ultrasound brought more transparency. She confessed, "I was testing you the last time I was here when I said I was a Buddhist. I wanted to see if you were judgmental."

The advocate grinned as she welcomed Lexi's honesty.

Lexi went on to say her attendance at the Buddhist meditation sessions was true, although she had only attended twice. She added, "Religion-wise, I don't really consider myself to be *anything*."

Lexi indignantly voiced she still couldn't tolerate Christianity's legalism. "I feel there's no peace to be found in a judgmental religion of *do* this and *don't do that!*"

The advocate explained Christianity isn't meant to be a rule book. "Even the *purpose* of the Ten Commandments is to establish a moral standard and, in this respect, act as a schoolmaster to teach how much we need Christ to live righteously. Without Him, we either remain unrighteous or self-righteous. Knowing our need for a Savior God, 'the Law has become our guardian *to lead us* to Christ, so that we may be justified by faith'" (Galatians 3:24 NASB, emphasis added).

She continued, "Jesus summed up the Ten Commandments. 'You shall love the LORD your God with all your heart, with all your soul, and with all your mind.' He added, 'You shall love your neighbor as yourself' (Matthew 22:37, 39 NKJV). Only Jesus could perfectly live up to this, while our own fallible lives reflect a gross inability to measure up. Only a spirit-filled life can enable living godly lives."

This brief discussion was life-changing for Lexi. It was a new thought to regard the law as schooling us in the impossibility of living up to the Commandments on our own. Even if it were true that we'd never lied, stolen, or committed adultery, etc., our *thought* lives would fail the moral standard. Because our thoughts cannot be perfectly managed, it reveals the spiritual need for a Savior.

Lexi and her advocate discussed legalism, which is trying to follow the Christian rules without surrendering our lives and hearts to Him. Legalism loses significance when we know we are not saved by our obedience to the Ten Commandments, nor by good works. We are saved by placing our faith in and believing Jesus is God in the flesh who came to earth to die to pay the penalty for our sins and give us the gift of resurrected life. The advocate shared a Scripture with Lexi: "For by grace you've been saved by faith and that not of yourselves; it is the gift of God, not of works, lest anyone should boast" (Ephesians 2:8–9 NKJV).

After a hearty discussion highlighting grace as the heart of Christianity, Lexi was ready to receive Christ into her life. Still a bit "wobbly" as a new believer, she still had not ruled out abortion. She was alone, and she had no support from the boyfriend who obnoxiously told her, "Kill it!"

Despite her anger at him, she was vacillating. "It's really not the right timing for a baby; I'm halfway through my second master's degree." Then she would shift, "But at my age, I might never be able to get pregnant again."

"Lexi," her advocate said, "give yourself permission to slow down! Take your time in walking through this process—pray, ask God what to do, and He will make it clear."

Lexi took the advice and spent a few days at a friend's cottage to pray and ponder the crossroad. Though she and the boyfriend were coldly estranged, the advocate's care and concern had become a major source of support. When Lexi returned from the short retreat, there was a positive movement toward giving life to her baby, whom she *just knew* was a boy. Lexi was now attaching *personhood* to the child she was carrying, a good sign that needed reinforcement.

Her ultimate decision involved a real person.

It was time to cast a vision to strengthen Lexi's grasp of reality. Her ultimate decision involved a *real person.* "Lexi," the advocate began, "one day you will look lovingly at your beautiful child, and you'll smile when you say to him, 'You will never know what I went through to bring you into this world. But you were worth it and still *are*!'"

Weeks flew by, and Lexi made an appointment for a second ultrasound, which she hoped would clarify her ultimate decision. She came in as planned and lay down on the gurney—her long body overlapped the length. The nurse positioned her for the procedure to begin, and a few minutes later, her baby's imagery appeared on the screen.

"O my gosh!" Lexi exclaimed. "Look at his long, long legs. They're just like mine!" God used the length of a baby's legs as the game changer! In the span of a moment, an ultrasound had consumed Lexi's indecision. She quietly said, "I am going to keep my baby." And she did.

God used the length of a baby's legs as the game changer!

At term, Lexi's son was born, and a couple of months later, she brought her baby boy to the center and introduced him to staff. Visibly transformed by the choice she had made, she marveled that her baby had an easy, pleasant temperament. She laughed when she added, "Despite all the *stress hormones* during my pregnancy."

One year later, Lexi moved out of state. Another year passed, and her advocate at the center received a note from her. An excerpt reads:

> My "baby" continues to be an awesome child. He's two now and full of curiosity and the wonder of life. We have moved out of state to be closer to family, and I've found a wonderful church full of love for Jesus. I'm also singing in the choir.

Every client's life is unique. Many have had a past abortion, and some will have one in the future. Some come with sound Christian beliefs, while others mix spiritual beliefs with secular beliefs. Though issues and beliefs are at times relative, we continue to speak truth in love.

Guiding the Client to Truth: Client Scenarios

1. The Client: *Blame-Shifting Beliefs*

"Why did God let me get pregnant?" asked the angry nineteen-year-old battling a crisis pregnancy. Her skewed theology had easily entered the mix to avoid responsibility. She repeated, "If there's a merciful God, why did God let me get pregnant?"

The advocate replied, "God has created and established physical laws in the universe. If you drop a pen (the advocate demonstrates), it falls to the floor. That's called the law of gravity. There are also *biological* laws God has established. When a sperm and an egg unite, a baby results. So how can any of us blame God, who already clearly established the way things work, along with His guidelines for sex in the Bible?" (Discussion.)

At times the advocate opts for another analogy to enlighten understanding: "When we see a street sign that posts a twenty-five miles per hour speed zone, and a car accident occurs by speeding at one-hundred miles per hour, who is responsible? Is it the lawmakers or the driver?" (Discuss briefly with client.)

The advocate continued, "We know that God, as a lawmaker, does not sin. He desires, for those who are single, the protection of living within His guidelines; one of those is abstinence before marriage. Despite not following His guideline, it doesn't change His love for you. In fact, He wants to walk through this situation with you. Will you let Him do that?"

If the client is interested, proceed to a Gospel presentation: "The good news for all of us is that God invites us to know Him. Can I show you a little booklet that explains this?" If appropriate, the advocate can begin with her testimony (or excerpt) and proceed to the Gospel message.

2. The Client: ***Presumption of Belief***

Likely, the quick-fix remedy of abortion voids the threat to her status quo.

The client announces to her advocate, "I'm getting an abortion, and since my God is a forgiving God, He will just have to forgive me." The client's statement lacks understanding about a relationship with God. Instead, it's a demand for grace based on a sense of entitlement. She is presuming upon God's grace. *Cheap grace*, some have called it.

Yes, if she is a believer, albeit a misguided one, then her sins have been wiped clean. The client seems to acknowledge that the Cross provided forgiveness from her sins. However, she isn't recognizing God's disdain for legalism that implies human good works provide merit enough to earn forgiveness of sins and salvation. Her heart is darkened to her own beguilement. God cannot be manipulated based on the thought that He owes her because she received His costly gift of salvation. (Somewhat like a *gotcha*.)

The presumption is self-focused. It is also manipulative. As she seeks her freedom independently of God, He could allow her to experience hardness of heart. The forgiveness of sins provided at the Cross becomes more elusive. Because of His unchanging love for her, God desires to be there for her, to walk through her situation with her, to forgive and grow her through the process.

What is driving her to abort? Likely, the quick-fix remedy of abortion voids the threat to her status quo. She has yet to learn that "fixing [her] eyes on Jesus" will enable her not to "grow weary and lose heart" (Hebrews 12:1, 3 NIV). Living in estrangement from Christ can never bring her peace.

NOTE to advocates: This client, though she recognizes the great mercy of God, is making demands of Him. This reflects self-focused entitlement. This may be a reason to question the authenticity of her salvation. Explore this. If the advocate is convinced she has made a bona fide commitment to Him in her past, then surely this client needs a recommitment to get back on track with Him. Explore her willingness.

---

3. The Client: *Guilt-Producing Beliefs*

Casey had just had her pregnancy confirmed and was struggling with the next step to take. During earlier weeks, suspecting she was pregnant, the father of the baby abandoned her. Currently, his whereabouts were unknown. Although Casey had finished three years of classes at a well-known university, she was having difficulty making it to the finish line to complete her degree. Her job background was also inconsistent.

She needed someone to believe in her.

Casey's first trip to the pregnancy center both confirmed the pregnancy and brought her to a renewed relationship with Christ. She needed someone to believe in her and found comfort by calling her advocate occasionally or dropping in unexpectedly. She was needy, and the spiritual conversations boosted her young faith and strengthened her will to carry her baby to term.

When Casey's baby boy was born, she returned to the center so the staff could meet him. A few minutes later, seated in her advocate's office, she glanced lovingly at her tiny son in the baby carrier. When she glanced back at her advocate, guilt swept across her face, and she blurted, "To think I almost aborted him!" (The accuser of the brethren was taunting her again with an option she had rejected: aborting the baby.)

"Casey," the advocate began, "through very difficult circumstances, didn't you choose to give life to your baby?"

"Yes."

"You have also rededicated your life to God and repented from living outside of God's best guidelines for you."

Casey nodded.

"So, don't you think it's time to simply love your darling baby and enjoy him? Remember, even Jesus was tempted but did not sin!"

That Jesus was also tempted had never occurred to Casey. It was a truth that visibly lifted her burden of guilt. It is the advocate's great privilege to speak on God's behalf.

4. The Client: *Peace—Mindset or Emotion?* (Isaiah 9:6)

When a client transitions from believing Christian precepts are true to making a decision to become a follower of Jesus as personal Savior, she receives God's gift of peace.

Ann, a pregnant client, spoke about needing peace amid her anxiety. The discussion began with her advocate asking, "So you're feeling the need for peace?" The advocate related to the expressed need by sharing her testimony. "In my own life, I was searching for peace also. I was always baffled when I heard Jesus was called the Prince of Peace. I knew that prior to His crucifixion, the Bible says He sweated blood the day before. How could He be called the Prince of Peace and then sweat blood?"

Peace is a mindset—a thought, not a feeling.

The client acknowledged the contradiction.

The advocate continued, "Later, I would realize peace is a mindset—a *thought*, not a feeling. For instance, we know Jesus, aware he would soon be dying on a cross, fixed His mind on the joy ahead." The advocate located the verse in Hebrews and invited the client to read. "As you read this, what do you think is 'the joy' Jesus believes lies ahead?"

The client read, "For the joy set before him he endured the cross, scorning its shame, and sat down at the right hand of the throne of God" (Hebrews 12:2 NIV).

The advocate discussed "the joy set before Him" with her client. "Jesus, about to be killed, experienced joy because He believed in the eternal redemption His death made possible. This belief, this mindset, brought Jesus peace despite the great suffering involved."

A discussion followed regarding choosing God's will for her baby despite the client's present suffering. "When choices are pleasing to God, you'll experience the joy of following His will!"

....

The following illustration can be used as a teaching tool with clients. It will help them understand how thoughts and emotions interplay with one another and can lead to positive choices.

What the mind believes rouses the emotions felt. An advocate explains to her client that thoughts of distress lead to an interruption of peace. She explains, "As your faith in Jesus matures and you believe He is walking through your situation with you, you experience greater joy and peace. I'll give you an example of how that happens.

"Let's look at the way our emotions align with what we believe. Let's say that you're alone in your house, working at your home office located in the basement. It's late and it's dark, and suddenly you hear the screen door banging furiously. It prompts quick thoughts. You recall hearing about a recent neighborhood break-in a few months prior, and the thought heightens your anxiety. *Is someone trying to break in?* After a minute, the banging stops. You flick off the lights and tiptoe toward the door. Your emotions have reached a 'ten.'

"Suddenly, you hear a howling gust of wind, and the door furiously bangs again. This time, however, you feel confident you're not dealing with a break-in. What you had initially thought no longer fuels your anxiety, and your emotions lower from ten to zero. Your newfound peace is now attached to the credible belief that the storm had caused the banging door. You are safe. The assessment your mind has made normalizes emotions." The advocate pauses a moment before asking, "How do you think this story ties in with your unexpected pregnancy?"

The advocate continues, "Today you may be experiencing anxiety based on emotions about your pregnancy situation, but your anxiety will diminish when you believe God desires to be with you and walk this out with you. It's a situation where He's calling you to turn to Him and trust Him with your life. He has the answers and wants you to trust Him. Do you ever think about spiritual things?" (A simple question, but it launches spiritual discussion.)

✎ **NOTE:** Chapter 4 gives a detailed account of the importance of personal testimony. Chapter 5 describes specifics to prepare one's personal testimony.

After some discussion, the advocate could ask, "May I share something personal from my own life?" She might begin: "In my own life, I remember a time when I was experiencing quite a challenge!" (This could be a *topic* or *situation testimony* giving credit to God for getting you through some ordeal. This could also be the right timing to share a situation that led to receiving Christ into one's life—a *salvation testimony*.)

5. The Client: ***Suppressor of Truth***

Thinking people do wonder about God—even those living a lifestyle dismissive of Him. (In which case, we can help her revisit the spiritual aspect of her life.) Biblically, we know God has already imprinted an awareness of something or Someone greater than oneself. Even when we choose not to give God due recognition, we bear His image. Without His indwelling Spirit, we remain incomplete image bearers.

Thinking people do wonder about God—even those living a lifestyle dismissive of Him.

There have been times when, at the beginning of the client session, the client states that she believes in God but "isn't religious."

"Oh, that's interesting! Tell me how you would define *religion.*" After a short discussion, you might explain, "Scripture tells us everyone knows in their heart there is a God. However, we can also become *suppressors* of the truth (Romans 1:18). Sometimes people suppress awareness of God by denying His ability to work in our lives. Others hope to push Him from consciousness. Yet when a crisis comes, the suppression is often weakened by desperate feelings. When crisis dislodges Him, they may reconsider the Savior."

We also see clients who say they haven't made up their minds about what to believe, yet, by the end of the session, after thoughtful discussion, they receive Christ. All along, a client may have genuinely *wanted* to believe but simply needed encouragement.

6. The Client: ***Procrastinator***

When the advocate shared her testimony with a young Mongolian client in her twenties, the client responded, "Someday I'm going to look into religion more." (A kairos moment—do not forego sharing.)

The advocate replied, "You don't have to wait until someday. Did you know that God already knows you by name (Isaiah 43:1)?"

The client's head jerked back, and her mouth gaped open with unfeigned shock. "What? You mean He *knows* my name?" (A kairos moment.)

"Yes, He not only knows your name but has reserved a *secret name* for you in heaven." (This knowledge always seems to intrigue the client and inclines her to listen.) "Undoubtedly, God's secret name for you fully expresses your special uniqueness as a person. Scripture says, 'And I will give [them] a white stone, and on the stone a new name written which no one knows except him who receives it' (Revelation 2:17 NKJV). Here, God is speaking only to the believer. The white stone stands for innocence and freedom from guilt because Jesus has paid the price for His spiritual children.

"Much like a caring parent who has given her child an endearing nickname, the name God has chosen is also endearing. It will surely capture the very essence about a person to reveal special qualities of character He's instilled." (Briefly speak to this idea with your client. For instance, ask if she ever had a nickname.)

During this pivotal moment, demonic activity often stirs. Be patiently discerning.

As the advocate and client began to tangibly connect through the discussion, the advocate offered to share a little booklet. Picking up the Gospel tract, she proceeded to share points of the Gospel, then explained how the client could go deeper in her personal relationship with Him through yielding her life. (*The ask* refers to asking the client if she would like to pray the prayer of salvation to receive Jesus into her life.)

"Would you like to say a prayer to assure you Christ is in your life personally?"

During this pivotal moment, demonic activity often stirs. Be patiently discerning. For instance, one client said, "I'm afraid of not following through if I make this decision." Fear comes from the Enemy. Her statement may also reflect a flesh pattern of inconsistency. Either way, the response needs to be addressed, such as: "Scripture tells us God gives us the desires of our heart. If you have the desire to follow Christ, even when you sin, just confess that you have slipped off track and thank Him that He welcomes your return."

7. The Client: ***A Broken Seeker***

The client's words were riddled with pain: "My broken heart feels like having a broken rib. Everything appears fine on the outside, but it hurts with every breath."

How could our troubled young client have known she had been prayed for that very morning? The prayer-warrior staff had prayed for all appointments that day, for our clients' openness to the transforming love of a Savior.

The advocate listened to the young woman's pain. She resembled Isaiah's description of a "woman forsaken and grieved in spirit" (Isaiah 54:6 NKJV). Plainly, she needed God's presence in her life. The advocate described the love story between the Savior and those who respond to Him. In her pain, He was wooing her closer until she received the gift of a Savior who died a torturous death on her behalf to bring acceptance with God. Through her emotional pain and drawn to the hope of salvation, God had won her attention. The message of the *spoken* Gospel had met her longing. Restoration had begun.

The Ask

Captured in the moments of sacred silence is an ancient doorway that leads to truth.

After an advocate explains the Gospel to her client, they are at the point of "the ask," referring to the prayer of salvation. Sometimes the ask is initially met with *sacred silence,* a deeply quiet pause heavy with the decision set before her.

- Be still and refrain from filling the void with idle talk. "Be still and know that I am God" (Psalm 46:10 NIV).
- During silence, pray. "In the name of Jesus, I break down the strongholds in her life so that she can be free to worship You."
- Allow the client ample time to respond to the invitation to receive Christ.

Captured in the moments of *sacred silence* is an ancient doorway that leads to truth. One that bids entrance to the Savior, a passageway to a kingdom.

We are "the called out" ones—*ecclesia,* the living church called to spread the Good News of the Gospel.[10] Jesus, our High Priest, appoints us as His "royal priesthood" (1 Peter 2:9 NIV) to serve others. And so we pray, "Lord, fill me to the brim with your Spirit that I may speak into lifetimes."

Chapter Three

Lifting the Veil of Unbelief

Father, use us to share Your love with others that they would know (experience) the Bridegroom.

(Prayer based on 2 Corinthians 11:2 NKJV)

God has planned a celebration for every believer! As a *future* event, Jesus, as the betrothed Bridegroom, will wed His church in heaven's "marriage of the Lamb." (Revelation 19:7) We can be assured: "These are the true sayings of God" (v. 9).

The marriage supper that follows will take place on earth, during the millennium after Christ's return. For now, as believers, we, His church, enjoy the unity of our betrothal to Jesus. The term *betrothal* in Jewish law is "to contract an actual though incomplete marriage. . . . In strict accordance with this sense, the rabbinical law declares that the betrothal is equivalent to an actual marriage and only to be dissolved by a formal divorce."[1]

For some, the Bridegroom entered our earthly lives through an arduous path, fraught with detours and resistance. For others, the walk has been unhindered, fluid and free. Despite the pathway, each of us was drawn into a covenant with Him of committed love. In the moment of "I do," we receive Jesus, our Groom, and the veil of spiritual darkness lifts. Our covenant is sealed, and words spill freely, "I will shout and sing your praises for all you are to me—Savior, Lover of my soul!" (Psalm 71:23 TPT).

> Let everyone who hears this duet join them in saying, "Come." Let everyone gripped with spiritual thirst say, "Come." And let everyone who craves the gift of living water come and drink it freely. "Come." (Revelation 22:17 TPT)

In the moment of "I do," we receive Jesus, our Groom, and the veil of spiritual darkness lifts.

"I do" removes the veil by personal consent and, a new destiny joins with the life of her Bridegroom.

Unveiling Brings Revelation

We, who know our Bridegroom, find salvation too wonderful to be confined. We call to others, "Come." Our invitation to His kingdom extends to our center's clients. The young woman wrapped in neediness and parched by spiritual thirst, craves living water in her search for *something more*. She has walked through the thresholds of our centers. She has stepped down the aisle of our hallways, led to an ordinary-looking room bidding entrance. Soon the opportunity presents a transformational question: "Would you like Jesus to be part of your life?" "I do" removes the veil by personal consent and, a new destiny joins with the life of her Bridegroom.

Every believer's covenant with Jesus is a love story in special spiritual union with others of one mind, heart and spirit. As followers of Christ, we enter a joyous matrimony with the Lover of our souls. With lifted veil, we now see Him clearly and discover new depths of understanding.

NOTE: The word *veil* means "to hide or to cover," thus, the *unveiling* refers to "revelation."[2]

Today, clients still replicate the walk to the altar of self-surrender. A sacred decision to embrace Christ as Savior will reach forever through eternity.

Your Client's Greatest Need

This hope we have as an anchor of the soul, both sure and steadfast. (Hebrews 6:19 NKJV)

Lenora had lived with dysfunction all her life—an angry father, angry Marine brother, and angry boyfriend. As a teen, she was deserted by her mother, who left the home in the middle of the night with two younger siblings—abandonment under the cover of darkness. Soon afterward came the traumatic breakup with an abusive boyfriend and her discovery of pregnancy.

"Do you feel you have support from anyone?" the advocate asked. "No, even my best friend, or should I say, my *former* best friend, who's twenty-five years old, is having an affair with my father!"

Would we even think of sending this client on her way after pregnancy confirmation and a fistful of referrals? There is so much more to pour into this languishing soul! So much more than abandoning her to the regret of a belly swelling with life. Though she is unaware of *how* anything can change for the better, it is the love of Jesus she needs—the Savior of the world who offers a "firm foundation to grow upon."

The advocate could connect with the young woman's despair. By sharing her testimony, she revealed she, too, had lacked a sure foundation for her life. "Quite frankly, without Christ in my life, I was incapable of making the wisest choices for my life."

As the advocate shared her real-life story, she won the client's attention. Immediately following the advocate's testimony, Lenora responded. "That's *exactly* what I need for my life. A foundation!"

When the advocate shared the Gospel message, the throne of God drew near. She presented the Gospel through a spiritual tract, and, faced with the decision of praying the prayer, Lenora responded eagerly to receiving Jesus.

Lenora's decision was so much more than she could have asked or imagined. Inviting Christ to be the new foundation for her life freed her faith to soar. Before leaving the center, Lenora received practical and spiritual resources that would stabilize some of the challenges ahead. An ultrasound was also scheduled. Yet, by far, the greatest resource Lenora had received was Christ—the "anchor for the soul" (Hebrews 6:19 NIV).

Removing the Veil of Unbelief

> For even to this day that same veil comes over their minds when they hear the words of the former covenant. The veil . . . is only eliminated when one is joined to the Messiah. (2 Corinthians 3:14 TPT)

The spiritual conversation was underway when Jan, a twenty-three-year-old client, suddenly blurted, "To tell you the truth, I've tried, really tried, to read my Bible. But it seems every time I start to read, I can't understand any of it. It's so confusing to me!"

When one turns to the Lord, the veil is taken away.

Immediately, the Holy Spirit imparted His message to the advocate: "A veil is over her mind."

God's revelations of the Spirit are only discovered by an illumination by the Spirit (1 Corinthians 2:14 TPT). It was time to address Jan's confusion. "Jan, was there ever a time when you invited Christ to take control of your life?"

"No, I never have." (This confirmed the *veil over her mind.*)

"May I show you a verse that has given me greater understanding for my own life?"

The client was open, and the advocate picked up the nearby Bible and read 2 Corinthians 3:16 (NKJV) to her. "Nevertheless, when one turns to the Lord, the veil is taken away." This time, spiritual revelation was possible. Jan was seeking, and the Spirit was meeting her needs.

More discussion followed regarding the veil. This included the advocate's testimony, which spoke of the worldly life she had led before knowing Christ, yet He had never forsaken her. It was a transformative thought that her life could be different. With renewed hope, Jan listened attentively and before leaving the center, she yielded her life to Jesus. The veil of spiritual blindness had lifted.

A Couple's Unity with God

A center visit confirmed to Jesse that she was pregnant. Although she was single, she welcomed the news. "My fiancé and I are getting married in just four days!" she chirped happily.

The advocate congratulated her on the upcoming plans. "That's wonderful, Jesse. Marriage is such a God-honoring event."

Jesse took the detour. "Yes, my mom has been asking me for some time to attend church with her, and even my fiancé has said he'd like to get baptized." (The kairos moment.)

"Sounds like your fiancé is open to a greater spiritual experience!"

"Yes, he's very spiritual." (Spiritual can mean different things to different people.)

The advocate homed in on the comment. "As an adult, getting baptized is reflective of one's deeper step with God since Scripture says, 'Repent and be baptized.'" (Discussion followed to include repentance and baptism)

NOTE: Repentance involves confession of wrongdoing and turning away from sin. Baptism is an outward manifestation of an inner change of heart. It witnesses to one's willingness to bury the old self. Denominations practicing submersion into the baptismal waters illustrate burial. Rising from submersion illustrates the new, resurrected life with Christ.

"Jesse, since you are getting married in just four days, would you like to be more personally and spiritually unified with your fiancé?"

"Oh yes!" she replied enthusiastically.

The advocate explained Scripture's "triple-braided cord" proverb that many Christians have used as symbolism applicable to the relationship between the husband, the wife, and the Holy Spirit. "When God is invited to be part of a marriage, we have assurance of His presence through life's trials," she said.

"In the Scripture verses from Ecclesiastes 4:9–12, we read of powerful encouragement to assure us of spiritual unity in marriage."

The advocate had her client read the passage: "And if one can overpower him who is alone, two can resist him. A cord of three strands is not quickly torn apart" (v. 12 NASB).

The advocate asked, "What do you think that can mean for a marriage?" (It means withstanding life's challenges with the help of God.)

The advocate chuckled when she shared, "Jesse, in my own life, you might say that I've 'done marriage' *with* Christ and 'done marriage' *without* Christ, and I can tell you *with* Christ is better!" She spoke of the difference Jesus makes in sustaining the unity between a husband and wife. "God affects everything—even readiness to forgive each other when issues arise."

The soon-to-be bride became animated, her words enthusiastic with the idea that Christ could join their marriage union to empower their harmony.

The advocate presented the Gospel message, and the unveiling of salvation came with the encouraging words from the Bridegroom whose glory is seen in the everyday life of a husband and wife in harmony with Him. "Did I not say to you that if you would believe you would see the glory of God?" (John 11:40 NKJV).

"Did I not say to you that if you would believe you would see the glory of God?"

John 11:40 NKJV

Historical Significance of the Veil

> Jesus cried out again with a loud [agonized] voice, and gave up His spirit [voluntarily, sovereignly dismissing and releasing His spirit from His body in submission to His Father's plan]. And [at once] the veil [of the Holy of Holies] of the temple was torn in two from top to bottom; the earth shook and the rocks were split apart. (Matthew 27:50–51 AMP)

On the Day of Atonement, all priests were forbidden entrance to the sacred Holy of Holies where God's presence dwelled. Only the high priest could enter to make the blood sacrifice of an unblemished lamb. (Other days of the year, sacrifices were offered in the courts outside the temple.) Because the high priest never entered the Holy of Holies without bringing a blood sacrifice, it served as a reminder of the sin that separated humanity from God.

On the day of Christ's death on the Cross, His blood sacrifice had opened the way for our salvation: "[We] who once were far off have been brought near by the blood of Christ" (Ephesians 2:13 NKJV).

J. Vernon McGee described it this way:

> When the temple of Solomon was erected, the veil was perpetuated in the temple, only it was larger and more elaborate . . . Josephus tells us that it was four inches thick . . . wild horses tied to each end of the veil, after it had been taken down, were not able to rend it asunder. . . . The veil was a prophetic picture-parable of the humanity of Christ—a silent symbol of the Incarnation. As long as the veil hung in its place, it separated God and man. . . . When Christ expired, the veil was rent, telling out in a symbolic way that

> the way into God was now open, and that it required nothing short of the death of Christ.[3]

The yearly atonements for sin had foreshadowed something far greater. When we receive Jesus's gift of dying on the Cross for our sins, we are forgiven. A meaningful relationship with Him is now possible. Through Jesus, we are reconciled to God.

In the Greek, *reconciled* (*katallasso*) means a "one-sided enmity." Since God has already reconciled Himself to us through Christ's blood sacrifice, any hostility is our own.[4] Responding to His sacrifice on the Cross brings His reconciling peace.

> And you, who once were alienated and enemies
> in your mind by wicked works, yet now He
> has reconciled. (Colossians 1:21 NKJV)

Tetelestai: Sin's Sacrifice Completed!

Jesus's death on the Cross enabled the debt of sin to be fully and eternally paid. "So when Jesus had received the sour wine, He said, 'It is finished!' And bowing His Head, He gave up His spirit" (John 19:30 NKJV). The Greek word *tetelestai* (translated "it is finished") connotes "to bring to an end."[5] Therefore, he fulfilled Scripture and dealt with sin's debt.

Historically, *tetelestai* is a significant word of interest. Familiarity with the Roman penal system deepens our understanding.

> When a Roman citizen was convicted of a crime, he was thrown into prison. A "Certificate of Debt" listing all his crimes was nailed to his cell door so that anyone passing by could know what he had been accused of and the penalty assessed. When the prisoner had served his sentence and was released from bondage, the indictment was taken down from the door and the judge who had put him in prison would sign the indictment and write across it the word TETELESTAI. . . . He could rest in safety and security because the word TETELESTAI guaranteed his deliverance and his liberty. The charges for those crimes could never again be brought against him.[6]

"So when Jesus had received the sour wine, He said, 'It is finished!'" (John 19:30 NKJV). Freed from the penalty of sin on the merit of Jesus Christ, the believer is acceptable to God. He views us through the perfection of Christ's blood sacrifice.

A closer examination of *tetelestai* and its Greek perfect tense adds impact to Jesus's utterance. The perfect tense in Greek "is used to describe an action or process that (1) has been completed and (2) has produced results that are still in effect at the time of writing."[7] The

Greek word *tetelestai* declares that the event of dying on the Cross was completed in the past, but the redemptive effect continues. That is, we have the assurance that the sin debt has been completed and will continue to be completed.

> Having wiped out the handwriting of requirements
> that was against us, which was contrary to us.
> And He has taken it out of the way, having
> nailed it to the cross. (Colossians 2:14 NKJV)

Following the intake's format, the advocate asked the client, "Have you ever experienced an abortion?"

"Yes, one," Terry replied—eye contact suddenly shifting.

"Are you doing okay now?"

"Let's just say, I have learned to cope with it."

"Tell me more about that."

"Well," she began, "whenever the guilt returns, I go to confession. To be honest, I end up going all the time. I find the need to confess it repeatedly."

Confessing a past sin repeatedly may alleviate momentary anxiety, but it reveals distrust of God's forgiveness as a once-and-for-all event. It's as if Terry kept snipping a weed above the surface of the ground, but it kept regrowing because the unseen root was thriving. Yet the penalty of the sin had been paid in full over 2000 years ago. The debt was paid. When Terry received Christ, God removed sin "as far as the east is from the west" (Psalm 103:12 NIV). (The post-abortion Bible studies most centers offer can help clients receive the forgiveness of Christ and the freedom He intended from all sin—to include abortion.) Terry's recovery led to fully grasping what Jesus did: "I am writing to you, dear children, because your sins have been forgiven on account of his name" (1 John 2:12 NIV).

"Your sins have been forgiven on account of his name."

1 John 2:12 NIV

NOTE: Scripture does not specifically tell individuals to forgive themselves. Advocates sometimes hear a client say, "I know God forgives me, but I can't forgive myself." More questions arise from a client's lack of self-forgiveness. Does she believe the Cross was sufficient to pay the penalty for sin? (Ask her.) Does she struggle with the inerrancy of God's Word? (Ask her.) Does she believe she is an "overcomer" like the Word says, or does she remain a victim of her past, unwilling to receive God's healing? (Ask her.)

Be bold but gentle when you say, "It's time to put an end to punishing yourself. As an act of will, are you ready to accept Christ's forgiveness and reset your life?"

Be bold but gentle when you say, "It's time to put an end to punishing yourself. As an act of will, are you ready to accept Christ's forgiveness and reset your life?"

The client must arrive at the point of recognizing that Christ paid a heavy price for her sins. If she continues to punish herself through guilt and condemnation, she chooses to pay her own reparation and discounts Jesus's sacrifice on our behalf. (Satan loves us to diminish the Savior's sacrifice.) "Beating oneself up" about a past confessed sin is like saying reparation is still needed. It is a lie from the Enemy of Our Souls.

All sins—past, present, and future—are covered by the blood of Christ. Some ask, "Why not continue to sin if past, present, and future sin have already been paid for?" Because surrender to Jesus exchanges the fleshly desire to sin with the heart's desire to follow Him.

> Delight yourself also in the LORD, And He shall give you the desires of your heart. (Psalm 37:4 NKJV)

Terry would later enroll in the center's post-abortion Bible study, and, for the first time, she deeply embraced the meaning of the Cross and the forgiveness Jesus offered. The crisis of belief played havoc until she grasped the implication of *tetelastai*. When the mind understands, emotions engage with belief. Indeed, the sin debt is *finished*.

Muslim Client: Unveiling the Mind

The advocate's love, patience, and perseverance become the tinder to kindle a godly outcome. Such was the story with Nora, a Muslim woman in her thirties with a small baby. She was a PhD candidate attending a nearby university. Through her citizenship in the Middle East, her embassy provided her with a monthly stipend. Because the family's income was limited, she had enrolled in a material needs program at the center that provided for monthly needs of diapers and baby items. (The program was a precursor to parenting classes entitled Earn While You Learn.)

The first day Nora arrived at the center, she was dressed in the weighty folds of a brown burqa with a traditional head covering called a hijab. Her advocate felt quietly intimidated by the visual cultural divide. As she got to know the bright, friendly woman, their differences no longer felt menacing.

Defensive barriers between the women were replaced by enjoying open discussion that included religious beliefs. At the time, the center offered monthly visits for material goods, so they met often. (This compensated for her embassy's meager monthly stipend for living costs.) Occasionally, her husband accompanied her and initiated aggressive conversations about the virtues of Islam. Aware of the center's affiliation as Christian, he was harshly adamant when speaking of the Muslim's view of Jesus. "Jesus didn't die on the Cross! It was Judas." His conclusion was that God would never let His own Son die in such a manner.

At such times, Nora became quiet.

When Nora arrived at her appointments alone, it assured greater freedom of discussion. This time, Nora's advocate spoke of how she, too, had once believed Jesus was "just a prophet—not God." This seemed to perk a cautious interest in knowing more.

Nora ventured to say, "We believe in Jesus too."

NOTE: In Islam, Jesus is not regarded as God. According to the Quran, he wasn't crucified, so no resurrection occurred. Muslims concede to belief in the historical figure of Jesus while asserting He too is a Muslim who will one day return to judge the world.[8]

Nora continued visiting the center regularly, and, one day, instead of a burqa, she arrived in Western fashion, dressed in slacks and a blouse. The hijab remained. Several more months passed, and this time, Nora arrived without the traditional hijab on her head. In its place was a small black felt hat.

When the advocate mentioned liking her hat, Nora giggled. However, at Nora's next appointment, she arrived without the hat. (The advocate refrained from comment.)

Another month passed, and Nora appeared wearing the small black felt hat again. This time, the advocate smiled and mentioned the change. "I see you're wearing your hat again, Nora."

"Yes," Nora laughed. "My hair was a mess!"

Did the on-again, off-again head covering visibly reveal a personal struggle to free herself from the dictates of custom in her country? Though suspect, reasons were unknown. The good news was the emerging open-mindedness detected by the advocate. Though the head covering had been a cultural choice, the advocate had viewed it as analogous to the veil covering the unbeliever's mind. As such, it was taking a progressively "diminished form," a tangible hope reflecting Nora's veil of spiritual darkness was subsiding. *Something* was happening. Nora also was freer with questions that explored different avenues of thought.

The veil of spiritual darkness was subsiding. Something was happening.

Easter was approaching, and a new film was making its debut which presented Jesus's life, death, and resurrection. The advocate sensed the gentle nudge of the Lord to invite Nora to view this feature film. She extended an invitation to the matinee, and Nora readily accepted. A few days later, they met at the theater and watched the film. Nora, fascinated by the Easter story, wept as she viewed Jesus's suffering.

Afterward, Nora's advocate encouraged her to tell her husband she had viewed the movie. She cautioned her to select the right timing. A few weeks later, Nora visited the center again for resources. She smiled when she said she had told her husband she'd seen the film.

"What did he say?" the advocate asked.

"He told me, 'I also went to see it!'"

The two women laughed.

Another month swept by, and Nora came to the center again—this time, her final visit before returning to her country. Her coursework was now completed, and she had recently received her doctorate. She was tearful as she confessed that she and her husband had been arguing that morning. Though she avoided specifics, the advocate spoke of the way Jesus understands what we are going through and will meet us during our greatest times of need. "He desires to comfort us. He wants to be a part of your life."

This time Nora appeared to listen from genuine need rather than intellectual interest.

Sorrow had created its unique path to seeking—and finding—Him.

At the close of the appointment, Nora revealed her decision to invite Jesus into her life. As she prayed a prayer inviting Jesus to take control of her life, she again began weeping softly. Sorrow had created its unique path to seeking—and finding—Him. By the time the prayer had ended, Nora was sobbing uncontrollably. Often when a Muslim converts to Christianity, God breaks mighty, spiritual strongholds. Dramatic conversions result.

When Nora's tears began to subside, the advocate asked what had touched her, and a shadow of a smile appeared as Nora wiped her eyes. "Jesus has forgiven me."

The covering upon her head had been removed months before. But now, on this sacred day, came the glorious lifting of the veil.

Helping Your Client Restore Purity

> You draw near to those who call out to you, listening closely, especially when their hearts are true. Every godly one receives even more than what they ask for. For you hear what their hearts really long for, and you bring them your saving strength. (Psalm 145:18–19 TPT)

Barely twenty years old, Rochelle arrived at the center for a pregnancy test, which was negative. During the intake section, regarding faith background, the client said she attended church regularly with her parents. She also said she prayed a lot. Though Rochelle believed the Bible to be true, the advocate learned the woman had never made a commitment to Christ.

As the interview intake progressed, Rochelle revealed a hurtful situation that occurred two years prior. At the time, she was a virgin, and her intent was to remain a virgin until marriage. However, one night during a date, her suitor pressured her to have sex with him. She gave in. Rochelle cried bitterly as she spoke of the shattering experience. "I had wanted to be the bride who saved her virginity for her future husband. And now everything is ruined!"

The advocate learned the incident had not only led to Rochelle's immediate feeling of guilt but also led to a promiscuous lifestyle. As the young woman spoke of the sexual encounters that had since followed, her eyes were downcast. The destructive weight of her shame had brought a sense of hopelessness. "What's the difference if I have sex now? I've already lost my virginity." (A kairos moment.)

The advocate, saddened by Rochelle's trauma, responded. "Thank you for sharing your feelings with me. Because of your desire to be a bride who saved her virginity for her husband, this must be a continuing grief for you.

Tearfully, Rochelle nodded.

"If it's okay with you, I'd like to share some thoughts about the purity you had desired to bring to a future marriage. You could say this is God's perspective. Did you know that in Scripture Jesus refers to Himself as the Bridegroom, and when we ask Him into our lives, we are called His bride?"

"No, I didn't know that."

"Yes, it's true," the advocate continued. "Though your previous desire to stay pure for your future husband is an honorable desire, receiving Christ into your life as your Bridegroom enables the truest of purities. He knew all along your heart's desire to be a virgin for your future husband, and He has already forgiven your acting out your disappointment. He desires His purity to be part of you, to indwell your spirit with His Spirit."

The advocate also addressed the guilt Rochelle felt from her promiscuous lifestyle. "Let's look up Luke 1:74–75 and read it," she said.

> "To grant us that we, Being delivered from the hand of our enemies, Might serve Him without fear, In holiness and righteousness before Him all the days of our life." (NKJV)

(They discussed the passage.) "Rochelle, this is good news for us! When we decide to be followers of Christ, He imparts His holiness and righteousness to dwell within us—in our spirit. When we become His followers, these are the defining traits of every believer. On the Cross, when He paid the penalty for our sins and exchanged our sins for His righteousness, Scripture tells us that He made sins become as "white as snow" (Isaiah 1:18 NKJV).

The young woman's expression was caught somewhere between awe, relief, and thankfulness. Finally, she managed to say, "I never knew that."

The advocate used a spiritual tract to share the Gospel with Rochelle, and, at the end of the booklet, without hesitation, Rochelle prayed to

"For you hear what their hearts really long for, and you bring them your saving strength."

Psalm 145:19 TPT

receive Him. God had used her burden of guilt to bring awareness of her need for a Savior.

> And we know that all things work together for good to those who love God, to those who are the called according to His purpose. (Romans 8:28 NKJV)

NOTE: Before leaving that day, Rochelle was given referrals that would serve to assist her practically as well.

"When wisdom wins your heart and revelation breaks in, true pleasure enters your soul"

Proverbs 2:10 TPT

Revelation Unveils Truth

> Nevertheless, when one turns to the Lord, the veil is taken away. (2 Corinthians 3:16 NKJV)

A Bible commentator noted: "Paul uses the metaphor of a veil to illustrate the inability of the Israelites to see the end of the fading glory under the Old Covenant, a veil that is removed in Christ. In doing so, he emphasizes the liberating power of the gospel, which unveils the minds of believers, allowing them to reflect the glory of the Lord with unveiled faces."[9] When the veil is removed, deeper knowledge comes. Truth brings an encounter with the falsehoods we've been believing. It prepares us for the ultimate commitment of saying "I do" to Christ, the eternal Bridegroom.

> When wisdom wins your heart and revelation breaks in, true pleasure enters your soul. (Proverbs 2:10 TPT)

The advocate had just asked the intake question about marital status. Sandy responded enthusiastically. "My boyfriend and I are living together. It's really like we're married already—we just don't have the piece of paper."

"I'm sure it can seem a lot like marriage. How long have you been living together?"

"For years. In fact, we have five-year-old twins, and I think we're expecting again." (Pregnancy test results were pending.)

"And you and your partner are doing well and still care about each other?"

"Oh yes." She smiled.

"Okay, Sandy, I've got to ask you something!" the advocate replied amiably. "Since you apparently care for each other and the two of you have children together, help me understand the reason you've chosen not to marry!" (The advocate avoided saying, "Why aren't you married?" since the word *why* causes defensiveness.)

The client replied, "We've talked about marriage, and, frankly, I wouldn't mind being married! Though he's agreeable about marriage, he keeps procrastinating about lining it up, getting the license, and all. I think he's the one who should take the initiative, not me!"

Saying "I Do" to Christ, the Bridegroom

The advocate replied, "I'd like to share a story with you—a true story. There was a dear couple who lived together for years. They shared a beautiful home together; they shared meals together; they shared bank accounts; they shared cars, and they also shared a bed. In every way, they appeared to be a married couple. Yet, they had never said, 'I do.' Since their commitment to one another had never been authenticated, the simple fact was they were not married."

Sandy nodded agreeably. "I hear what you're saying, and like I said, I wouldn't mind getting married, especially with another baby coming. I know you are Christian here. I'm a Christian too, but I haven't paid attention to my faith for a long time." (A kairos moment.)

"Is that something you would like to change in your life?" the advocate asked.

NOTE: This is an important follow-up question to a client's statement about being distant from one's faith.)

"Yes, I've been wanting to make some changes," Sandy said. "When I was a child, we always went to church, and I'd like to get back to what I believe."

NOTE: She is summing up her faith with church attendance, not a relationship with Christ.

"My fiancé is *supposed to be* a Christian too," Sandy added.

"In my own life," the advocate responded, "it took years before deciding to take that leap of faith and commit my life to Christ. We can believe in Christ; we can even know all about Christian doctrine but still withhold saying 'I do' to Jesus. It's the difference between dating and marriage; the latter involves greater commitment. So, Sandy, I ask you, would you be ready today to say 'I do' to Jesus? It means 'I do' want to follow You through a personal relationship with You."

"Yes, I want to do that. Thank you for challenging me."

That afternoon, Sandy committed her life to Christ.

Addressing Abstinence with Your Client

Nearing closure, the advocate said, "Before you leave, we need to talk about something that may be difficult. That is, God's desire for *abstinence* before you marry. Even if you're already pregnant, the abstinence issue doesn't change because we're talking about a *heart attitude of truly following God and guidelines that will deepen your relationship with Him.*" (Discussion.) "This will be challenging because the two of you have already been living together. Your fiancé has been dragging his feet about the marriage license, but there's something that may speed up his timetable!"

The advocate suggested the client share her new commitment to Christ with the boyfriend. "Share that you have made a decision to follow Christ, and as an unmarried person, you have the desire to live by God's guidelines." The advocate added, "I know your heart is truly to follow Christ, but your decision may also warm up motivation for a marriage license!"

The women chuckled. Sandy left soon afterward, expressing how excited she was to tell her partner about her new commitment to Christ.

Several months later, Sandy called her advocate to share an update. She said that when she returned home that day, she and her fiancé had a long talk. She shared her recommitment to Jesus. She said this led to his getting back in touch with his Christian faith. "Just a couple of days ago, we got married," she exclaimed. "Right now, I'm calling you from the airport because we're taking a flight to visit my family and celebrate!"

Saying "I do" to our Bridegroom untethers the beauty of our following Him.

> Even though you were once distant from him, living
> in the shadows of your evil thoughts and actions,
> he reconnected you back to himself. He released his
> supernatural peace to you through the sacrifice of His
> own body as the sin-payment on your behalf so that you
> would dwell in his presence. And now there is nothing
> between you and Father God, for he sees you as holy,
> flawless, and restored. (Colossians 1:21–22 TPT)

"And now there is nothing between you and Father God, for he sees you as holy, flawless, and restored."

Colossians 1:22 TPT

God's Timing for Client Restoration

The walk "down the aisle" of faith may take a while before saying "I do" to our Bridegroom. An advocate shares coming across a former client's email she had answered six years prior. With an adventurous spirit and hoping the email address was still valid, she decided to reach out to the former client for an update. At the time of her visit to the pregnancy center, Shelly was single, abortion-vulnerable, and a "cultural

Christian." At the time of the initial visit, she was not ready to commit her life to God. Although the Gospel message was shared with the client, the session had been little more than a sprinkling of God's Word. Shelly was non-committal, and the spiritual topic was dropped.

Now, curious to know what path Shelly's life had taken, the advocate sent her a brief but friendly email. The following was Shelly's reply.

> Hi! I got your email. Thank you! I had a baby boy five years ago and you guys played a huge part in that. Yes, I am in love with him though he sure knows how to push my buttons. I also had a baby girl a couple of years ago.
>
> Life is very busy but so rewarding. My heart is to homeschool the children and I pray every day that they grow up to be champions for Christ.

Our part is praying for our clients, sharing the Gospel, and trusting Jesus with the outcome.

Though Shelley had not shared a testimony of conversion, biblical truths shared six years before had taken root in an obviously softened heart. Jesus had not let go of her despite her earlier lack of readiness during her center visit. As advocates, our part is praying for our clients, sharing the Gospel, and trusting Jesus with the outcome. God says His Word "shall not return to Me void, But it shall accomplish what I please, And it shall prosper in the thing for which I sent it" (Isaiah 55:11 NKJV).

Satan would have us believe clients who aren't ready to yield their lives will *never* be ready to do so. The Enemy of Our Souls desires to convince us that, in the first place, we're likely wasting our time. Satan's falsehoods must not only be rejected but also exchanged with God's truth. We must tirelessly partner with our Savior, the Son who "came to seek and to save the lost."

NOTE: We keep practical resources available if the client is interested in taking them. This includes Bibles and Christian resources as well as a list of churches and faith-based support groups like MOPS (formerly Mothers of Preschoolers, now called MomCo for Mom Community), women's Bible studies, medical and non-medical community referrals and resources, information on furthering education, and even available scholarship opportunities, etc.

Beyond First Impressions of Your Client

So, then faith comes by hearing, and hearing by the word of God. (Romans 10:17 NKJV)

"So, then faith comes by hearing, and hearing by the word of God."

Romans 10:17 NKJV

"I have to get an abortion!" Leslie sounded adamant. A petite college girl with dark, shoulder-length hair, she wore a black T-shirt with white lettering on the front. It read, NAUGHTY GIRL. As the client walked toward the chair in the counseling room, the back of the T-shirt was now visible. It read, EVIL ONE.

Leslie's pregnancy test confirmed what she said was her greatest fear. She was pregnant. Since the father of her baby had suspected she was pregnant, he had already abandoned her. She said she felt angry about his lack of support for her.

Unknown to her, it was Jesus she needed, not an unsupportive boyfriend. The God who loved her desired to walk through the situation with her. Based on the messages advertised by the woman's T-shirt, her advocate thought, *There's next to zero chance she'll be interested in the Gospel.*

At ease with the advocate, Leslie's stress level came with a burst of words. "My mother already told me, 'If you get yourself pregnant, I want nothing more to do with you—you're out!'" Feeling she was unable to rely on her mother's help had reinforced her thoughts of abortion.

Much discussion followed, mingled with questions on the intake form. Finally, it was time for the advocate to introduce the topic of faith. "Leslie, do you ever think about spiritual things?"

"Oh yes," came the unexpected reply. "I used to go to a Catholic church with my mother in our country—in fact, she made us go to church all the time! She's so religious, she'd be furious with me if she found out I was pregnant. She always warned me, 'Don't you get pregnant. If you do, you need to get an abortion!"

The advocate asked, "So although your mom is 'religious,' she's okay with an abortion?"

"Yes, that's what she told me." (Always refrain from criticism.)

"Leslie," the advocate continued, "you said that while growing up, you and your mother went to church all the time. That must mean you know the family priest well."

"Oh yes, we sometimes invited him to dinner!"

"I have a thought that might prove helpful. When you go home next month for the summer, arrange a meeting with him. After you disclose the pregnancy, ask if he would be willing to break the news to your mother with you."

"Yes, that's good . . . I could do that!" Leslie replied.

"This is a difficult situation you're in, and with no support from your boyfriend, you'll need the support of your mom and your priest."

The client nodded her head.

"Leslie, you're also going to need God's strength for this situation, and He *wants* to walk through this with you! Are you open to getting your relationship with God back on track?"

NOTE: Sometimes it's unclear whether a commitment or recommitment is taking place. But this is not essential to know. God knows whether she is praying to dedicate or rededicate her life.

That day, the young woman yielded fully to Jesus. Her ability to see the truth had been obscured by a lifestyle lived apart from Christ. Though Satan had whispered many times, "*You have to get an abortion,*" his lies thrive only by the power we give them.

Satan's lies thrive only by the power we give them.

The outcome: As planned, Leslie met with the family's priest to disclose the pregnancy. The priest was supportive of continuing the pregnancy, and he accompanied her to break the news to the mother. Through his encouragement, the mother accepted her daughter's pregnancy and became supportive. God's plan of love and forgiveness had triumphed!

Witnessing to the Boyfriend

> Also, I say to you, whoever confesses Me before men, him the Son of Man also will confess before the angels of God. (Luke 12:8 NKJV)

It is always a special joy when a couple arrives at the center anticipating only a pregnancy test and then receives Christ into their lives. So it was with Hannah, who was twenty-one years old and accompanied by her boyfriend, Jarrett. As the intake and the pregnancy test with Hannah proceeded, Jarrett waited patiently in the waiting room.

When the pregnancy was confirmed, Hannah was elated. "My boyfriend is going to be so happy!"

When we began to discuss the spiritual aspect of her life, Hannah shared that a lot of people had talked to her about God, but she had never made a commitment to follow Him. (A kairos moment.) The advocate shared her personal testimony, which deepened Hannah's understanding that our faith is applicable to "real life." The Gospel followed and a few minutes later, the client prayed to commit her life to the Lord. Afterward, she spoke of her boyfriend's spiritual beliefs, and concluded, "I think he is a Christian."

"Whoever confesses Me before men, him the Son of Man also will confess before the angels of God."

Luke 12:8 NKJV

With Hannah's permission, Jarrett was invited to the counseling room. Both were happy about the confirmation of pregnancy. Because Hannah had asked her advocate to tell Jarrett about her commitment to Christ, Hannah's decision was shared. Jarrett's eyebrows rose, yet he looked unmistakably pleased (kairos).

The advocate asked if Jarrett if he had ever made the decision to ask God into his life. He replied, "No, but I used to attend church as a kid."

"Tell me more," the advocate said gently. A discussion followed, bringing assurance that Jarrett agreed with Christian beliefs.

When the advocate briefly shared her testimony, he responded, "Getting to know God really interests me." Soon, he, too, prayed a life-changing prayer of commitment.

Hannah and Jarrett discussed with the advocate the practical outworking of their faith. For instance, the new commitment to Jesus included following the Bible's guidelines for abstinence until marriage. It was also discussed that compliance could be especially challenging since Hannah was already pregnant.

"The fact that Hannah is pregnant really doesn't enter the abstinence issue because the real issue is following God as He has prescribed for persons not married. This is a heart attitude of being true to who you now are: believers," the advocate said.

They agreed they had the desire for their relationship to be "right" before God.

NOTE: At times, when a center offers a male mentor to meet with the boyfriend, the offer has been declined. If not at odds with your center's guidelines, this may suggest the same advocate who met with the girlfriend will now invite her boyfriend to join the latter part of the session. Other than inviting Christ into one's life, the boyfriend is the singular, most significant component influencing a choice for life. At times a topic testimony will illustrate the way God saw you through a difficult situation. Depending on the person, at times a female advocate is less intimidating to the boyfriend, and he readily interacts. Ask for God's discernment as you navigate Gospel sharing with a couple who has come to the center.

No More Cheap Grace

Now then, we are ambassadors for Christ, as though God were pleading through us: we implore you on Christ's behalf, be reconciled to God. (2 Corinthians 5:20 NKJV)

Grace is never cheap. It comes at great cost.

If a client were to say, "I feel so guilty; I've done a lot of bad things," *cheap grace* would reply, "Oh, that's okay, we all do bad things in our lives, but we have a forgiving God!"

Grace is *never* cheap. It comes at great cost. Jesus sacrificed His life on our behalf so we could receive forgiveness for our sins as well as His resurrected life and eternal life with Him. Cheap grace makes light of the Cross and the heavy penalty paid for the debt of our sins. Cheap grace dismisses the repercussions of sin. It neglects the need for the raw repentance of turning away from sin to follow the Savior.

Instead of cheap grace, when a client speaks of feeling guilty (a kairos moment), readily affirm the authenticity of valid guilt. In fact, the presence of genuine guilt reveals a sensitive conscience. The advocate could say, "We have all done things that we're now ashamed of. But even the most outrageous sins have been paid for at the Cross. In spite of ourselves, God loves us and wants to give us new life."

The situation is ripe for presenting a *topic testimony* to the client. "I, too, had a lot of sin in my life, and a tremendous ingratitude to Jesus was one of them. Before becoming a believer, I shamefully dismissed the greatest sacrifice in the world. I callously thought, *What's such a big deal about His dying for us? We've all heard about soldiers on the battlefield who have thrown themselves on a grenade to save others.* Then one day I read that when Jesus chose to go to the Cross for us, He accepted the sin burden for every human being who has ever lived, is currently living, or *will* live. Collectively! The weight of this cumulative sin must have been unbearable—only the Son of God could choose to endure it. It cost Jesus dearly to pay the penalty for our sins. His sacrifice enabled us to be washed of our sins. It enabled an eternity with Him. For the first time, I felt emotional pain for what He had gone through. For the first time, a deep sorrow penetrated my sin-filled life. It created in me a great gratitude for His love."

The advocate's honest sharing moves the discussion into the arena of the Gospel message. Near the end of reading the tract, she adds, "God removes our guilt. Scripture says, our sins can become *white as snow* (Isaiah 1:18). Do you feel ready to invite Him into your life? It means a time for yielding your life, your sins, and even your guilt to Him?"

"Yes!"

Client Restoration Brings Godly Choices

For You, Lord, are good, and ready to forgive,
And abundant in mercy to all those who
call upon You. (Psalm 86:5 NKJV)

When a single and pregnant client is convincingly a Christian, despite having wandered from her relationship with the Lord, a spiritual discussion may lead her to rededicate her life. By revisiting the client's lifestyle choices, a discussion can help reset the client's spiritual life. In no manner does this insinuate scolding her for past unwise choices. The intent is to restore.

In no manner does this insinuate scolding her for past unwise choices. The intent is to restore.

Reviving Your Client's Faith

Revive us again, O God! I know you will! Give
us a fresh start! Then all your people will taste
your joy and gladness. (Psalm 85:6 TPT)

When the advocate believes her client is a believer but not living to honor Christ, then "the talk" (not a scolding) must lovingly proceed. Often, the advocate finds the off-track Christian client appreciates help and encouragement with getting her life back on track with the Lord.

A Backslidden Client and Her Boyfriend

Meri, a nineteen-year-old from Nigeria, arrived at the center accompanied by her live-in boyfriend. They were seeking confirmation of pregnancy. When the test registered positive, she responded sweetly by saying she would keep her baby and take online college courses. (She could apply her college scholarship to do so.) During our faith discussion, she spoke of the closeness she had enjoyed with Jesus as a child. She also related a harrowing experience when she was twelve years old.

"About one hundred Muslim men with rifles invaded my village and were killing everyone. When they found me in the house where I had hidden, a man came up to me, and when he pushed the tip of the gun hard into my forehead, he shouted, 'Are you a Muslim?' I said, 'No, I am Christian.'"

God has a special plan for your life, and because He loves you, He longs for you to return to Him.

When the man aggressively demanded she convert to Islam, she became aware of a white light near her shoulder that periodically appeared to her. (She told the advocate she rarely shared this with others because she knew it sounded "crazy.") "This light always has brought comfort to me. As he kept shouting, the light gave me courage to say, 'I cannot convert. I am a Christian.'"

Then she closed her eyes tightly. She was waiting for him to kill her. "But nothing happened! After things were silent for a very long while," she said, "I opened my eyes and saw the men were gone!"

Hearing this, the advocate said, "My own faith has never been tested to the point of death like yours. Meri, God has a special plan for your life, and because He loves you, He longs for you to return to Him."

Meri said she was aware that the sexual relationship with her boyfriend interfered with truly following Christ. She confessed that she missed Him and said that she was ready to return to the Lord. After praying to rededicate her life to Christ, she asked if the advocate would be willing to speak to her boyfriend about Jesus. "I want my boyfriend to believe like I do," she said.

Because Meri wanted to be unified spiritually with her boyfriend, she was excited when the advocate agreed to speak with him. With Meri's approval, the advocate asked Jason, who was sitting in the waiting room, to join his girlfriend so that the "three of us could talk." As Jason entered, he smiled at Meri and looked expectantly at the two of them as if to ask, "Now what?"

The advocate spoke first. "Meri told me that I can share with you. She just rededicated her life to Christ. She also indicated she would love having a stronger, spiritual unity with you."

The boyfriend nodded pleasantly as the advocate proceeded.

"In my own life, I didn't accept Christ until I was in my thirties." The advocate continued to share her salvation testimony.

Turning to the boyfriend, the advocate asked, "Do you have a faith background, Jason?"

He nodded yes.

"I would love to hear more about it. Would you be willing to share?"

He was smiling as he recalled the memory. "Sure. I'm *supposed to be* a Baptist because about eight years ago, my Baptist grandmother brought up a discussion about God, and that led to saying a prayer to ask God into my life." His love for his grandmother seemed obvious. He chuckled amiably as he proceeded to dismantle the significance of what he had just shared. "I kept telling her I wasn't ready to say a prayer, but she kept pressuring me, and you don't say no to Grandma! So, I prayed just to please her."

"Jason, would that mean you didn't actually ask God to come into your life?"

He grinned—nodding his agreement. After explaining the Gospel to him, the advocate asked, "Right now, are you feeling genuinely ready for inviting Christ into your life. I mean *sincerely* without any feeling of, 'I have to do this?'"

Their eyes met and, the young man, looking more solemn, answered quietly, "Yes. I feel I'm ready now."

The advocate retold the Gospel, and in the gentle moments that followed, a young man's life-changing prayer became the delight of the God who waits patiently.

In the gentle moments that followed, a young man's life-changing prayer became the delight of the God who waits patiently.

Stories of God Surprises at Your Center

> Now to Him who is able to do exceedingly abundantly
> above all that we ask or think, according to the
> power that works in us. (Ephesians 3:20 NKJV)

When God promises to achieve infinitely more than our greatest request, this tells us that *God surprises* are in store. We constantly pray for God's interventions at the center, and He loves to deliver! Surely, He knows His God surprises give us the needed boost of enthusiasm for keeping our spiritual outreach motivated. Below are real-life examples that reflect God *entrusts us*—even with life's anomalies.

1. The GPS Versus God's Map: "Go ahead and make all the plans you want, but it's the Lord who will ultimately direct your steps" (Proverbs 16:1 TPT).

When a center embraces a willingness to share the Good News with others, God matches freedom of opportunity with the extraordinary.

A twenty-eight-year-old woman showed up at the front desk. Her disappointment was obvious when she learned that she had not arrived at an abortion clinic. Shocked and puzzled, she explained, "I was so careful when I entered the abortion clinic address into my GPS. This doesn't make any sense," she said. "Why did I end up here? I can't understand it!"

The staff member attempted to put her at ease. "Hey, it's okay that you're here. We can even do a free ultrasound for you today. We don't do the procedures, but we see many clients who are thinking about abortion and make us their first stop for pregnancy confirmation."

Because the center had an unscheduled two hours available, an ultrasound appointment could be offered if her pregnancy test registered positive. The client opted to remain at the center. An intake and options counseling took place. God's intervention presented an opportune moment to present the Gospel message to her. Although she listened well during the intake, she made no commitment. Yet, for now, God's plan had been fulfilled. She had heard the timeless message of the Gospel and was left with much to ponder.

2. God Controls Radio Airwaves—Knobs Too! When a center embraces a willingness to share the Good News with others, God matches freedom of opportunity with the extraordinary.

One day, a man called the center from out of state and, with no introductions, said, "I was just now searching for a good radio station in my car. Suddenly, I'm hearing some woman talk about religious things. I think her name was Beth . . . something like Beth Moore. She was talking about God, so I tried to change the station. When I turned the knob, the station wouldn't budge so I kept listening until she quit talking." There was a pause before he said, "Uh-h-h-h, you people there are Christian, right?"

The staff member confirmed they were.

He asked, "Well then, how do I get saved?"

After the volunteer shared the Gospel, this man prayed to receive Christ over the telephone.

3. No Coincidences. "God always makes his grace visible in Christ, who includes us as partners of his endless triumph" (2 Corinthians 2:14 TPT).

Still another God surprise served to remind the staff of God's sovereignty over the center and with its clients. God orchestrates events beyond happenstance.

One early morning a staff member at a pregnancy resource center was seated in her car at a drug store's parking lot. She had just turned on the engine to leave when she heard knocking on her car window. Looking up she saw a young woman appearing to be very ill and weak.

She quickly lowered her car window in response and listened to the young woman telling her she wasn't feeling well. She also apologized for asking but inquired about a ride to her workplace. "My cleaning job is just a mile from here." Though the staff member was not in the habit of giving rides to strangers, the woman's fragile appearance was compelling. It led to offering to take her to work.

Along the way, the stranger told her the reason she was ill. "I'm pregnant." The staff member shared that she worked at a pregnancy center, and when she mentioned its location, the amazed passenger said she had visited "that very center" recently. She also shared during her visit to the pregnancy center that she had committed her life to Christ.

Through the generous provision of a ride, this new believer was learning about God's personal and continuing involvement in her life. She also shared that just a few weeks before, a kindly, older man had spoken to her on the sidewalk near her home and asked her if she was homeless. Though she told him she wasn't homeless, he proceeded to give her his business card. He was a pastor from the nearby church, a large, non-denominational church, well-known in the area. Ever since then, she had begun to attend his church and joined their Bible-based program for mothers of preschoolers.

These are *God-incidences*! We constantly witness God's provision because He loves to respond to our individual needs. As we invite His Spirit to freely move, we offer a salvation opportunity to clients and a sense of purpose that constantly brings blessings to the staff. As a team serving Christ, the continuing adventure of supernatural living fuels our passion.

"God always makes his grace visible in Christ, who includes us as partners of his endless triumph"

2 Corinthians 2:14 TPT

NOTE: At times clients seem out of touch with themselves—with little self-awareness of seeking God to fill life's void. The seeker can be identified in simple ways, like her response to the question "Have you ever felt a longing for more fulfillment in your life?" Nodding her head yes has become a frequent prelude to deeper spiritual discussion.

A Center's *Rhema* Moment

Rhema, according to *Strong's Concordance*, is a word or words "said or spoken, an utterance."[10] Aligning with *logos* (the written word), rhema occurs when the written word "pops out" at you to speak in a personalized way to you. It can also occur when you hear words spoken by another person that especially connect with you, bringing insight and application to your life.

Whereas the written Word of God (the logos) is the actual message, rhema is the enhanced "communication of the message."[11]

> I would have lost heart, unless I had believed
> That I would see the goodness of the Lord
> In the land of the living. (Psalm 27:13 NKJV)

"Before coming to this center, I had made two appointments at the abortion clinic," Mardi told her advocate. "I canceled both at the last minute but ended up scheduling a third appointment. The Sunday before my appointment, I asked God to help me by giving me His *personal answer* for my situation. That Sunday I decided to go to church and was floored at the pastor's opening remarks. 'Choosing life for a baby, not abortion, is the best decision a person can make.' He added, 'It is a godly decision.' My pastor also shared his sermon notes had not included mentioning abortion, so he didn't know why he was talking about it." Her eyes danced when she said, "He didn't have any idea why he was saying it. But I did!"

God's response to Mardi was a rhema word, a precise message spoken directly to her need. Now, with a firm decision to carry her baby, Mardi had come to the center for referrals, an ultrasound, and an inquiry about the Earn While You Learn program.

God's response to Mardi was a rhema word, a precise message spoken directly to her need.

She was filled with excitement as she shared that she "was seeing the power of God in her life like never before." Recognizing that He personally had spoken through her pastor had deeply touched her. "I have reset my life," she said.

Mardi's story is really God's story, a reminder of His faithfulness and His love.

God's Gift to Advocates: A Crown of Rejoicing

> For what is our hope, our joy, or crown of
> rejoicing? (1 Thessalonians 2:19 NKJV)

The driving energy behind lifting the client's veil of unbelief is not from trying to earn a crown in heaven but from the *kingdom heart* we share with Christ. Nonetheless, it is exciting to realize that those who are willing to share Christ with others will personally receive a special gift born of His pleasure—the soul-winning crown. We relish the thought of one day placing the crown worshipfully at Jesus's feet as our hearts fill with gratitude for His enablement.

> I have been entrusted with the stewardship [of
> the Gospel]. (1 Corinthians 9:17 NKJV)

[God has] no greater joy than to hear that my
children walk in truth. (3 John 1:4 NKJV)

To walk in truth means her life will never be the same.

Our calling is to step away from our comfort zones and step into faith zones where we are wholly reliant upon Him. Jesus entrusts us with the special stewardship of Gospel-sharing to match each life with God's purpose. An often-repeated phrase from an unknown source says, "The two most important days in your life are the day you are born and the day you find out why."

As vessels of the living Christ, our joy finds completion when a client's "veil of unbelief" has been removed. To walk in truth means her life will never be the same.

Chapter Four

The Testimony

Father, I desire to be Your servant, "fully mature and perfectly prepared to fulfill any assignment" that You give to me.

(Prayer based on 2 Timothy 3:17 TPT)

Every believer has spiritual testimony. The testimony is a story that bears personal witness to the truth of the Gospel—that God saves us through the death, burial, and resurrection of Jesus Christ. It is God's story, yet it is our story—fused together in Spirit and life for the continuing experience of redemption.

The Influence of Your Salvation Story

Someone once asked, "What could be better than a story about following a God who lived 2000 years ago and has radically changed my life today?" Though a good story stokes interest, research validates that it impacts the listener's emotions, enhances openness, and achieves connection. "Stories generate empathy at the chemical level," one source says. "It's hard to learn someone's story and not feel connected to them. The oxytocin we get from stories helps us care, whether we like it or not."[1] Oxytocin, a neurotransmitter, affects emotions.

Another source cited the science found in a research review:

> Oxytocin has a positive impact on social behaviors related to:
>
> - relaxation
> - trust
> - overall psychological stability
>
> The hormone has also been shown to decrease stress and anxiety levels when released into certain parts of the brain.[2]

Sharing one's story encourages reciprocation.

Sharing the stories from our personal testimonies quickly lowers barriers to communication. Sharing vulnerably from one's life story can enhance credibility and create bonding with the other person. When the advocate turns storyteller by sharing her testimony, this impacts decisions. Time and again, clients, reticent about sharing deeply, open up after hearing the advocate share personally about God experiences in her life. Sharing one's story encourages reciprocation. This dynamic helpfully plays to the limited time of the client session to "get things rolling." In short, sharing one's testimony brings fresh sincerity between the listener and storyteller.

What's the difference between sharing sound, medical information with clients instead of sharing information through a story? For example, we can speak of how God is present during our personally difficult circumstances but tell a riveting story of God's rescue through a genuine hardship, and the listener hears truth, not a "teaching!"

A communications professor shared,

> Solid information in any form is good . . . "But that's not necessarily enough." A vivid, emotional story "can give that extra push to make it feel more real or more important." If you look at the times somebody's beliefs have been changed . . . it's often because of a story that "hits them in the heart."[3]

Likewise, sharing a spiritual slice of life prompts a rapport that glides into the Gospel message.

Generational Footprints

Tell your children about it, Let your children
tell their children, And their children
another generation. (Joel 1:3 NKJV)

A stranger called the pregnancy resource center and introduced herself. "Hi, my name is Charlotte. I am calling to say *thank you* to this center for changing my life! Twenty-two years ago, I arrived at your center at a loss for what to do with my pregnant teenage daughter. At the time, I thought, *She's too far along for an abortion.*"

The caller also mentioned the advocate and said, "She made me realize I first needed to get my own life back on track with the Lord. She shared the Gospel message and the assurance that God would see me through. I rededicated my life to Him."

She continued, "My daughter eventually came to faith also. After her baby girl was born, she went back to school and earned her high school diploma. Afterward, she pursued further education. A few years later, she met and married a wonderful Christian man. The 'little baby' grew up too, and she is now in her twenties. My granddaughter has become a strong Christian woman—passionate for the Lord. I just want to say thank you for touching generations of my family!"

The client's transformative experience began with an advocate who was willing to share her faith. This impacted an entire family's legacy through three generations.

Your Witness Shapes New Destinies

Many clients return to the center to express thankfulness for the help they have received. They come with the certainty that their advocates and other staff truly care. The bonding exceeds "professional kindness" extended. When we take the time to share our stories in the form of a life incident through a testimony, a neurological ignition lights up our connection. The compassionate care received remains a resounding message of God's love for them as reflected by the advocates. The memory of their caring advocates may craft a pivotal point of choosing life for their babies. And when they do, they often return, legacies in tow, still warmed by the love they received.

Compassionate care remains a resounding message of God's love.

The *intentional* willingness to share Christ gives birth to new destinies. Sharing the Gospel is not reserved for an anointed few who so naturally introduce faith into a conversation. God calls *all believers* to share His Good News. Even when we feel inadequate, He longs for us to trust Him to lead with the hope He abundantly offers.

As we stay alert to God's leading, He will open opportunities for spiritual discussion. We approach each client with expectancy and the certainty that God will enable a kairos moment to intervene. An advocate commented, "I've experienced times when I'm near the end of the client appointment and realize I haven't shared the Gospel. I silently petition His help: 'Oh Lord, please provide an entry for sharing You.' Once again, I find myself in the neighborhood where the kairos moment dwells. God provides the perfect, spiritually led moment to introduce Himself to a client who sorely needs Him."

The Advocate: Commissioned by God's Authority

> Then Jesus came close to them and said, "All authority of the universe has been given to me. Now wherever you go, make disciples of all nations." (Matthew 28:18–19 TPT)

As believers, we are charged with the task of going into the world and making disciples. In the case of the pregnancy resource center, the *world* is approaching us! Jesus bestows a divine authority to the believer with each spiritual mission assigned and, with it, His enabling power.

Pastor Terry Eckersley, senior pastor at River Network Church in the United Kingdom gives clarity to the difference between biblical power and biblical authority.

Jesus bestows a divine authority to the believer with each spiritual mission assigned and, with it, His enabling power.

He describes power, from the Greek word *dunamis,* as rooted in the English word *dynamite.* "It means energetic power, explosive power, or a demonstrative power."[4] On the other hand, authority, *exousia* in the Greek language, means the "right, privilege given to someone by another."[5] For clarity, Pastor Eckersley cites the example of a traffic policeman. The policeman doesn't have the *dunamis* power to literally (bodily) stop traffic, but he can stop traffic through his authority power, *exousia,* which grants him a delegated right to do so.

As believers, God has granted us *delegated authority* to use for His purposes. He empowers us for the task to be His witnesses who draw the unbeliever to Himself. The call to the Great Commission involves a transfer of authority to God's own. Matthew 28:19 cites the commissioning, yet the prior verse enhances our understanding. "All authority has been given to Me in heaven and earth." The next verse begins with, "Go therefore" (Matthew 28:18–19 NKJV).

Prior to the words "Go therefore" is the assurance of God's authority delegated to us. It assures the believer that God equips us for the mission. *Believing* His words motivates us to proceed. God's power is shared with us as well. Acts 1:8 assures us, "But you shall receive power when the Holy Spirit has come upon you; and you shall be witnesses to Me" (NKJV). It's like saying, "May the kingdom building begin!"

Overcoming the Enemy of Our Souls

> And they overcame him by the blood of the Lamb and by the word of their testimony, and they did not love their lives to the death. (Revelation 12:11 NKJV)

The tools of warfare to overcome the Evil One are by "the blood of the Lamb" and "by the word of their testimony." This is a description of *power* through the shedding of blood at the Cross that atoned for all sin. It released Christ in resurrection power. There also exists the power of our testimonies—made possible by embracing the gift of salvation and filling us with new life. In the same breath, the power of the advocate is prominently linked to both. The words of our testimonies would be non-existent without His shed blood on the Cross. There would be no forgiveness of sin, no removal of barriers between Christ and us, no miracle of resurrection, no redemptive application of Jesus's spilled blood. *Every* salvation testimony is *inseparable* from the Cross.

After the advocate shares her testimony, she transitions to the client. "Right now, you are faced with some hard choices, but I want you to know, there's spiritual strength available. Do you have an interest in going deeper with God and allowing Him to comfort and bring strength to you?" Other times, advocates have said quietly, "I can't imagine going through all that you're going through, but by leaning on God, you'll be able to get through it. Do you ever think about God?"

At the right time, a personal testimony reassures, "God is present in this situation." The following is a personal testimony by the author. Many times, one's story isn't told in its entirety but highlights the excerpts relevant to a client's life. Because a client doesn't expect a candid peek into the advocate's life, the occasion is met with attentiveness. "As you hear a story unfold, your brain waves actually start to synchronize with those of the storyteller," says one science journalist. "It can even shift our core beliefs . . . when we 'come back out of the story world into regular life.'"[6] Much like our being affected by a good film, the client is drawn through emotions and chemistry when she engages in your story.

Because a client doesn't expect a candid peek into the advocate's life, the occasion is met with attentiveness.

Kay's Testimony

Before Christ:

I remember saying to a friend of mine, "If I join your organization, I'll end up divorcing my husband." I ended up joining the local chapter. The organization was a national, feminist organization I knew would give me the momentum I needed for leaving an unhappy marriage. I had reached a point of weariness in my self-centered attempts at finding happiness. The only solution, I concluded, was divorce, "wiping the slate clean" from sin by starting over again. The mindset would later adjust to the revelation that Jesus had wiped the slate clean more than 2000 years ago. However, his costly gift of salvation still waited to be received.

Two years after the failed marriage, fresh expectations moved forward. A new husband, a relocation to another state, and my ready-made family of four children was poised for adventures to come!

Let's insert a "bookmark" here.

....

When I was growing up, my dad was a career Air Force dental officer and my mother a gifted homemaker who loved to entertain. Our family attended church every Sunday, yet I knew nothing about a personal relationship with God. College conveniently afforded the opportunity to skip the past routine of church attendance, which I happily did. However, on campus at a liberal university, vigorous discussion took place regarding religion—faith was casually dumped into the blended category of philosophy and "religion."

Later, as a young married person, I responded to the nearby university's flyer announcing new courses offered. I was drawn to enroll in the course entitled Demythologizing the Bible and Reinterpreting it by an Existential Point of View. I immediately enrolled, but at the end of the semester, God was as distant as ever. All the world religions claim to have the truth, and I concluded that truth is simply unknowable. Regarding Jesus, I settled on the idea that He, along with other prophets, was an "enlightened being," not God.

....

Remove the bookmark.

Prior to the new marriage, my husband-to-be and I agreed to my taking a furlough from teaching. It seemed a fair concession with family adjustments to new schools and children's chaotic sports schedules. Though initially optimistic about the plan, idling through long daytime hours took its toll. How much cleaning can one do? I was used to rising early, and the house was in ship-shape by mid-morning. Idle afternoons nudged a renewal of thoughts from the past. *Is this all there is?* (Wifehood, motherhood, grandmotherhood, then death?) Unknown to me, the dark musings reasserted unfinished business with God.

Pivotal Point:

Seeking something more had returned to its haunt. Or had it ever left? The setting was early morning. God's presence moved quietly through predawn hours as sleeplessness coaxed me from the comfort of bed covers. At 4:30 a.m., I brewed coffee. Soon my new husband would be early out the door with coffee mug in hand. I had not shared my lingering discontent. *What husband wants a depressed bride*? I also wondered, *Why am I not at peace with a life I have changed completely?*

The tipping point had arrived—the kairos moment—this one of God's making.

Wandering thoughts tightened into an acute awareness of God's presence. His pursuit felt strangely tangible. The tipping point had arrived—the kairos moment—this one of God's making. Apologetics bypassed to bring a sinner to a personal encounter with God. My response came shaped as a prayer that had taken a lifetime to say. "God, if there is anything you could *possibly* want in my life, you can have it." A surge of daylight suddenly burst through the window—like light filling my soul to banish the darkness.

After Christ:

At the time, I was unaware my prayer was called a prayer of surrender. I hadn't grasped the meaning of this shift to my life. New life had dawned with a bonus of peace, but much lay ahead. God's guiding wisdom awaited discovery. His Word awaited reading. His revelations awaited receiving. I had met the Living God. It was now time to *know* Him.

I began reading books with genuine spiritual meaning.

I felt a sense of unmistakable optimism.

God brought mature Christians into my life who spoke to a deeper Christian life.

I was irresistibly drawn to the Bible and a Bible-believing church.

I excitedly purchased a Bible commentary to enhance understanding.

Two years later, I was discipled by a staff member of Campus Crusade for Christ (Cru), which eventually led to ministry opportunities.

New life had dawned with a bonus of peace.

> Yes, he's always loving and kind, and his faithful love never ends. . . . Tell the world how he broke through and delivered you from the power of darkness. (Psalm 107:1–2 TPT)

Inserting Your Testimony into the Intake

You will find you can pick and choose parts of your testimony that are applicable to the discussion with your client. During the client intake, the details you learn about your client will cue which excerpts from your testimony you will pull to share.

For instance, based on my testimony, I have often shared these excerpts:

- The process of uncovering truth based on understanding the Bible. (Sharing some of C.S. Lewis's teachings.)
- Recognizing the difference between living as a cultural Christian rather than with a relationship with God.
- The Before Christ period: Failing to find peace through knowledge instead of a relationship with Jesus. Example: Enrolling in a secular university's course, Demythologizing the Bible, only magnified my distance from God. The answer all along: knowing Jesus.

"Tell the world how he broke through and delivered you from the power of darkness."

Psalm 107:2 TPT

The Testimony: Prelude to the Gospel

> "Don't worry about defending yourselves or being concerned how to answer their accusations. Simply be confident and allow the Spirit of Wisdom access to your heart, and in that very moment he will reveal what you are to say to them." (Luke 12:11–12 TPT)

The following four examples of one's testimony can be inserted after various client statements. Addressing the client's statement serves as a prelude into the Gospel message.

NOTE: The responses to each client statement can vary. Keep in mind *relating* to her.

1. Client: "I want to study different religions first. Then I'll decide."

Advocate: "I can save you the trouble because that's exactly what I did! I studied the world religions so I could be informed but discovered there is no other religion that has a god willing to sacrifice his life so we could spend eternity with him. All religions, other than Christianity, are based on man's attempt to *earn* salvation rather than receiving salvation as a gift from God. Attempts of earning salvation pose an awkward question: 'How can we be sure we've done *enough* to earn our way to heaven?'"

As the advocate looks intently at her client, she asks, "Would *you* know how many good works would satisfy God to earn your salvation?"

The advocate turns to Ephesians 2:8–9. After reading the Scripture, she asks, "What do you think this Scripture is saying?" (These verses refute good works lead to salvation.) The advocate adds, "Only Christianity is based on what Christ did for us and not what we do for Him to be saved. This is freedom. Can I share my personal story with you?"

2. Client (Buddhist background): "Though I've regarded Jesus as enlightened, I'm not sure He's God."

Advocate: "That question baffled me for a long time, though I was brought up attending church."

NOTE: If you cannot relate to what your client is sharing, you could simply state, "That's an interesting point of view."

Jesus claimed to be more than enlightened. He claimed to be God.

Continuing, the advocate says, "At one point in my life, I had concluded Jesus must only be a prophet. He was a good man, an enlightened person with great wisdom. Did you know even the Dalai Lama said Jesus was a holy man? The Dalai Lama said: 'My attitude toward Jesus Christ is that he was either a fully enlightened being or a bodhisattva.' A bodhisattva, in Buddhism, is someone who has pledged to devote their life to achieving enlightenment and serving all other beings."[7]

Despite the Dalai Lama's reverence, Jesus claimed to be more than enlightened. He claimed to be God (Colossians 1:15–18). When discussing the Dalai Lama's views, insert a valid question: "Since Jesus claims to be God, does a holy person lie?"

(Client ponders question.)

Advocate: "What do you think—could Jesus still be a holy man and yet be a liar?"

(Discussion)

Client (doesn't answer directly): "There is so much sin in my life; I don't know what to think!"

Advocate: "I can relate to that because there was a lot of sin in my life also. I felt so empty inside. Do you ever feel that way?" (Be intentional about bringing the client in.) The advocate could also respond, "Before I knew Christ, all my sins loaded me with condemnation. Do you ever feel a sense of condemnation?" (Slow down. After asking a question, wait for input and further discussion.)

If your client has experienced condemnation, point her to Romans 8:1. "Let's look up this verse."

The client reads: "There is therefore now no condemnation to those who are in Christ Jesus" (NKJV).

Advocate: "This statement is meant only for followers of Christ. So, when we receive Jesus's gift of dying on the Cross to pay for our sins, the believer is no longer under sin's condemnation. Can I share my personal story with you?' After sharing the testimony say, "This isn't about following Christian doctrine but following a personal Savior." Ask the client, "Are you interested in finding freedom from condemnation?"

"There is therefore now no condemnation to those who are in Christ Jesus."

Romans 8:1 NKJV

---

3. Client: "I am a Catholic."

Advocate: "What I'm about to share with you is neither Catholic nor Protestant. It's biblical and life-changing. I know what I'm about to share is true because I've personally experienced it. You say you were brought up in the Catholic faith, so I'm sure you know the basics of Christian faith—like we are sinners and Jesus died on a cross to pay the penalty of our sins. (Wait for client's affirmation before proceeding.) As a Catholic, you are familiar with the Easter story—Jesus died, was buried in a tomb, and on the third day, He was resurrected from the dead."

(The client nods to indicate knowledge of Easter.)

Advocate: "Based on Jesus's death on a cross, He invites us to go from knowledge of His sacrifice for us to inviting Him to take control of our lives. Wouldn't you agree there's a difference between learning about Jesus versus making a commitment to follow Him? It's like the difference between dating and marriage. May I share my personal story with you?" (Testimony.) After sharing, ask if you can show her a little booklet (tract) that "has been meaningful to me. It explains the personal decision of receiving Christ." If she agrees, go through the booklet and just before the salvation prayer, ask, "Do you have an interest in having Christ come into your life?"

NOTE: Various tracts are available—one is entitled *I'm a Catholic.* Also, inform the client that all Scriptures in the pamphlet are cited in the Catholic Bible.[8]

....

"*Wealth and honor come from you; you are the ruler of all things.*"

1 Chronicles 29:12

4. Client: "I can't afford a baby."

Advocate: "The fact that you're thinking about finances shows you're a responsible person. Tell me more about your financial concerns."

Client responds that she has no medical insurance.

Advocate: "If your pregnancy and delivery did not have to be a financial challenge to you, would you then consider having your baby?"

Client: "Yes."

The advocate shares resources to provide the help she needs. The advocate says, "Even though you have need of these resources, this is not your greatest need. Let me show you a verse that's applicable to your financial situation. It's in 1 Chronicles 29:11–12." The advocate locates the Scripture and the client reads: "Yours, LORD, is the greatness and the power and the glory and the majesty and the splendor, for everything in heaven and earth is yours. Yours, LORD, is the kingdom; you are exalted as head over all. Wealth and honor come from you; you are the ruler of all things" (NIV).

Advocate: "What do you think the verse is saying to you?" (All wealth is from Him.)

Follow with personalizing the verse cited. "God is in control of all wealth. Do you believe God is personally aware of your situation?" (Discuss.) "I have seen Him bring people through tough financial situations by providing better jobs, housing, even a car. God knows your needs." The advocate shares a topic testimony—how God addressed a financial need in her life. If the client is willing, proceed to sharing a spiritual tract with her like *Would You Like to Know God Personally?*

As believers who have personal stories of meeting Christ personally, we know every testimony represents God's intervention in a life. Sometimes He intervenes suddenly; other times it's more of a slow pivoting. Either way, interfacing with Him personally deepens intimacy.

Thoughts That Hinder Faith Sharing

Case One. Advocate's thought hindrance: "I don't want to be pushy and offend my client."

> With meekness you'll be able to carefully
> enlighten those who argue with you so they can
> see God's gracious gift of repentance and be
> brought to the truth. (2 Timothy 2:25 TPT)

Women seem to be especially leery of being viewed as pushy. They fear this may label them as fanatics. This fear causes reticence toward sharing one's faith. The truth is, when witnessing to a client, it's rare to offend her by sharing your testimony. Based on the website reviews, most are drawn to the kindness and peace they witness at the center.

It's rare to offend her by sharing your testimony.

Case Two. Advocate's thought hindrance: "I don't want to share my testimony. It involves so much pain!"

If something from the past is too private or painful to bring out in the open, someone can share generically rather than disclosing specifically. For instance, "When I was in college, I went through a traumatic situation that made me question everything. I was in a lot of emotional pain and knew I couldn't handle it by myself. I began thinking about God, etc."

NOTE: Not wanting to share may indicate additional healing needed. Though it may not be enjoyable to share a difficult circumstance you've experienced, it need not be overwhelming after inner healing.

Case Three. Advocate's thought hindrance: "I don't want to create an opportunity to be rejected and have the established bond blow up."

If sharing something from one's personal life destroys the bonding, then the bond is likely mischaracterized.

A testimony bursts with redemptive power. Transparent personal stories present an *example* of humility to clients. Humility comes from recognition of God's involvement in our lives. An advocate's personal story of salvation or a story of God's intervention (topic testimony) leads the way. As God guides you, stay alert to the kairos moment of intervention.

Every personal testimony applauds God and His intervention.

Case Four. Advocate's thought hindrance: "It feels too self-focused to be telling a story that's all about me."

This thought comes from an exceptionally humble person. However, the advocate would surely agree that every personal testimony applauds God and His intervention. One must keep in mind the objective. It involves using story (testimony) as a headwind to bring about a spiritually tangible influence. When hearing a personal story, a client engages. The testimony will prompt additional conversation. (If the client is quiet after the sharing, ask, "Can you relate to any part of that?") Testimonies often break the ice and quickly crumble defensive barriers.

Your openness will encourage your client to come to terms with God in her life.

Case Five. Advocate's thought hindrance: "I grew up in the faith, and as far back as I can remember, Jesus was in my life. Frankly, my testimony is not very dramatic. It feels sort of boring."

First, no testimony can be diminished since each represents the miracle of God's intervention in a life. Even those who grow up in the faith must realize that not everyone who grows up in a Christian household chooses a relationship with Christ. Each conversion is a tribute to a personal response connected to a very personal pursuit by our Creator. Because trials are part of life, excerpts from the testimony can include the topics: how God saw you through; how God kept you afloat despite trauma, pain, or doubt. The richly meaningful testimony is a treasure poised to share the gift of salvation.

If there was a sinful or dry period in which you wandered from the faith, share this with your client. Your openness will encourage your client to come to terms with God in *her* life. How God wooed you to return is intriguing. His unwavering love that finally connected to your life brings a punch of victory.

The Topic Testimony

When speaking about a testimony, this can refer to a salvation testimony or topic testimony. The topic testimony is confined to a specific issue and how faith led to victory. Example: "I loved my job, and when I lost it, I was devastated! But God had other plans for me." Other topic testimony examples:

If you had wandered from your faith, what influenced your return?

If you had not wandered from the faith, but something caused you to doubt or go deeper with God, describe the situation. If you were doubting, what brought you back to faith as a strengthened believer? If you went deeper with God afterward, describe the encouraging details.

If brought up as a Christian, what event(s) occurred when your faith transitioned from merely borrowing family beliefs to taking personal ownership of believing?

"I've Always Been a Christian" Is Not a Testimony

Julie, interested in advocacy at the pregnancy center, was interviewed by Morgan, the client services director. When asked to share her testimony, Julie was transparent. "Frankly, my testimony lacks inspiration. I grew up in a Christian family who regularly attended church and loved the Lord, so I've always been a Christian."

Julie added that she had never wandered away from her faith and had tried to make decisions in her life based on following Christ. Morgan said, "No one is born a Christian. When someone is brought up in a Christian home, there inevitably comes a time when a distinction is made between one's parents' faith and one's own. In other words, there's a point at which ownership is taken. Do you recall a time when you made your family's faith your own?"

Julie pondered the question before speaking. "Well, there was this small episode when I was away at college. I remember stepping out of an elevator at my dorm and noticed a man doing repair work on the adjacent elevator. He abruptly asked, 'Do you have assurance you're saved?' I responded, 'Yes, by faith, I know I am saved.' That was it. Only later did I realize that by this one encounter, I felt a great uplift of encouragement. The memory is vivid."

The director said, "It's vivid because it was significant. That's when you took ownership!"

Julie's face brightened. "Yes, that's when I owned it."

We can learn from "the elevator story" and adapt our growing up in the faith to a meaningful testimony shared with clients. Here is the testimony Julie shares with clients:

> I was raised in a family with a rich Christian heritage. I believed the doctrine that they believed, and I followed Christ just as my family did. Soon after leaving home for college, I remember an incident I still think about decades later! I was on campus and had just walked out of an elevator when I noticed a man doing repair work on the adjacent elevator. He looked at me and asked me a question. "Do you have assurance you're saved?"
>
> I answered, "Yes, by faith, I know I am saved."
>
> If I were to describe that incident in spiritual terms, God was having me "bear witness" to my faith. Not to my parents' faith, not to the faith of my spiritual tradition but to *my* faith! This explains why this fleeting encounter felt so encouraging. It was the first time I declared ownership of my beliefs.

The elevator story recounts a defining moment of ownership.

The elevator testimony transitions to the arena of the Gospel message:

> The question the elevator man asked me, "Do you know if you are saved?" is a question *all* of us need to answer. *Do we know for sure we're saved?* To spend eternity with God, we've invited Him into our lives.

(This is a place to pause for discussion with client, then proceed to the Gospel.)

NOTE to the advocate trainee: When an individual has been brought up in the Christian faith, God seems to provide a defining moment, or even a defining frame of time, to bear witness to one's *personal* faith—this definitive time installs legitimacy. The elevator story recounts a defining moment of ownership.

"Our heart is restless, until it repose in Thee."

St. Augustine

A Testimony from a Bible Story

St. Augustine once said: "Thou madest us for Thyself, and our heart is restless, until it repose in Thee."[9] In the Bible, there's a well-known story about a woman who had a restless heart until she met Jesus as Savior. Retelling her story is powerful for the client who's having difficulty dealing with the sins she's committed. We learn Jesus's perspective of loving forgiveness and second chances. The Bible-based story involves a woman who stops at the home of Simon, the Pharisee, whom Jesus is visiting.

This woman's reputation follows her everywhere. Simon has heard about her, and he doesn't respect her. She's an uninvited guest at the Pharisee's home, yet she's motivated to see Jesus. His non-judgmental response resonates with all who have sinned. Retelling the woman's story reminds us that lives pocked by sin are redeemable through a relationship with Jesus.

> And behold, a woman in the city who was a sinner, when she knew that Jesus sat at the table in the Pharisee's house, brought an alabaster flask of fragrant oil, and stood at His feet behind Him weeping; and she began to wash His feet with her tears, and wiped them with the hair of her head; and she kissed His feet and anointed them with the fragrant oil. Now when the Pharisee who had invited Him saw this, he spoke to himself, saying, "This Man, if He were a prophet, would know who and what manner of woman this is who is touching Him, for she is a sinner." (Luke 7:37–40 NKJV)

"But to whom little is forgiven, the same loves little."

Luke 7:47

Weeping, the woman continues to wipe the feet of Jesus with her hair as she cries. The scene of this reputedly sinful woman crying at Jesus's feet triggers the Pharisee's condescending thoughts. Jesus, reading his thoughts, confronts Simon. "I say to you, her sins, which are many, are forgiven, for she loved much. But to whom little is forgiven, the same loves little" (v. 47).

Centuries later, the power of this story resonates. Hearts still warm when hearing Jesus's mercy toward a penitent sinner.

The Bible as Mentor

1. Client Situation: A client, who says she is a Christian, is angry at her ex-boyfriend for abandoning her during pregnancy. She is unwilling to forgive him.

The advocate discusses how detrimental unforgiveness is to the client's emotional well-being. She asks her client, "Do you believe anger and happiness can co-exist?"

"No," the client answers.

The advocate then asks, "Then are you saying you're willing to allow unforgiveness to damage *your* well-being?"

"I see what you mean," the client responds.

The discussion proceeds to speaking of Jesus's forgiveness of those who crucified Him. "Father, forgive them, for they do not know what they do" (Luke 23:34 NKJV).

The client responds, "But they *did* know what they were doing! And my ex-boyfriend knew what he was doing when he walked out!"

This leads to discussing that although Jesus's enemies were well aware they were torturing and killing Him, they were ignorant of what they were doing. The advocate explains, "They had no clue about His love for them nor His death to atone for their sins. It's also true your ex-boyfriend knew he was abandoning you, but, for him, 'not knowing what he was doing' meant he was unaware of God's provision for him to handle an unforeseen pregnancy."

The advocate, as believer, has the great privilege of speaking on God's behalf.

The advocate continues, "Your issue is different than your boyfriend's issue. In your case, you also 'do not know what you do' because you're rejecting the peace God would provide to you through forgiving your ex-boyfriend. Both are spiritual issues."

The client concedes, and the advocate asks, "Are you willing to extend the same forgiveness to your boyfriend's sins that Jesus extended to you for your sins?"

2. Client Situation: A client cannot forgive herself over past sins.

Jesus is challenging those ready to stone a woman to death for her adultery. (The partner is nowhere in sight.) Jesus says to the band of accusers, "'He who is without sin among you, let him throw a stone at her first.' And again, He stooped down and wrote on the ground" (John 8:7–8 NKJV). Whatever He writes on the ground, perhaps their sins, causes them to leave. Jesus turns to the woman and says, "Neither do I condemn you; go and sin no more" (John 8:11 NKJV).

If the client is not a believer, she can still learn about the authority and goodness of Jesus. He doesn't shame the woman nor even scold her. He shows love for her by the intervention on her behalf. He creates the opportunity for a fresh start. 'Go and sin no more.'"

The advocate continues, "Jesus doesn't make it complicated. He has intervened for you and for me by forgiving all of our sins by dying on the Cross for us." The advocate moves to a pointed question. "Would you like to receive the forgiveness of God personally?"

3. Client Situation: A client feels guilty about wandering from faith.

Jesus knew Peter would return and ultimately grow deeply in his faith.

The apostle Peter's story resonates with many. He reminds us of ourselves, who start with good intentions yet don't always follow through. Peter boasted to the Lord of his great allegiance, yet soon afterward, by an act of self-protection, he denied knowing Christ. (Luke 22:33–62). Impetuous Peter wasn't in tune with his capacity to sin. God enabled him to get in touch with his weakness of the flesh. The transgression humbled him in preparation to better serve God.

The advocate says, "When we are not aware of our propensity for sin, we have less gratitude to God for what we have been saved *from.* Before Peter's betrayal, Jesus had told him, 'And when you have returned to Me, strengthen your brethren' (v. 32). No scolding, despite Jesus's foreknowledge that Peter would fail Him. Jesus knew Peter would *return* and ultimately grow deeply in his faith. We all make mistakes like Peter did. How do you feel about doing a reset of your relationship with God?"

The Testimony: A Witness to God

One of the best definitions of success in witnessing was written by the late Bill Bright, founder of Campus Crusade for Christ (now known as Cru). "Success in witnessing is simply taking the initiative to share Christ in the power of the Holy Spirit and leaving the results to God."[10] By witnessing, we share about the character of our Savior, Jesus Christ, the Gospel message, and His personal significance for our lives.

The disciple John was an eyewitness to the Lord. He wrote about the crucifixion of Jesus in a detailed account that included mentioning a soldier who pierced Jesus's side with a spear to be certain that He was dead. It was John who said, "He who saw it has borne witness—his testimony is true, and he knows that he tells the truth—that you also may believe" (John 19:35 ESV).

Because John was the one who saw Jesus being pierced, he was the one bearing witness. Similarly, our personal testimonies bear firsthand witness so the client *also may believe.* A testimony speaks to the character of a God who loves us. Unlike John, we are not eyewitnesses to Christ's life and death; however, our personal experience of Christ continues through interactive prayers and His Word. Significantly, as followers of Christ, we are appointed to lead others to believe.

God Himself has a testimony about His Son, Jesus.

If we accept the testimony of men, how much more should we accept the more authoritative testimony of God that he has testified concerning his Son? . . .

This is the true testimony: that God has given us eternal life, and this life has its source in his Son. Whoever has the Son has eternal life; whoever does not have the Son does not possess eternal life. (1 John 5: 9, 11–12 TPT)

Focusing on Truth, Not the Counterfeit

Keep in mind, it's not necessary to know everything about another religion to effectively witness Christ as the Savior. Though knowledge about other religions is never discouraged, if you have questions about it, simply ask your client. Seeking understanding about others' beliefs shows respect, and people usually enjoy explaining what is familiar. For the most part, however, keep the focus on the Gospel rather than any counterfeits to salvation.

It's not necessary to know everything about another religion to effectively witness Christ as the Savior.

When FBI agents learn to detect counterfeit bills, instead of studying the counterfeit bills, their laser focus is on memorizing every nuance about the genuine currency.[11] We also do well to focus on the genuine faith: Christianity and the Gospel of Jesus.

This means there's no need to be intimidated to silence if the client states, "I am a Buddhist," or "I am a Hindu," or "I am a Muslim." Refute the fear of "What do I say?" and reply cordially, but only briefly featuring *the counterfeit.*

"That's interesting. Did you grow up in that faith?"

"Oh yes," said a Muslim client.

"My family is Muslim, so, of course, I am also Muslim."

The advocate entered the moment's opportunity. "In the Christian faith, I love that our God is a *personal* God. I value the freedom of choice to follow Him because it shows Him my heart for Him. We believe Jesus is a personal God, and so He cares about our feelings for Him."

It's fine to ask, "Do you attend services at the mosque?" If she doesn't, this leads to a discussion.

Advocate: "In our faith, we sometimes have 'cultural Christians'—perhaps similar to 'cultural Muslims' who aren't close to the faith. I was once a cultural Christian, affiliated with the Christian faith but not a true *follower of Christ.*" Ask the client, "Do you think of yourself as a cultural Muslim or practicing Muslim?" This can lead to a significant discussion about faith.

Journey from Muslim to Christ Follower

Some centers offer a service of free material needs for the clients, such as clothing, baby equipment, diapers, etc. Today, many centers offer resource referrals instead. Fatima's story took place when the pregnancy center offered monthly visits for material resources.

When Fatima first visited the center, she arrived with three young daughters. Her emotionally abusive husband, again in a rage, abandoned the home. Fatima was an attractive woman, a non-practicing Muslim, who wore Western-style clothing. Left with no financial resources, she sought help from the center. She told her advocate she had visited the nearby mosque to find help, but they were not sympathetic.

"What did you do wrong that your husband would leave you?" someone there had asked.

Feeling desperate, she left immediately. "I know the Christians will help me. This country was founded on God!"

At the pregnancy center, the fear of being pregnant was settled by a negative pregnancy test, but Fatima's visits would continue monthly to pick up diapers and baby clothing.

An outgoing person, Fatima enjoyed spiritual dialogue, which resumed every visit. Though she had difficulty believing Jesus was God, she occasionally would give a shoutout saying, "I love Jesus!"

One day Fatima responded to the advocate's invitation to attend church. That Sunday they sat side-by-side in the pew as the pastor spoke about forgiveness. Midway through the sermon, Fatima began sobbing—producing visible shaking that continued as the service drew to a close.

There, on the gravelly shoulder of a busy city thoroughfare, a Muslim woman prayed to receive Christ.

After the congregation had left, Fatima began to settle down. The advocate leaned closer, "What was it that touched you during the sermon?"

Fatima replied, "I must forgive my husband!"

The next morning, Fatima called her advocate with excitement in her voice. "I had a dream last night about Jesus! He came to me! He wore a long white robe, and, in the dream, there were two roads. One was dark and shadowy, and the other one was full of light. Jesus held out His hand to me, and when I took His hand, we walked together toward the road of light."

"Oh, Fatima!" the advocate said. "I think your dream has a special message. Now that you're fully awake, would you like to ask Jesus to come into your life personally?"

"Yes!" Fatima said. "Let me pull over to the side of the road first!"

There, on the gravelly shoulder of a busy city thoroughfare, a Muslim woman prayed to receive Christ. She began attending church regularly and, in a few months, was publicly baptized.

In the years that followed, Fatima would meet a Muslim man who was a nominal, non-practicing Muslim, hardworking and kind, with a love for children. Since she told him she would only marry a Christian man, he began to attend church with her. Months later, he received

Christ as his Savior. Eventually, they married at the church, and the entire congregation joyfully celebrated with them.

Testimony and Gospel sharing focus on an intentional fortitude, not a spiritual question asked by a client.

Intentional Gospel Sharing

Be ready in season and out of season. Convince,
rebuke, exhort, with all longsuffering and teaching.
For the time will come when they will not endure
sound doctrine. (2 Timothy 4:2–3 NKJV)

To be ready *in season and out of season* means spiritual fruit can be produced at any time. We must stay alert to the moments for gathering the harvest!

All Christian centers have probably experienced opportunities to enter spiritual discussions with their clients. Some are more intentional than others—looking for openings for sharing spiritually with clients. Testimony and Gospel sharing focus on an *intentional fortitude,* not a spiritual question asked by a client. The more passive approach cancels opportunities to witness.

More About the Topic Testimony

The *topic testimony* has its place in the counseling room. It can be powerfully used in lieu of or with the *salvation testimony* prior to presenting the Gospel.

The salvation testimony is a story about initially "entering into" a personal relationship with Christ and receiving the forgiveness of sins. The topic testimony is a God story that is personally experienced but involves a specific topic that bears personal witness to God's faithfulness. The topic could be an event of answered prayer, a fear that was overcome, a special unexpected joy revealing God's intervention, a forgiveness issue God addressed, or a challenge through which God met you at your point of need.

Topic Testimony of Forgiveness

Why highlight forgiveness in a book about evangelism? Without forgiveness, spiritual growth becomes stunted. Even in the advocate's life, any event of anger and unforgiveness can quench the life of His Spirit and inhibit the life of her spirit.

Client's situation: Soon after Anna arrived in the United States, she discovered she was pregnant. When she contacted the boyfriend back home with the news, his response was to sever all communication with her. Weeks later, the distraught young woman came to our center for help. We stabilized the situation by offering emotional support and resources, but most importantly, we introduced her to the love

Forgiveness is a matter of the will, not emotions.

of Jesus. Her new relationship with Him motivated her to join the Bible-believing church of one of the volunteers who spoke her native language.

Anna grew in her faith rapidly. Her baby daughter was born, and Anna, having been college-educated in her country, found a job with a good company. Life went well for a couple of years until she received a startling phone call.

Afterward, Anna contacted the center, saying she "needed to talk" to her advocate. After arriving for the appointment, she shared the disturbing news. Her daughter was now three years old, and, shockingly, the child's estranged father now wanted to establish contact. During his phone call to her, Anna learned he had only recently disclosed to his parents that he had a child living in the United States. His parents wanted to meet their granddaughter. To Anna, the notion was inconceivable. She felt outraged. "How can he possibly think that he, along with his parents, can just walk back into our lives after he abandoned us."

Anna was deeply troubled, and, as a Christian, she acknowledged she needed to forgive. But how? She *wanted* to forgive, but, "It's impossible to change my feelings," she said.

The advocate explained forgiveness is a matter of the will, not emotions.

After intense discussion, Anna chose to forgive the father of her child. Following her advocate's guidance, she prayed and confessed her anger and unforgiveness. Most significantly, it was helpful to know forgiveness isn't dependent on feelings but on the will to obey God and *deciding* to forgive.

When Anna left the center, she felt renewed in God's strength, restored in His peace, and free to pray for her child's father. In time, her ill feelings about him eased. The next year, she returned to her country to work remotely for her American company. She and the father of the child were eventually able to assume a civil co-parenting arrangement that served the best interests of their daughter.

NOTE: It is comforting to a client to be reminded that even Jesus was betrayed. He fully understands every emotion she's contending with. Yet Jesus extended grace to His enemies, forgiving and praying for them. We must choose to declare forgiveness of another person—entrusting feelings to a God who is able to catch them up to our forgiveness decision.

A Powerful Prayer of Forgiveness

- It is helpful to identify on a scale of zero to ten the intensity of your negative feelings. (No denial!) For example, "Lord, I confess I'm at a ten. I'm feeling outraged because ___________"
- In prayer (and perhaps to other believers), openly elaborate, telling God all the precise details behind the hurt and unforgiveness you are *feeling*. Though your unforgiveness may feel justified by the unfairness of the wrong done to you, with God's love and guidance, we don't have to stay in bondage to bitterness.
- Because God asks us to give up our rights, we release the right to remain angry or bitter. In the power of the Holy Spirit, confess your willingness to release justification of your right to be angry and not forgive. In the power of Jesus's Spirit, we acknowledge our own sin debt and express thankfulness that God holds nothing against us. Our debt is paid in full.
- Speak your forgiveness aloud: "God, because you, Jesus, died for all my sins and forgave me, by your power, as You are my witness, I now forgive _______ for _________." By words spoken aloud, you will know that you have entered the act of forgiving despite conflicting, even pervasive, negative feelings.[12]
- Pray for those who have offended you.

NOTE: Keep in mind that forgiveness does not necessarily imply reconciliation, particularly if past misdeeds subject the victim to harm.

The way of love frees us from hateful and negative feelings that keep us bound in emotional chaos.

Freedom from Lingering Negative Emotions

The Scripture commands us to pray for our enemies (Matthew 5:44). The way of love frees us from hateful and negative feelings that keep us bound in emotional chaos.

You do not have to keep forgiving for the same offense, even when a negative feeling returns. Instead, *stand on* the forgiveness you initially declared. Jesus said, "Let your 'Yes' be 'Yes,' and your 'No,' 'No'" (Matthew 5:37 NKJV). This means once you have forgiven the offense, walk in the forgiveness you have declared. If your anger recirculates into experiencing negative feelings again, praise the Lord that, through Him, you forgave the offense. If hatred and anger are smothering your declaration of forgiveness (quenching the Spirit), ask Jesus to refill you with His Spirit to live *from* His resurrected life that indwells you. This includes continuing prayers to free us to agape love the other person.

A Topic Testimony: Sexual Sin

Peace from knowing Christ is worth everything.

Client situation: Tammy, the twenty-year-old client, was visibly worried she was pregnant. When the result of her pregnancy test was negative, she said, "I dodged the bullet this time!"

Her concerned advocate asked, "Is your sexually active lifestyle really worth the anxiety every month? Have you considered what you'd do if you had been pregnant?"

Tammy admitted that her lifestyle caused constant worry about pregnancy.

The advocate said, "God has a different plan designed for you. It avoids the worry and anxiety you continue to experience." As the advocate spoke of God's plan for sex, she said, "I think God knew what He was talking about when He said sex is confined within the boundary of marriage. It's not that He thinks sex is bad—He invented sex! But He also knew that sex could bring heartache outside of His principles. We see that a lot here." (Discussion.)

The advocate continued, "In the counseling room, I witness the 'tears and fears' that come from single women finding out they're pregnant. God wants to save us from this turmoil of pregnancy outside of marriage along with its rampant sexually transmitted diseases. Most of all, He desires us to draw closer to Him."

The advocate shared her testimony, then led into the Gospel. "Peace from knowing Christ is worth everything. Would you like to know more about God's plan for your life?"

The client was open, and after hearing the message of the Gospel, she responded by accepting Christ into her life.

Months later, the client emailed the advocate to share the impact God had already made.

> So much has changed since I came to the center. It has amazed me how much happier and how much more fulfilled I feel since I made that decision. Your prayer for me that day meant so much to me! You prayed God would fill the longing in my heart that comes from Him . . . and He has! I have also started dating someone new and, from the beginning, I told him I'm not interested in having a sexual relationship until marriage. That's when I learned he's also a Christian and willing to wait. It's so good just to talk and get to know the person! I feel so much more cared for, knowing someone is willing to spend time with me without the expectation of sex.

The Option of Adoption

The following story illustrates how to use a biblical topic testimony with a client despite the absence of personal, relatable experience. Unlike her client, who was adopted at a young age, the advocate was raised by natural parents. Yet the topic of adoption, based on the Bible, provided a relatable discussion.

Leigh, a twenty-two-year-old client, shared openly with her advocate: "I took the morning-after pill, but it didn't settle well, and I threw it up!" Several weeks later, the absence of her menses led her to take a home pregnancy test. Stunned by the positive reading, she took a repeat test, then another, and another. Positive, positive, positive. Each test relentlessly declared the same shocking news.

Leigh called the pregnancy center, and after learning of its medical-grade pregnancy tests, she made an appointment. With another repetition of a positive test, the "bad news" apparently began to lose its impact. The client calmly said, "My boyfriend is very caring and supportive of whatever I do." She added, "I'm sure my parents will come around."

When her advocate introduced adoption as an option, Leigh disclosed, "I was adopted." Her uplifted tone of voice seemed to recognize adoption as a suitable choice because of her personal experience. Leigh's initial inclination toward abortion weakened as she rethought this new alternative. After all, *she* had been given life by her birth mother. There was much to think about. The moment compelled spiritual discussion.

Endorsing the option of adoption, the advocate said, "Leigh, thank you for sharing about your adoption! Adoption, in the eyes of God, is *really* a lofty concept! Did you know in the book of Romans in the Bible, all believers are called the 'adopted children of God'? It's significant because, at the time the book of Romans was written, a natural parent could lawfully disinherit a natural child, but, by law, they could not disinherit an adopted child."[13]

"I didn't know that!" Leigh replied with genuine surprise.

"This resonates with Scripture. When we become God's adopted children by entering the faith, there's new meaning to the words, 'I will never leave you nor forsake you'" (Hebrews 13:5 NKJV).

When we become God's adopted children by entering the faith, there's new meaning to the words, "I will never leave you nor forsake you."

Leigh's eyes widened. As if imparting a secret, she whispered, "I want to get closer to God."

Leigh's words created a defining moment, offering an opportune time (kairos) to share the Gospel message. "Leigh, for anyone to be a part of God's adoption plan, it means He is our Father, and we are His child. We've entered His family through a relationship with Him. Can I share more about that with you?"

Leigh, touched to learn of adoption's unique place in the heart of God, was open to hearing more, and together, they went through a Gospel tract. At the close of the session, Leigh committed herself to the care of her loving, *adoptive* Father.

What About Spiritual Disinterest?

Client disinterest happens from time to time for different reasons. Keep in mind that despite some clients being *initially* dismissive of spiritual topics, we often see them respond with increasing interest, especially after hearing the advocate's personal testimony. Continue to ask God's discernment before you bail prematurely from the conversation. (If you feel relieved at the closure of a spiritual discussion, it's suspect that you're prematurely bailing!)

Silently pray for the Lord to create a moment of entry for your testimony. As you proceed through the intake form, stay alert to His bringing the right moment.

The Quiet Client

Miraculously, when an advocate shares personally, we often witness client expressions softening.

Clients come from varied backgrounds. Sometimes a client appears cordial, which can be mistaken for openness to the spiritual message. Other times, a client can act flippantly or be quietly insular. This can tempt the advocate to refrain from sharing a salvation or topic testimony, thinking, *She won't be interested.* Miraculously, when an advocate shares personally, we often witness client expressions softening as they become receptive to an advocate's personal story.

It's tempting to land on early impressions. "My client's quietness feels like resistance." Although the way she presents can *feel like* disinterest, this may or may not be the case. Continue to be friendly, and don't be surprised if your quiet client perks up when you begin to share your personal story. Her curiosity is drawing her interest, and, likely, she feels special because of an advocate's willingness to share so personally. This is adamantly contrary to the world's counseling model. The advocate is free from such restrictions, and outcomes of rapport bear out the wisdom of sharing a personal testimony and the peace found in Christ. In the process of listening, the client will draw applicable inferences for her own life. For instance, she may infer, "Can my life find the peace she has found?" If the client is a genuine seeker, this becomes more evident.

The Outcome Is in God's Hands

An Eastern European woman came to the center, accompanied by her husband. After the test confirmed Marlena's pregnancy, she readily expressed dismay and her need to seek an abortion. With two graduate degrees and a job she enjoyed, Marlena wondered aloud how she could handle her work plus care for a third child. Spiritually, she had been raised in an Orthodox religion in her country but had no prior understanding about a personal relationship with Christ. She also seemed overwhelmed with the financial challenges of enlarging the family, especially since her husband was temporarily out of work. "In my country, people don't normally have more than two children," she insisted.

When the husband was asked about his thoughts, he abdicated by giving her full responsibility. "I'll support any decision she makes." His response forfeited the support she needed.

She responded tearfully, "I just don't know how I can manage another child with my work demands!"

"God has answers for you," the advocate responded, "and He wants you to trust Him. God can work out solutions even when things seem impossible." It was important that the woman connect emotionally with the life of her baby, and the advocate spoke of the baby's siblings. Your five- and three-year-old will so enjoy this new baby. You can't imagine the joy this little life will bring to all of you! The advocate went on to mention the fourth baby she had carried, which was an unexpected pregnancy. She spoke of the laughter and enjoyment he had brought to their family.

God can work out solutions even when things seem impossible.

As the session progressed, the advocate shared her testimony with the couple. The client remained noncommittal. (Disengagement from the spiritual aspect of the session can occur when abortion is still under consideration. Most, if not all, recognize abortion is outside of God's will.)

A few days later, the couple returned for the wife's ultrasound procedure. The baby's imagery was animated, and the client became tearful, though still undecided. The family was planning to travel to Eastern Europe the following month to visit their extended family. When they were again available, the advocate sent an email to Marlena and said she had been praying for her. Marlena promptly replied:

> I just wanted to update you on our progress and let you know that you were right—God is helping us in difficult situations! First, right after I learned I was pregnant, I told my manager at work. She told me she would give me a salary increase and allow me to work from home twice a week to keep me happy! We will always remember you as the person who guided us in the right direction. I'm glad we met, and it helped us not to make a mistake. Thank you.

The advocate responded to Marlena's encouraging email by reinforcing her decision for life. At the end of the email, she included a prayer of salvation.

The excerpt:

> Marlena, when you feel ready to do so, you may want to consider the prayer I've included. It is a special prayer that would begin a deeper relationship with Christ. He will make a difference in your life! [Following this was the special prayer of salvation that thanked God for dying on the Cross for her sins and took the step of inviting Christ into her life.]

Marlena did not respond right away. It was two years later when the advocate received an email with an attachment. A picture of Marlena's beautiful family of five. The youngest child was a toddler boy held in Marlena's arms. Between the mother and father were two older children, a boy and a girl, both smiling. The final sentence of Marlena's message still brings delight. "I want to tell you I prayed that prayer you sent me. Our family has now found a church, and we are all attending!"

A Spiritual Legacy Brings Glory to God

One day an advocate received a call from a client who had visited the center ten years prior. The client, Janice, explained that she had casually shared her salvation testimony with one of the pastors of a large area church where she volunteered. This led to his invitation for her to speak at their staff retreat the approaching weekend.

While preparing her testimony, she recalled her first visit to the center that had been key to becoming a follower of Christ. She also thought about the advocate who had met with her. When she called the center, she discovered the same advocate she had met with years before was still there. She made an appointment to bring the ten-year-old son, the one saved from abortion.

The Holy Spirit is with us in the counseling room.

Janice arrived at the center and introduced her son—a handsome, well-mannered child. Later she shared unknown details from her earlier time of crisis. When the center first saw her, she had just left an abortion clinic without having the procedure. "I just couldn't go through with it despite their attempt to persuade me."

When she arrived at the center, she'd had no idea it was a Christian ministry. In fact, she said, "I would never have come if I'd known that! For years I stayed clear of Christians because, as a teen, I'd been violated by a churched person. During the session the advocate completely touched and softened my heart when she said to me, 'Even if you decide to go through with the abortion, we will be here to help you with counseling, prayer, and the healing process.' Since I knew abortion was contrary to her values, I was taken aback by her kind response. She didn't judge or make me feel like a horrible person for considering an abortion. Instead, she showed me God's mercy and grace. With her answer, she showed me the love of Jesus Christ. It was like God Himself speaking what I needed to hear."

Before the session ended, Janice had surrendered her life to Christ, and when she left the center that day, she said she felt acutely aware of two things: "First, I knew that my situation would work out, though I had no idea *how*! Second, I knew I was not going to abort my baby."

As we pray to invite God to move freely behind the doors of our centers, His Spirit inspires opportunities for changed lives. He is the One we serve expectantly, knowing He is with us in the counseling room.

Witnessing Despite Intimidation

Ministering to others is a calling from God. It is not necessarily dependent on spiritual gifts currently powerful in your life. Perhaps God wants to develop abilities in you that you've never imagined. Like sharing your faith boldly. Like being an active listener. Like presenting the Gospel to a stranger. Like developing sensitivity to the Spirit's prompt.

God's plan for you is in motion. There is nothing more exhilarating than seeing a life changed for eternity.

God's plan for you is in motion. There is nothing more exhilarating than seeing a life changed for eternity.

A Well-Known Speaker Overcomes Intimidation

When we fit our will into God's will, we proceed by faith, and feelings begin to acclimate to our decision. Sometimes the advocate in training is intimidated by the sharing-your-faith aspect of ministry, yet knows God desires her participation. Be patient. He is developing you into His plan.

Priscilla Shirer, though called to speak at stadium-sized women's events, is one who proceeded by faith. It was an uphill battle for her. When she spoke to an audience of thousands of women, the stage fright was overwhelming. For a long time, she hoped she would eventually "just get over it," she said. When that didn't happen, she spoke with a mentor who said, "This kind of fear (the kind that refuses to leave) is not a mere emotion to deal with but a spiritual stronghold to demolish."[14]

Priscilla recognized she would have to fight for freedom from this fear, and speaking God's Word aloud became her spiritual armor. Scripture says, "Our sufficiency is from God" (2 Corinthians 3:5 NKJV). Of this, Pricilla wrote,

> We've got new guests to entertain. Their names are Competence and Adequacy. They come directly from God's Spirit (2 Corinthians 3:5–6) bringing peace, assurance and joy.

Whatever God has called us to, He will equip us to carry out His mission. Growth entails stepping out of one's comfort zone.

"Our sufficiency is from God."

2 Corinthians 3:5 NKJV

When meeting with single pregnant clients at the center, at some point, we address the sin of living a lifestyle outside of God's will. An advocate's testimony ordinarily includes areas of living sinfully that have been overcome through Christ. Hearing this, the client's defenses begin breaking down. This leads to transparency and the client's admission that she has missed being close to God or would like the peace she sees in believers. Many speak of a grandmother who helped initiate their faith walk. These grannies made a significant impact by taking their grandchildren to church with them.

Some clients confess to not living "very much like Christians," but at the end of the session, they indicate readiness for change in their lives. Still others may respond, "I'm just not ready now," which can reinforce self-awareness of where they are, spiritually. It provides fodder for self-examination.

A Volunteer's Letter of Encouragement

Over the years, not having come from an evangelical background, an advocate named Mary expressed growing closer to the Lord as she shared her faith with clients. As a seasoned advocate, she wrote the following letter to encourage the advocates in training.

> An amazing, life-changing journey occurred the day I decided to go through the center's training to become a client advocate. During your training, you will often hear that the Holy Spirit is present in the counseling room. To hear this both fascinated and encouraged me, yet at first, I couldn't quite grasp what that might look like.
>
> Part of your training practicum will involve your observing seasoned advocates while they meet with clients. It was in those moments I first truly saw God at work here. A client, in what appears to be a bleak and hopeless life situation, often feels like abortion is her only answer. She may change her mind when her advocate non-judgmentally encourages and offers practical resources to assist her needs.
>
> Time and again I have had the privilege of watching a client's carefully constructed wall of protection crumble when she hears the Gospel message. The Holy Spirit powerfully guides the words of the advocate to meet what the client has need of hearing. Do all clients change their minds? Sadly, no, but, at the least, they leave the center having heard a personal God loves them and a Savior named Jesus died to atone for their sins. We trust the Holy Spirit to take it from there.
>
> My own faith has been incredibly strengthened because of the ministry at the pregnancy resource center. How could

it not be? I have seen the power of prayer before meeting with each client. I have experienced the Lord guiding my words when meeting with a client, prompting me to uncover topics that need to be touched on. He also presents the opening to share my personal experiences in a meaningful way. I have grown through a deeper grasp of how much our God unconditionally loves us and orchestrates our lives in a way that draws us nearer to Him. Clients do not show up in our office by accident but by divine appointment!

As you progress through the training and the practicum that follows, I encourage you to let it all soak in but not let yourself become overwhelmed. God does not call the equipped but equips the called. He is faithful!

I look forward to meeting each of you as you join our volunteer team.

In His love,

Mary

"I have had the privilege of watching a client's carefully constructed wall of protection crumble when she hears the Gospel message."

The heart of the letter is captured by words of Scripture: "In the same way you received Jesus our Lord and Messiah by faith, continue your journey of faith, progressing further into your union with him! Your spiritual roots go deeply into his life as you are continually infused with strength, encouraged in every way" (Colossians 2:6–7 TPT).

Chapter Five

Preparing Your Three-Minute Testimony

Father, our souls open up to You for "presenting the truth to everyone's conscience in the sight and presence of God."

(Prayer based on 2 Corinthians 4:2 TPT)

A salvation testimony is a uniquely tailored story about one's personal relationship with Christ. Every Christian testimony includes acknowledgment of oneself as a sinner and the receiving of God's forgiveness through His atoning death on the Cross, His burial in death, and His resurrection to life (1 Corinthians 15:3–6). Our testimonies reveal the spiritual growth that's taking place through God's Spirit when we receive the Gospel of new life. Self-focused living is called to yield to the process of renewal through dependence on the Holy Spirit.

Addressing Objections to Testimony Preparation

When advocate trainees are asked to write their personal testimonies, some express well-meaning resistance. "My testimony talks about *me*, but I'd rather focus on the client." Here, faulty thinking omits the fact that testimonies feature God as our centerpiece of faith. Without Him, there's no intrinsic renewal and no testimony is possible.

The testimony is a story of God's transforming love in our lives. It's a validation of the Savior's forbearing love, and praiseworthy changes in the believer's character belong to Him. Testimonies chart spiritual life transitions: before Christ, after Christ, and the pivotal point between.

Testimonies chart spiritual life transitions: before Christ, after Christ, and the pivotal point between.

Some have asked, “Why should I write down my testimony? I know my story, so I’ll just tell it!” The written testimony aims for timely precision and manages the tendency toward wandering thoughts and unnecessary details. It brings a well-ordered presentation and confines it to a three-minute presentation. It is well thought out to highlight the prominent features of a conversion.

Writing Your Three-Part Testimony

BC: Before Christ in my life

PP: Pivotal point of receiving Christ

AD: After Christ in my life (AD is *anno domini,* Latin for “year of our Lord”)

Writing your testimony can be a challenge when the timelines are blurred and your story is more a progressive revelation with unclear distinction between the time periods. The pivotal point of conversion isn’t clear, yet you recognize something spiritual has happened in your life. Know that it is acceptable not to have clear-cut sections between the BC, PP, and AD. Describe evolving perspectives associated with your “coming into a more personal relationship with Christ.” Describe changes in perspectives as God was drawing you to Himself. In the case of blurred timelines, especially the pivotal turning to Christ, write your testimony with a strong contrast between the BC versus AD.

Before Christ Time Frame

This is the “tell it like it is” time frame in your life when you were basically focused on yourself, your goals and interests with no compelling interest to grow spiritually. This period in your life may include what one hopes to get out of life or achieve in life to “make this world a better place.” Within this window frame, a transitioning may have begun—perhaps an existential pondering like, *Is there any deeper meaning of life beyond the here and now?* Activities help to fill the inner emptiness yet are never enough to satisfy the remaining inner void.

Activities help to fill the inner emptiness yet are never enough to satisfy the remaining inner void.

This period of life, prior to pivoting toward the spiritual, is simply a “tell it like it is” story of one’s life before the move toward a personal relationship with Christ. It presents a contrast to the later life period of pursuing a deepening experience of Christ. It involves an account of mainline beliefs prior to salvation. What was the source of your identity? This may include achievements, family name, education, wealth, etc., and how you viewed your purpose in life. How did you pursue happiness or find temporary peace? What problems did you struggle with? What were your thoughts about God and Christianity? As you detail your written testimony, include life goals during the BC stage of life and what significance success held for you.

The Pivotal Phase: A Distinct Turning Toward Christ

Sometimes a definitive turning point occurs that's clear. An event spurred your desire to be closer to God or your interest in God was initiated by the death of a significant person, a great disappointment, a failed relationship, or a great triumph. Perhaps the turning point was in the form of a prayer that invited God to take control or a traditional altar call. It could also include a positive response to "Would you like to pray a prayer of salvation?" The pivotal point comes with a heightened awareness of spiritual need that prompts yielding one's life to God.

The pivotal point comes with a heightened awareness of spiritual need that prompts yielding one's life to God.

If you were gravitating toward God, what did a greater God focus look like? This stage might entail your desire to pray more or read the Bible more, or may include a sense of growing peace. Essentially, this period of life involves a shift of heart attitude toward God. His personal revelation can be subtle but creates impact.

After Christ Time Frame

This is the period in which one enjoys a peace founded in God, growing and learning as the relationship with Christ deepens. Though the exact time of this change may be elusive, new motivations and attitudes, new spiritual coping mechanisms, new joy, thankfulness, and strengthened traits of character are unquestionably taking place. Other noticeable changes occur, such as a change in heart attitude, how one acts or reacts, perspectives, beliefs, approaches to problems, etc.

Enrichment comes by God's purposes taking shape, perhaps coordinated with a growing awareness of a spiritual gift imparted. Be specific. Conclude with how God is leading you *now.* (If you quote a favorite Scripture, explain why it's meaningful to you.)

> And this is the testimony: that God has given us eternal life, and this life is in His Son. He who has the Son has life; he who does not have the Son of God does not have life. (1 John 5:11–12 NKJV)

Showtime!

Though writing about our spiritual journey has been focused on three different stages—BC, PP, and AD, there is a fourth period regarding your testimony. After your salvation story has been written and is ready to go, it is now spiritual showtime. Share your miracle of new life through Jesus's Gospel message.

Well-known Pastor J.D. Greear of Summit Church has said, "God's call on your life is a call to use you in his mission. God chose you to make you an eternal blessing to someone. That's good news for those of you who feel like God only has enough grace to save you—and that's it. But that's not how it works. God is like a spiritual tornado. He never pulls you in without also hurling you out."[1]

Tips for Testimony Preparation

Rather than sharing the entire testimony, you may use excerpts of select sections tailored to a client's situation.

As you write your testimony, begin by asking God for His wisdom and guidance. Think of an initial statement that will grab the listener's interest. Follow with paragraphs that unfold smoothly and lead to an ending that culminates in a satisfying closure. If you use Scripture as closure to the testimony, use only one, and be sure to express its significance.

Consider your testimony as versatile. From time to time, rather than sharing the entire testimony, you may use excerpts of select sections tailored to a client's situation.

As you begin, pray and ask God's help before writing. Other considerations include the following:

A written "three-minute testimony," when double-spaced, is about one and a third to one and a half pages. As you begin, pray and ask God's help before writing. After the testimony is written, read it aloud. Perhaps reread it in another day or two for edits.

Other considerations for testimony preparation include:

- Generally, "write the way you speak" (conversationally).
- "Don't be overly negative or positive." (Overall, strike a positive tone.)
- "Don't criticize or name any church, denomination, organization, etc."
- "Think about your listeners. Avoid overly religious terms."
- "Practice telling your story until it becomes natural."[2]

In addition, avoid words that may not be familiar, such as "saved," "born again," or "slain in the Spirit," etc. If you were a child when you became a believer, tell what Jesus means to you now, and describe the turning point of assuming "ownership" of your faith as a practicing adult.

The Apostle Paul's Testimony

1. The Apostle Paul's BC

After becoming a follower of Christ, the apostle Paul voraciously shared his testimony.

Paul (Saul) was a Pharisee. A well-educated man, he considered himself a Jew of all Jews because he was "circumcised the eighth day of the stock of Israel, of the tribe of Benjamin, a Hebrew of Hebrews; concerning the law, a Pharisee" (Philippians 3:5 NKJV).

Saul, later also known as Paul, was a "genuine Jew by birth, not a proselyte. Furthermore, he was of the elite stock of Israel, directly descended from Abraham, Isaac, and Jacob. Calling himself a Hebrew of the Hebrews, Paul's "family retained Hebrew customs and spoke the Hebrew language."[3] With his distinguished Jewish heritage, Paul was a zealot who "scrupulously observed the external demands of the Law and fanatically tried to wipe out all opponents of Judaism."[4]

Before knowing Christ, Paul was known for his ruthless, treacherous targeting of Christ followers known as people of "the Way."[5] (See Acts 9:2 and other references in Acts.) Paul sanctioned the cold-heartedly murders of countless persons of faith, but it was one man, in particular, whose death was haunting: Stephen. As he was being stoned, the martyr's last words were unforgettable. "Lord, do not charge them with this sin" (Acts 7:60 NKJV).

Because Paul was savagely hateful in his persecution of Christians, no one could have imagined he was redeemable. Yet God had other ideas! Paul's conversion story is one of the greatest examples of testimony sharing in the Bible. After becoming a follower of Christ, the apostle Paul voraciously shared his testimony, whether speaking to an ordinary person or a reigning king.

NOTE: As an ethnic Jew born in Rome, Paul was a Roman citizen. Though his parents had given him the Jewish name of Saul, it was common to be given a Roman name as well. Fourteen years after his conversion, "Saul" began his God-designated mission to the Gentiles and began using his Roman name of Paul.[6]

If the apostle Paul were to write his BC testimony today, perhaps he would write:

> There was a lot of over-the-top sin in my life before I knew Jesus. I had justified stalking and was responsible for persecuting and causing the death of many Christians. I felt these Christians were rebelling against the religion of our forefathers. Hatred saturated my every thought of them because, to me, they were a cult! I'll never forget this one

> guy named Stephen though. I hated him, but I felt oddly unsettled by his death. I'd never witnessed anyone violently dying and, at the same time, praying for those killing him. We were his enemies!

2. Paul's Pivotal Point (PP) of Conversion

After Stephen's martyrdom, Paul was traveling to Jerusalem with a small group. His plan was to capture them and then force them to return to Damascus for trial. When a bright light suddenly appeared, it was so overwhelming it knocked Paul to his knees and blinded him. He heard a voice,

> "Saul, Saul, why are you persecuting Me?"
> "Who are you, Lord?"
> The Lord answered, "I am Jesus, whom you are persecuting; it is hard for you to kick against the goads." (Acts 9:4–5 NKJV, paraphrased)

Though a goad was a prod used for animals, the message was clear to Paul. God was prodding his stubborn resistance—a vain and pointless losing battle. The kairos moment prompted Saul's surrender.

> "Lord, what do You want me to do?"
> "Arise," Jesus commanded, "and go into the city, and you will be told what you must do." (Acts 9:6 NKJV)

We note that the Lord did not give Saul full disclosure. Always, He desires that we trust Him.

Those who were traveling with Paul led him by the hand to where God arranged a meeting with Ananias—a devout believer but distrustful of Saul. Yet when God called him to meet Saul, Ananias took a step of faith to obey and meet the murderous, infamous Saul.

When Ananias saw Saul, he addressed him respectfully as "Brother Saul"—a common salutation when one believer greeted another. Saul explained that God had appeared to him, and as the two men began to pray together, scales miraculously dropped from Saul's eyes. He was filled with the Spirit of God, and his sight was restored.

If the apostle Paul were to write his PP testimony, perhaps he would write:

> I was on my way to find Christians living in Damascus—I planned to bring them to Jerusalem, where they'd go on trial and be condemned to death. I thought they deserved it! As I was walking, a sudden light appeared. It was so bright that I was completely blind and fell to the ground. Although others were with me, I was the only one blinded.

The voice I heard called Himself Jesus and asked why I was persecuting Him—"kicking against the goads," He called it.

In my heart, I knew God was speaking to me, and I also knew exactly what He meant. I had been resisting Him by persecuting people of "the Way."

Although my sight was gone, I began to see things more clearly than ever. I knew it was time to stop running from God, and so I asked, "Lord, what would you have me to do?"

3. The Apostle Paul's AD

Author John Piper captures the grace God extended to Paul: "Grace is not simply leniency when we have sinned. Grace is the enabling gift of God *not* to sin. Grace is power, not just pardon."[7]

When God extended grace to Paul, He enabled Paul to become a champion for Christians and one of the greatest evangelists in the early days of Christianity. God's grace allowed Paul, as a new creation in Christ (2 Corinthians 5:17), to make extraordinary impact. His Spirit-filled life and inspired writings have prevailed through the centuries.

When God extended grace to Paul, He enabled Paul to become a champion for Christians and one of the greatest evangelists in the early days of Christianity.

After Paul's personal encounter with God, Paul lived as His chosen vessel—the bearer of His name before the Gentiles, kings, and children of Israel. His dramatic conversion had transformed his heart, attitudes, and mission in life. His new motivation for his life is reflected by his words:

> That I may know Him and the power of His resurrection, and the fellowship of His sufferings, being conformed to His death. (Philippians 3:10 NKJV)

Paul is speaking of experiencing Christ personally by fellowshipping in His suffering, by a change and conformity in his character by the power of the Spirit. The verb *know* means to know personally, not merely intellectually. Paul had met his Savior, and the rest of his life became a deepening of his relationship with Him.

If the apostle Paul were to write his AD testimony today, perhaps he would say:

My life has completely changed! After I was blinded for three days, God used Ananias to pray with me and restore my eyesight; God touched my heart as well. He forgave me of my sinful past and awakened in me a fervent desire to follow Him. Whether Gentiles, kings, or anyone else, God has given me a supernatural love for others. Jesus is God incarnate. Because He extended His love and His grace to me, all is rubbish compared to knowing Him and experiencing His love. I've had my share of suffering—shipwrecks, hunger and thirst, beatings with rods, stoning and other perils, but I will never forget His words: "My grace is sufficient for you." I know His words are true because I've experienced it. "Strength is made perfect in weakness" (2 Corinthians 12:9 NKJV).

Sample of an Advocate's Written Testimony

Introductory statement: In the counseling room, the advocate begins her testimony with a riveting statement to win the listener's attention. "God had personally prepared a rescue plan for my life. It was so radical, it still fills me with wonder."

Next, she describes her before-Christ days.

BC: "Somewhere in the middle of my college years, I decided my sinful choices disqualified me from a life with God. What on earth would God want with *me?* I was raised in a Christian home and knew right from wrong, yet I had chosen my own way. Fitting in with others was important to me. I was aware of my sinful lifestyle and certainly felt shame at times. I didn't feel comfortable walking into a church. I felt like an impostor among people who belonged there. So, I tried to block God out of my life."

How could she walk so closely with God and have such a sinful past?

Transitioning to the pivotal point of her testimony: "After I married and began to have children, I realized I could no longer ignore God. That wouldn't be fair to my children. I enrolled them in Sunday school, and though I attended church, I felt like I was going through the motions. During that time, I started spending time with my next-door neighbor, also a new mom. Cathy was different than some of the Christians I'd met. She spoke of Jesus like she knew Him. She relied on Him in a personal way. She read her Bible and talked about the strength she found in day-to-day stresses. There was something different about her. When troubled about something, she sought to know God's will. 'Therefore, do not be unwise, but understand what the will of the Lord is' (Ephesians 5:17 NKJV). As I spent more time with Cathy, I was convinced I wanted whatever it was she had found but thought my past prevented getting close to God. One day, as if she were reading my mind, Cathy told me about some sinful choices she had made earlier in her life."

Pivotal point: "I was stunned. I could hardly believe my ears. *How can she walk so closely with God and have such a sinful past*? Cathy then explained the Gospel."

- "God created me to be with Him and have eternal life.
- "Sin separated me from God, His fellowship, and the eternal life He offered.

- "God loved me so much that He sent His only Son to be sacrificed for my sins, which would then restore my fellowship with Him.
- "Jesus died for my sins, but He didn't stay in that tomb. He rose from the dead in new life and gave me new life in Him.
- "That day I responded to God. I acknowledged Jesus as my Savior and asked Him to take over my life."

AD: "Ever since asking Jesus to take control of my life, my eyes were opened, and I recognized His presence everywhere. The past is forgiven, and He has given me the desire to avoid sin. Yet I know if I sin, I am forgiven. And when I find myself living too independently from Him, I know the door is open to draw closer without condemnation."

"The past is forgiven, and He has given me the desire to avoid sin."

A Seasoned Advocate Encourages Testimony Sharing

Dear advocate in training,

Soon you will experience one of the greatest joys possible as a believer—sharing Christ in the power of the Holy Spirit. And you will be ready! You present any subject matter after thoughtful organization. Your carefully prepared testimony can be of immediate and effective use in nearly every witnessing situation—at times extracting select portions as you witness.

By presenting your personal story and how God has touched your life, others will be encouraged toward making a personal decision to invite Christ into their lives.

As you share, positive responses will come—such as your client's life-changing decision to receive the gift of salvation. (With often a positive impact on the pregnancy decision.) Occasionally, you'll be used of the Lord to "expand your territory" to present the Gospel message to the client's boyfriend or husband. There have also been occasions when an informal translator—a neighbor, friend, or relative of an English learner (EL) client—has been used to translate the Gospel message in the counseling room and then decided she also wants to pray to receive Christ!

On one occasion, a young woman interviewed for an internship with the ministry. When asked about her faith background, her mistaken belief that good works could secure her salvation became apparent. After more discussion, she was convinced that only Jesus could assure her of salvation, and she prayed to receive Him into her life. You'll find that working at a pregnancy resource center is always an adventure.

In the counseling room with a client, you will hear about the personal circumstances that brought her to the center. As she speaks, listen

The spiritual truth she has heard can be the genesis of a later decision.

to her tone, her expressions, and for what is not said as well as what is said. Listen for pain behind her words and know that God, all the while, is wooing her to His amazing love. God's desire is to become her strength to fortify her "righteous decision-making." Even if the client does not make a spiritual decision, the spiritual truth she has heard can be the genesis of a later decision.

If a client is not ready to accept Christ into her life, she is often availed of other opportunities that can fan interest. For instance, when enrolled in a parenting program, she could be asked, "With all the craziness going on in our world, do you know the greatest gift that a mother can give her child?" (The client always seems anxious to hear the answer.) "Faith is the answer! Helping your child develop faith through a relationship with God provides much security in life."

We know that a pregnancy brings a unique impact to life, yet a client often feels, in her fear, that pregnancy will negatively impact the rest of her life. She needs to hear, "Just slow down. You don't need to be in such a hurry to decide."

Keep in mind that whatever her specific reasoning, she often feels in survival mode. "It's either this baby's life, or it's my life!" The what-ifs begin a haunting chant.

"What if my parents throw me out of the house?"

"What if I never finish college?"

"What if I can't provide for my baby?"

"What if my boyfriend leaves me?"

Crisis spins everything out of control and puts security into a tailspin. This young woman needs God. ("Jesus, tender her heart so she is open to receiving you.")

The role of advocate includes creating a climate of safeness, of acceptance, of being there for the client's moment of need. Yet, I knew her *deepest* longing was connecting with Christ, the Source of all love. As advocates, we are given the privilege of pointing the way to Jesus, the Source of the greatest love in the world.

God is always faithful to lead us from one divine appointment to another!

Spiritual interest finds fruition when a client meets God in the counseling room or rededicates herself to God. Any intimidation felt about sharing one's faith loses strength by preparing a well-thought-through testimony, ready to make an impact on your client. After a decision to invite Christ into their life, clients are asked, "How do you feel?" Most often they respond, "I feel peace," or "I feel lighter." God equips and uses those willing to obey. And His kingdom continues to grow!

Thank you for your willingness to lovingly and selflessly serve these young women (and their partners) by sharing the greatest gift in the world with them: Jesus. He is always faithful to lead us from one divine appointment to another!

God bless you!

Chapter Six

Gospel Conversations

Father, with your help, we will continue to live our lives based on the reality of the Gospel of Christ, which reveals Him to others.

(Prayer based on Philippians 1:27 TPT)

Culture Versus Conscience

You live in the midst of a brutal and perverse culture. For you will appear among them as shining lights in the universe, holding out the words of eternal life. (Philippians 2:15 TPT)

The words of the apostle Paul are especially meaningful as we serve at our pregnancy resource centers. Cultural influences are in a violent surge to defy the sacredness of human life.

The "abortion solution" that's become acceptable to many is "brutal and perverse." Yet, for the post-abortive woman, far from an abortion solution bringing closure, her conscience outlives the procedure. One's conscience recognizes sin: "The requirements of the law are woven into their hearts. They know what is right and wrong, for their conscience validates this 'law' in their heart" (Romans 2:15 TPT). The aggressive intrusion to empty the womb leaves an aftermath of inward conflict between self-accusation and rationalization. Inner battles steal from one's peace, despite the culture's moral relativism.

Story of Abby Johnson

Author of *Unplanned,* Abby Johnson is a former director at an abortion clinic. She understands firsthand the aftermath of abortion. As a

Cultural influences are in a violent surge to defy the sacredness of human life.

post-abortive woman, she experienced a kairos moment when called to chaperone an abortion for the first time. Shorthanded staffing recycled previously held beliefs into a major turning point of her life. The "brutal and perverse" reality that comes with observing an abortion triggered an undeniable reality.

The horror of this experience led Abby to resign as director of the abortion clinic. God's plan for Abby has her in the public arena—a voice defending the life of the unborn. "Never trust a decision you don't want your mother to know about!" Abby says.

The redemption from her past through Jesus Christ has had a major impact in disclosing the evil of abortion and the money-driven agenda of the abortion industry. Abby's change of perspective has been transformative to her personal life and the lives of many others.[1]

Transformed by Truth

And do not be conformed to this world;
but be transformed by the renewing of
your mind. (Romans 12:2 NKJV)

"Be transformed," is in the "present, imperative, passive tense."[2] In other words, when we or our clients receive Christ, there's a continuous process, a transformative, ongoing process for renewal taking place. When Scripture declares us to be *transformed*, the passive voice means it is not something we ourselves do, but something done *to us.* We, as God's own, *receive* the Spirit's transformation in our lives. God is the change agent. He grows the fruit of new character that continues to ripen our development and our own voice to speak life into the lives of our clients. When she enters a new, personal relationship with Him, this will renew her thinking and likely preserve the life of her baby.

In the Greek language, *transformation* and *transfiguration* are the same word: *metamorphoo.* "The transfiguration of Jesus is also part of our destiny, for the same Greek word is used twice for believers being transfigured by the renewing of our minds and by the glory of Christ within us that will complete our transformation into Christ's image."[3]

Chipping Away at the Flesh

Michelangelo, famous artist and sculptor of the magnificent statue of David, once said, "In every block of marble I see a statue as plain as though it stood before me, shaped and perfect in attitude and action. I have only to hew away the rough walls that imprison the lovely apparition to reveal it to the other eyes as mine see it."[4]

When likened to Michelangelo's artistic process, God's method of transformation "sets His children free" by chipping away all that doesn't belong, such as sin that keeps us imprisoned. In Christ we have been liberated from the power of sin in our lives. "If anyone is in Christ, he is a new creation; old things have passed away, behold, all things have become new" (2 Corinthians 5:17 NKJV). All that *doesn't belong* is that which the Master removes. The intent for the crude chunk of stone is the Creator's masterpiece!

> *"If anyone is in Christ, he is a new creation; old things have passed away, behold, all things have become new."*
>
> 2 Corinthians 5:17 NKJV

God's Gift of Transformation

Courtney arrived at the center for pregnancy confirmation. Though she had grown up in a Christian home, she had never made a personal commitment to Christ. An earlier incident as a teen betrayed her trust in all Christians. She said, "Had I known this was a Christian center, I never would have made an appointment."

Courtney's salvation story involves an advocate at the center who lovingly shared her testimony with the message of the Gospel. Courtney spoke of her advocate after the baby was born:

> My advocate didn't judge me or make me feel like a horrible person because I was considering abortion. Instead, she reminded me of God's mercy and grace and showed me the love of Jesus Christ. I still get a knot in my throat when I tell this part of my story. When the advocate told me, "God has a purpose for your child's life," tears began pouring down my cheeks. She also said that after twenty-one days, the baby has a heartbeat. She spoke of Jesus, who loved me and said He would help me through this difficult time. She prayed with me and, that day, I received Jesus as my Lord and Savior.
>
> I felt this unbelievable peace. After leaving the pregnancy center, I canceled my abortion appointment, and nine months later gave birth to a beautiful daughter. This child has been such a blessing to my life and her siblings' lives as well. It's as if God sent her to unite and heal our family.

God's miraculous transforming power stripped away Courtney's stony heart, which kept her sin confined. That day God was the Master Sculptor who stripped away all that didn't belong and enabled freedom to serve God.

Building the Tabernacle: Spirit-Filled Ability

Those reticent about sharing their faith find encouragement in the miraculous story of God equipping people to accomplish a task He has appointed to them.

The tabernacle was the sacred meeting place for God's presence dwelling among His people. God's presence reigned in the beauty and glory of His sovereignty. According to Scripture, God commanded

By prayerfully sharing our faith with others, we discover that the more we share Christ, the more bountiful the harvest.

Moses to build a tabernacle—a demand of ability and giftedness of the artisans performing the work. Instead of calling persons who were already fit for the task, He called select individuals and provided an ample skill for the special work. One of the men, Bezalel, received the call but needed an infilling of God's Spirit to do the work. God met him at his point of need. Not only did God provide "wisdom and understanding" and knowledge, He also provided the skill for superior "workmanship" (Exodus 35:31).

Jesus said, "The Holy Spirit, whom the Father will send in my name, will teach you all things and will remind you of everything I have said to you" (John 14:26 NIV). The same God who equipped Bezalel is ready to equip us! "Jesus Christ is the same yesterday, today, and forever (Hebrews 13:8 NKJV).

As surely as the tabernacle artisans were given special gifts and skill to fashion beauty and glory to God, with certainty, we know God equips those called to the pregnancy center to serve women's needs, especially their need for a Savior.

The Advocate: Messenger of Good News

"How beautiful upon the mountains
Are the feet of him who brings good news,
Who proclaims peace,
Who brings glad tidings of good things,
Who proclaims salvation,
Who says to Zion,
'Your God reigns.'" (Isaiah 52:7 NKJV)

Everyone loves good news! Our family's good news, or a friend's good news, or our own good news spills freely from hearts and mouths. When followers of Christ hear the good news of someone's salvation, ready smiles reflect instant joy. This is because the heart of a believer shares the heart of an evangelist. If this seems questionable, consider this: Would it delight you if every person who walked through the center's doorway accepted Christ as her Lord and Savior?"

If you respond, "Yes," then you have the caring heart of an evangelist. No one needs a badge entitled, GIFT OF EVANGELISM to relish the Good News of Christ.

Once we realize we have the heart of an evangelist, how do we proceed? What about being filled with the Spirit to minister mightily to those who seek *something more*?

By prayerfully sharing our faith with others, we discover that the more we share Christ, the more bountiful the harvest. *Expansion* is part of the energy of creation. Scientists say that our universe is literally ever-expanding. Words such as increase, harvest, grow, and expand reflect a dynamic, never static, concept of life.

By sharing the Gospel, the faith of staff and volunteers at the center will catch the delight of changed lives. How can one *not* rejoice when hearing a departing client announce, "I came to this center for a pregnancy test, and I'm leaving with Jesus!"

Yes, good news is meant to be told!

Spirit-Filled for His Purposes

We are filled by the Holy Spirit by faith; then we can experience the abundant and fruitful life, which Christ promised to each Christian.

Preparing us for the appointed task is accomplished by an infilling of His Spirit. Thus, He declares, "Be filled with the Spirit" (Ephesians 5:18 NKJV). "Be filled" is something received *from* the Holy Spirit. When we desire to be filled with His Spirit, we confess our sins so we are not quenched of His Spirit. We thank God for forgiving our sins and ask his infilling by faith. We know we are asking according to His will since He has commanded us to be filled. We are spiritually ready to respond to the mission to which He has called us.[5]

Energized by the Spirit

> For it is God who works [Greek *energeo*] in you both to will and to do His good pleasure. (Philippians 2:13 NKJV)

> The same God distributes different kinds of miracles that accomplish different results through each believer's gift and ministry as he energizes and activates them. (1 Corinthians 12:6 TPT)

As we yield our lives to God, we pray that He will ignite our passions anew as we serve Him. "Lord, reboot my spiritual stamina—fill me to serve You that I may operate in the might (*energeo*) of Your Spirit."[6]

In service to our living God, we continue to pray by asking Him for the "energy" of His Spirit.

When God entrusted Peter with sharing the Gospel, he was energized (energeo) to minister to the circumcised (the Jews). Paul was also entrusted with sharing the Gospel—energized (energeo) to speak to the uncircumcised (the Gentiles). King David wrote, "I'm energized every time I enter Your heavenly sanctuary to seek more of your power and drink in more of your glory" (Psalm 63:2 TPT). In service to our living God, we continue to pray by *asking* Him for the "energy" of His Spirit. This surging power becomes a compelling response—like God's Spirit leading us to detect the kairos moment!

Passivity, a Death Knell

Passivity. What is it? Passivity suggests non-participation and, at its worst, complacency. Characterized by inactivity or flatness, passivity

Passivity means that if the client doesn't initiate a spiritual topic, there will be no discussion.

shrugs its shoulders at energeo—the divine energy of the Spirit. In the counseling room, its death knell counters everything God's Spirit desires to impact.

Passivity by an advocate means that if the client doesn't initiate a spiritual topic, there will be no discussion. If the abortion-vulnerable client comments, "I know God doesn't like abortion," a wise response is curbed. If an abortion-minded client says, "I wish I had more faith," passivity smothers kairos glory peeking through the shadows. It squelches the hope of the Gospel and fights God's desire to reach the lost.

We, as Christians, are called to walk by faith. "You do not have because you do not ask" (James 4:2 NKJV). Our focus in prayer must be to ask God for a transformative change of heart to reach our clients with his life and love. "Search me O God and know my heart" (Psalm 139:23 NKJV). Serving at the ministry, we know God cares about saving the lives of babies. He also cares about saving the lives of our clients through knowing Christ personally.

Understanding the Gen Z and Millennial Client

Anyone born between 1981 and 1996 (ages twenty-nine to forty-four in 2025) is considered a millennial, and anyone born between 1997 and 2012 is considered Gen Z.[7]

Zoomers (as Gen Z is sometimes called) and millennials, collectively called GenZennials, have diminished engagement with traditional religion, though many use the word "spiritual" to describe themselves. As an advocate, we must explore the client's personal meaning when she says, "I am a spiritual person." Respond with, "What meaning does the word *spiritual* have for you personally?" This opens the door to more discussion.

A study reported "most Gen Z (77%) consider themselves spiritual, and over half (51%) of millennials report feeling deep spirituality at least weekly. GenZennials . . . fluidly [combine] religious and nonreligious elements such as gratitude, fasting, prayer, art, affirmations, time in nature, and alternative practices (ie, tarot.)"[8] Your personal story of overcoming difficulties or receiving His gift of salvation offers the optimism of satisfying the client's spiritual void. According to a Gospel Coalition article,

> Gen Z is spiritually starved. The disorienting circumstances of the last three years—a global pandemic, countless mass shootings, the woke wars, a contested election, rapid inflation and widespread abuse scandals created a famine of identity, purpose, and belonging.
>
> . . . World rates for depression and anxiety grew by 25 percent during this period, Gen Z experienced a 33 percent

> increase. Now only 45 percent of Gen Z describe themselves as mentally healthy.[9]

Likewise, the study above revealed additional dire statistics:

> Over half of the US Gen Z (57%) and nearly half of the US millennials (46%) say they have experienced anxiety and depression symptoms. In a survey of over 23,000 people, nearly half (48%) of Gen Z and 38% of millennials reported being stressed or anxious all or most of the time."[10]

When a client contends with added stress from an unplanned pregnancy, there's often an acute awareness of needing more support. It creates readiness to listen. The advocate gently asks the client, "With your challenging situation, do you ever feel it's hard to get past the stress?"

Likely, the client admits an unplanned pregnancy is difficult.

Next, the advocate follows with a significant question: "How do you handle the stress?"

(The client's answer to this question is countered with a topic testimony by the advocate remembering "a situation where God came through, because that's what a God of great love does—He comes through!"

Gen Z is "starved for a peace that surpasses all understanding and that can still the waters of chronic anxiety," said the Gospel Coalition article. The article also reported that "Gen Z wants to be mentored, but they don't know how to meet older people. Only a minority actually have mentors."[11] Gen Zs long to connect, and when an advocate provides warmth, sincerity, and intrigue of storytelling through a personal testimony, the client begins dropping defenses. The shared experience of a story, whether teller or listener, is bonding. Gen Z is drawn by authenticity, perhaps a pushback to social media that entices the projection of perfect images online.

Though we may not have a specified spiritual gift of evangelism, per se, we are not off the hook!

But I Don't Have the Gift of Evangelism

Sometimes a misguided mindset becomes a major hindrance. "I'll leave evangelizing to those with the gift of evangelism, and since that's not my gift, I won't be sharing my faith." This belief, sometimes kept under wraps, is an offense to biblical truth. All believers have a spiritual mandate to share their faith. If this is part of a center's expressed mission, then, as advocates, sharing our Christian faith is part of God's calling.

As followers of Christ, the "image-bearer identity" proclaims us soul winners—"fishers of men." Though we may not have a specified spiritual gift of evangelism, per se, we are not off the hook! A soul-winning God desires us to reach out to others, to "fish" for souls as a team endeavor with Jesus. We're not to say, "I don't have the gift of evangelism" because we can still tell our testimonies and speak of the God of salvation. In fact, why not ask Him for the gift of evangelism in its fullness? God gives gifts as He wills, and, in the end, we can still manifest elements of all the gifts. For instance:

- If I have not received the gift of mercy, would this mean I must not or am *unable* to offer mercy to others? (No.)
- If I have not received the gift of exhortation (or gift of counseling), would this mean that I must not or am *unable* to offer good advice or sound counsel? (No.)
- If I have not received the gift for service, would this mean I must not offer or am *unable* to serve others—so that I'll never wash another dish that isn't mine or help clean up after an event? (No.)
- If I have not received the gift of teaching, would this mean I must not mentor or instruct? Does it mean I'm *unable* to teach anyone about anything? (No)
- If I have not received the gift of faith, would this mean I must not or am *unable* to place my faith in God with the challenges in my life? (No.)
- If I have not received the gift of discernment, would this mean I can never or am *unable* to discern nuances that lead me to truth? (No.)
- If I have not received the gift of evangelism, would this mean I am unable to offer my testimony and the Gospel message to others? (No.)

God will "make you complete in every good work to do His will."

Hebrews 13:21 NKJV

When God calls us to a mission, He will prepare us! Ask the advocate trainee, "Do you feel God has called you to serve here?" If an advocate feels called to serve at the center, then God will "make you complete in every good work to do His will" (Hebrews 13:21 NKJV).

Each spiritual gift has characteristics *adaptable* to God's calling for evangelism. Let's say you do not have a specific gift of evangelism, but you have the spiritual gift of teaching. It can typically be said of those who love teaching: A teacher loves to learn, then loves to talk about it. Teachers love to promote understanding and expand another's depth of knowledge. Sharing their personal stories of surrendering control of one's life to God promotes understanding and depth of insight.

A testimony is a story, and people love a good story. According to a PR expert citing researcher and cognitive psychologist Jerome

Bruner, storytelling makes a message more memorable than just using facts. He says:

> The neural networks ignited in our brains during a dream are the very same one that light up when we lose ourselves in a great movie or a compelling book—putting you right there in the action. . . . Authentic, realistic and human storytelling, with an element of drama, will strike an emotional chord every time.[12]

This means any facts about Jesus you include in a salvation testimony or a Scripture you bring to life through a story will be remembered in context of storytelling. This sets up the opportunity of inference for the client. That is, hearing the story of your testimony, a client is more inclined to infer, *If giving her life to God changed things for her, maybe God can make a difference in my life too.*

There's application for the other gifts as well. Consider the spiritual gift of mercy. With this gift, undoubtedly, the client will sense your compassion for her crisis. In recognition of your mercy toward her, she feels at ease and lowers defenses. Soon she's sharing from her heart. Her greater openness is the doorway to a Gospel presentation. God uses any spiritual gift you have for the sacred purpose to which He has called you.

God uses any spiritual gift you have for the sacred purpose to which He has called you.

Grace Empowers

> My message and my preaching were not with wise and persuasive words, but with a demonstration of the Spirit's power, so that your faith might not rest on human wisdom, but on God's power. (1 Corinthians 2:4–5 NIV)

The apostle Paul tells us grace was given to him to preach to the Gentiles. Though Paul was called to be an apostle, nowhere does Scripture indicate that he had been given all of the spiritual gifts. Yet, Paul, like the rest of God's children, received a measure of grace to proceed with God's mission.

> Grace alone empowers me so that I can boldly preach this wonderful message to non-Jewish people, sharing with them the unfading, inexhaustible riches of Christ, which are beyond comprehension. (Ephesians 3:8 TPT)

Non-Jewish people were not a familiar addition to Paul's relational orbit. Paul was a Jew, and the Jews hung around other Jews. At our centers, God has appointed us to interact with those from differing cultural and faith backgrounds.

Jehovah Jireh, one of the Hebrew names of God, refers to God's provision. Grace abounds whenever God is calling us to share Him. Our prayers shore us up in full-bodied faith to release the indwelling life of Christ. "But what if I feel intimidated?" Ignore your feelings and ask God to guide you. "Do it afraid," a well-known evangelist likes to say.

> And I pray that he would unveil within you the unlimited riches of his glory and favor until supernatural strength floods your innermost being with his divine might and explosive power. Then, by constantly using your faith, the life of Christ will be released deep inside you. (Ephesians 3:16–17 TPT)

Fishers of Men Through Christ

> Then Jesus said to them, "Follow Me, and I will make you become fishers of men." (Matthew 4:19 NKJV)

Our fishing expedition with Jesus begins with the Greek word *deute* (follow), "which is an adverb, not a verb, that means 'come here' and 'come hither.'" It is spoken along the lines of "Here, behind me!"[13]

The mission is already set, and He desires us to join Him. As we draw close to Him, we offer ourselves to His supernatural remake. Don't miss the understood subject of His words. "*You,* follow me." When we reread Matthew 4:19, we glean how relational evangelism is.

As we draw close to Him, we offer ourselves to His supernatural remake.

NOTE: *You . . . Me. I . . . you.* Our lives, our ministries, are accomplished in sync with the Master. We were created by Him to be part of His expedition. Let's jump "in the boat" and catch souls!

We belong to Him. Why wouldn't we desire to live in close association with the One we belong to? Jesus knows where the fish are biting, even those swimming in the depths of the sea in vast darkness. "Lord, bring those who need you to our centers that we may share You with them."

Because God enables us, we're up for the task. We become increasingly aware of His divine plan as we plumb meaning from His words. He says He "will make" us—a passive verb because Jesus is the One who does the equipping for action. How exciting to learn God is predominant in our outreach, and we are the receivers of His grace-filled abilities. We're an amenable recipient of a "twosome outreach" with the Lord. We don't have to muster up. He completes us and provides. As we receive from Him by faith, He mobilizes us to the soul-winning life. It's as if Jesus is saying, "When you come hither with me, I will remake you." Show your interest by going to Him. The Greek word for *make* (*poieo*) could be translated "create." Whatever we may lack, God can bring it to existence![14] Creating requires starting from scratch. This is bringing something from nothing! He is acting upon our new creation hearts to catch souls for God.

The Greek term for *fisher* "here doesn't refer to the Greek word for fish. . . . As a noun, the word means 'those of the sun' or 'sunners.'" The word translated as *fishers* also means, "of the sun" or "sunners" (*halieis*). Thus, from Matthew 4:19, listeners heard: "Here, behind me. And I will make you sunners of men."[15]

The linguist continues with a personal note:

> "I like the symbolism of bringing fish to the sun by pulling them out of the dark depths of the water. These ideas of a hidden future and bringing people to the light ties to many of Jesus's concepts: "Light" is knowledge. "Darkness" is ignorance. "Truth" is what is unhidden. "Seeing" is knowing and understanding.[16]

The believer's new life in Jesus is an expression of Jesus's divine purpose for her.

The believer's new life in Jesus is an expression of Jesus's divine purpose for her. Look closely at the verse *prior* to the command to fish for men.

> And Jesus, walking by the Sea of Galilee, saw two brothers, Simon called Peter, and Andrew his brother, casting a net into the sea; for they were fishermen. (Matthew 4:18 NKJV)

Let's reread the passage: "Casting a net . . . for they were fishermen." In our mind's eye, can we see Simon and Andrew casting fishing nets into the sea? At first, the passage seems merely to identify Simon and Andrew as fishermen. But don't miss the subtlety. "For they were fishermen" points to their casting a net because they are acting like fishermen and what do fisherman do? They fish!

We, as believers, are designated fishermen by Jesus. We toss our nets into the sea of lost souls—adrift and aimless. The "fish," who arrive at our centers assume a disguise. Some appear as a young pregnant woman, frightened and floundering, bereft in the current of crisis called "an unplanned pregnancy." The shores of new life are calling to her.

Encouragement for the Faint of Heart

Oswald Chambers, Scottish evangelist and author of *My Utmost for His Highest,* offers words of encouragement to those faint of heart about sharing their faith:

> When our Lord said to the disciples, "Follow Me and I will make you fishers of men," His reference was not to the

> skilled angler, but to those who use the drag-net—something which requires practically no skill; the point being that you do not have to watch your "fish," but you have to do the simple thing and God will do the rest."[17]

We toss our nets into the sea of lost souls—adrift and aimless.

Scripture often cites a condition with a promise to follow. Thus, we have "Follow Me" (the condition) and "I will make you" (a promise). It's as if Jesus is saying, "If you do this, I will do that." Because relationships strengthen when united in one accord, fishing for souls by sharing the Gospel draws us infinitely closer to the Master Fisherman.

What Is the Gospel Anyway?

> Christ died for our sins . . . He was buried . . .
> He rose again on the third day according to the
> Scriptures. (1 Corinthians 15:3–4 NKJV)

Sometimes, when a client is asked if she knows what the Gospel is, she responds, "Matthew, Mark, Luke, and John." As her advocate, you might respond by saying, "It's true that these four books of the New Testament are called the four Gospels and focus on Jesus's life and ministry. But the Gospel message itself refers to Jesus's death, burial, and resurrection—the Good News of salvation."

As fishers of men, we could transition into spiritual discussion. "Isn't it amazing to think that Christ's death and resurrection—2000 years later—can still hold significance for our lives today? I didn't discover that for myself until . . ." (Share testimony.)

Many of our clients are cultural Christians. Though familiar with Christian doctrine, they lack the greater understanding of a personal relationship.

To explain further, let's say that during Jesus's earthly life, He is called to a home where a woman has died. Let's imagine cancer has taken her life, and Jesus is led to the back room to see a lifeless body. With a voice of unmatched authority, He shouts, "Cancer be gone!" and the cancer instantly leaves her body. She is now disease-free, but her body remains dead. She still needs life. Jesus commands her lungs to be filled with the breath of life. And when He shouts, "Come forth!" she rises from her deathbed in response—healed from the disease, fully breathing, fully alive.

When we surrender our lives to Christ, He has freed us from humanity's "sin disease." Just as, "Cancer be gone!" freed from the person from disease, however, her cancer free body *still needs life.* We who receive the gift of the Cross are forgiven of all sin, including Original Sin, but we still need the breath of (His resurrected) life to live through us. This is exactly what the Gospel promises—the life of His Spirit. By sheer grace, God shares His triumph of the Cross with those He loves! Receiving the precious gift of His indwelling life, we join hearts with the apostle Paul who said:

> My heart spills over with thanks to God for the way he continually empowers me, and to our Lord Jesus, the Anointed One, who found me trustworthy and who authorized me to be his partner in the ministry. (1Timothy 1:12 TPT)

God fortifies us for His mission through our relationship with Him.

> And with great power the apostles gave witness to the resurrection of the Lord Jesus. (Acts 4:33 NKJV)

Healed of original sin, we now live by "bringing to death" the self-life and exchanging it with Jesus's life—the life of the Spirit. When our client receives Christ into her life, her choices have expanded to godly choices through God's Spirit. Though the way of our flesh (self-life) remains accessible, as we follow Him faithfully, sin becomes utterly distasteful to the believer. His Spirit, indwelling the believer's spirit, is in a 'partnership' with us—a *covenant,* in which Christ takes the lead. We are enabled to function from the new spiritual identity provided for us. The emphasis has changed. We now live from God's Spirit within.

In the quiet intimacy of engaging our client in spiritual discussion comes the dismantling of barriers keeping her from truth. Jesus is the centerpiece, and when one receives Him, His perfect sacrifice exchanges mortal unrighteousness for the righteousness of the Spirit of God. When received, the "new creation being" is "holy and blameless in his sight" (Ephesians 1:4 NIV). We enter acceptability through Jesus's sacrifice.

Isn't it amazing to think that Christ's death and resurrection can still hold significance for our lives today?

Receiving a New Self

> And if you are not joined to the Spirit of the Anointed One, you are not of him. (Romans 8:9 TPT)

> Be renewed in the spirit of your mind, and that you put on the new man which was created according to God, in true righteousness and holiness. (Ephesians 4:23–24 NKJV)

Without Christ, there can be no renewal. When we enter into new life with Him, the transformation process is now on jumpstart! Romans 8:9 contains "an unusual Greek clause that can be translated, 'If anyone is not joined to the Spirit of Christ, he cannot be himself.'"[18] We have a foundational *inability* to become our truest self when we are without Christ. "Who I am" (as God intended) is the self whose spirit is born again into Christ with new redemptive power. The self, according to God's original intent, is restored with new purposes, thoughts, and motivations for living. Thus, Satan's desire for repeat clients at our centers is greatly hindered by a client's committed rebirth into faith and a willingness to follow God's guidelines for her life.

If an unbeliever leaves the counseling room with the hope to improve her life choices without a relationship with Christ, at best, this is behavior modification, not transformation. Without God, our client cannot become "the best version of herself" because the genuine, truest self is one in relationship with Him, filled with His Spirit and infused with a new heart's motivation and ability. Only through Him can one hope to sustain a God-honoring life.

A case in point, found in Luke 15, is the familiar story of a wanderlust son who returns home. His life has neither been virtuous nor exemplary. He has consorted with ungodly people, squandered his early inheritance, and, stripped financially, is now working for a farmer feeding pigs. (Even touching a pig for a Jew was disgraceful and deserving of a curse, according to Old Testament law.) At the heart of every godless life is an old version of self. In the life of the returning son, however, we see a person who has stepped away from self's brokenness. His fractured self-will has been redeemed by the severity of a new humility through the confession of sin to the father who loves him. Like a child confiding in his parent, he speaks the unimaginable. "I have sinned against heaven and against you."

We have a foundational inability to become our truest self when we are without Christ.

The wayward son, like some of our clients, is ready for change. Perhaps the prodigal's story is akin to some of our own testimonies. Stories of those who live the repercussions of sinful choices when we were still defying God. In Luke 15:17, we learn the son "came to himself"[19] and returned home. That is, he came to his real self . . . the one God created him to be.

An advocate that God uses to lead her client to Christ will find no greater joy. Every new believer has "come to herself." She is changed from the client who entered your center only an hour before. The miracle of new life is delivered, and a Savior now governs her life by God's Spirit. "But how do we know," asks the trainee, "if a client has made a *sincere* decision to give her life to Christ?" By faith we accept her decision at face value. The issue of her sincerity is between her and God.

NOTE: Occasionally, the advocate suspects a client is people pleasing when she consents to pray to receive Christ, and provides an out by saying, "I want you to know there's no pressure here. You are free to pray to receive Him today or take the booklet home to think about it."

Helping a Client Understand a Relationship with Christ

Jesus answered and said to him, "If anyone loves Me, he will keep My word; and My Father will love him, and We will come to him and make Our home with him." John 14:23 NKJV)

A client who had never invited Christ into her life was striving to grasp the meaning of a personal relationship with Christ. To her, occasional prayers seemed good enough. Though she leaned toward a legalistic view of religion, her perspective had changed within a one-hour appointment.

To clarify the meaning of a personal relationship, the advocate said, "Think of a personal relationship with Jesus as His standing on the doorstep of your home. He has rung the doorbell, and you respond by opening your door. 'Oh, it's you, Jesus, coming to pay a visit!' This offers a recognition of Jesus, yet as you greet Him, you resist welcoming Him into the sanctuary of your home. Home is the relaxed dwelling place where you are 'completely yourself.' Perhaps the thought floats through your mind that you don't want Him to see you when you're completely yourself! Yet God, in His love for you, continues to pursue you."

The advocate continued with topic testimony about keeping one's distance from God. "I, too, kept my distance, even though He was intriguing, and I wanted to know Him but wasn't ready to make changes in my life. Strangely, I had a strong, 'inner knowing' that God wanted me as His own. It was like an intangible sense of His presence following me. I felt conflicted until I ultimately invited Him into the home of my heart."

Every new believer has "come to herself." She is changed from the client who entered your center only an hour before.

The Gospel Encounter

A young woman in her twenties arrives at the center for her scheduled appointment. Her youthful appeal and pleasant greetings to the staff disguise dark thoughts of terminating her preborn's life. At this battlefield for the life of her child, she hears about abortion risks, the emotional toll of an abortion procedure, and the life-giving options for her baby—parenting or adoption. She is nearing the tipping point when her advocate speaks of hope through a life-giving Savior. A God who rescues those in despair. Enter the Gospel encounter!

The Gospel: God's Method of Spiritual Growth

We desire the best for our clients. Their personal growth is part of it. One's greatest personal growth begins and ends with Gospel living. Here's how:

The Gospel refers to the death, burial and resurrection of Christ. His death on the Cross atoned for sins, making it possible to receive the gift of the Cross and a relationship with Him. As we live the Gospel intentionally, the Gospel journey is also applicable to clients with whom we share the good news of new life.

One's greatest personal growth begins and ends with Gospel living.

Death:

The client: Is the client willing to "die" to her self-life and surrender her life to Christ? Is she willing to bring "death" to her worldly solutions? Is she willing to say, "God, I can't handle this situation anymore. I give it to you so You can guide me"?

The advocate: Is the advocate willing to "die" to her self-life and bring death to intimidation regarding sharing the Gospel?

Burial: (Figurative)

The client: The client must be willing to say, "God, I know that You have a plan, and I am willing to avoid digging up my old ways and leave problems *buried* with You."

Is the client willing to bury her worldly lifestyle to follow Him? Bury her personal ambitions to walk out God's purposes for her life?

The advocate: Is the advocate willing to bury her fears and make a decision to step up to God's mission and share Christ with clients?

Resurrection:

The client: Is the client willing to invite the living Christ into her life to fill her daily with His new, spirit-filled life? Is she willing to say, "God, I know that You are the God of the impossible; You are a redeemer God, and I am going to trust You with this pregnancy"?

The advocate: Is the advocate willing to live a life of faith by sharing the good news of Christ and leaning on the Spirit who does more than we can ask or imagine?

The advocate often initiates faith sharing through her personal story of surrendering to Christ. "I know this is a difficult situation you're facing. In my own life I've discovered God's willingness to meet me exactly at my point of need." (She shares her testimony with the client). "I know He desires to be there for you, too, if you'll trust Him with your situation." "Can you think of a time when you were facing a difficult situation and things worked out?"

As the conversation flows easily to the client's spiritual background, the client admits she misses feeling close to God. The advocate asks, "Would you like to do a "reset" with the Lord to begin a deeper relationship with Him?" The question is first met with silence. (Learn to be comfortable with pauses so the "still small voice of God" (1 Kings 19:12 NKJV) can speak into your client's life.)

After a few moments, the client speaks. Her words sound firm. "Yes. I want to pray that prayer." That day, abortion took no prisoners! Her life, surrendered to God, was released from its stronghold.

She would later tell the advocate that in the days that followed, temptation intruded, but she was equipped with the Spirit of God to stay on course. Living in triumph finds strength a day at a time through a God who *reigns* in the life of His child.

Living in triumph finds strength a day at a time through a God who reigns in the life of His child.

A Splash of God's Glory in the Counseling Room

> I have fought the good fight, I have finished the race, I have kept the faith. (2 Timothy 4:7 NKJV)

Some clients—even after receiving the good news of the Gospel—continue to teeter between life and death for their unborn baby. As staff and volunteers, we pray for God's intervention in the incorrigible fight between flesh and spirit.

Author Gary Thomas, in his book *Holy Available* (previously published as *The Beautiful Fight*), tells of an Orthodox monk who pointed out that the phrase "the good fight" (2 Timothy 4:7) was a "strikingly Greek" expression. He said it was best understood as, "I have fought the beautiful fight."

How can a fight be called beautiful? Thomas pondered. He concluded, it's because "amid real transformation and sacrificial service, there is drama, passion, struggle, and vision—everything our souls need to feel alive."[20] Every life struggling for triumph in each individual situation is indeed a beautiful fight. Our spiritual outreach in the counseling room is also a beautiful fight, a struggle between light and darkness. In Him, we are equipped for the task. In Him, we await the "splash of His glory."

A Muslim Turns to Christ

After five surgical abortions, the Muslim client seemed oblivious to the high risk of carrying a sixth pregnancy to term. She declared, "I've decided to keep this baby!" She had never given birth, and at forty-five years old, she said she believed the chances of having a child could be narrowing because of her age.

Not wanting to inspire false hope, the advocate discussed the higher "possibility" of miscarriage after five abortions. "But I will say this," added the advocate, "I believe I worship the God of the impossible! Jesus is different from Allah because He is a God of miracles. Our God looks at you with such a tender love, and He wants you to draw closer to Him. He desires you to become His child."

The advocate proceeded to share her testimony. They talked briefly before the advocate asked, "May I share a little booklet with you that has meant a lot to me?"

After the advocate shared the spiritual tract with the client and discussed, this dear lady prayed to receive Christ. (Jesus's existence as a historical and enlightened prophet is part of Islam's doctrine. Muslims

Jehovah-Rophe, the God of healing, is the One still performing miracles.

believe He will return to judge the world. However, Islam rejects the redemption based on the sacrifice of Jesus on a cross as mankind's Savior.)

Before the woman left that day, her advocate asked if she'd like to pray. Again she said, "Because of many past abortions, there is a much greater risk of miscarriage with this pregnancy. But I worship a mighty God. His name is Jesus, and I'd like for us to pray about this if that's okay."

The woman excitedly submitted to the prayer. She left smiling broadly as if she had already forgotten the warning about a heightened threat of death for her baby.

NOTE: At times, we hold back from bold prayers, thinking, *It will ruin the client's faith if God doesn't answer the prayer explicitly.* Keep in mind that God can defend His own reputation. Though the odds for miscarriage were high, life and death are within God's realm. We don't have to protect Him by refraining from a prayer request that, in our perspective, is tinged with a questionable outcome.

Months later, our former Muslim client delivered a full-term, healthy baby girl. Our God answered our prayer with the new life of a mother and the sustained life of her child. Jehovah-Rophe (or Jehovah-Rapha). The God of healing! He is the One still performing miracles in response to an ordinary believer petitioning His throne for grace. What a great and merciful God we have.

Chapter Seven

Compassion in Action: How-Tos of Gospel Sharing

Father, in You is "spiritual wealth. . . like hidden treasure waiting to be discovered—heaven's wisdom and endless riches of revelation knowledge."

(Prayer based on Colossians 2:3 TPT)

One of the greatest earthly treasures ever discovered gained fast notoriety—a gem with an extraordinary weight of 45.52 carats. This famed diamond with a rare, deep blue hue was named the Hope Diamond because of ownership by a London banking family named Hope. The gem's final owner was Harry Winston, a New York gem merchant, who purchased the gem from the McLean estate. In 1958 the stone was donated to the Smithsonian National Museum of Natural History.[1]

Mr. Winston's manner of mailing was shocking. From a post office in New York, the jewel was enclosed within an ordinary brown, paper-wrapped package. It was sent registered mail, with insurance, to the Smithsonian Museum. The contents were received intact. Today this prized diamond attraction rests on a slowly rotating pedestal behind protective glass. Admiration endures among museum enthusiasts.[2]

Sharing the Treasure of Jesus

Humanity is drawn to beauty, and rarities are treasured. Jesus, as the Father's unprecedented gift, provides enduring value for our lives. Receiving Christ personally sows eternity into our hearts with a joy spilling freely. Before we know Him, lives resemble an ordinary, brown envelope with unremarkable value. With the entrance of the treasure, the "envelope" is transformed, sealed with God's purposes. We are appointed with the glorious destiny of delivering Jesus's message.

> To me, the very least of all saints, this grace was given, to preach to the Gentiles the unfathomable riches of Christ. (Ephesians 3:8 NASB)

As Christians serving at respective centers, we have received the personal treasure of Jesus's salvation. God's power mingles with our witness. We pray, "Lord, give me a heart for the client who has yet to know You. Guide me to a destined opportunity that deepens her knowledge of You. Tender her heart to receive You."

Beyond Gospel events, outreaches, and church opportunities, we can have a formidable impact at our respective centers by sharing *one-on-one* with clients. At every pregnancy resource center, the potential harvest walks through our doors every day.

The following research will encourage you to share your faith:

> 75 to 90 percent of new believers come to Christ through a friend or acquaintance who explains the good news on a one-on-one basis. Only 17 percent of all conversions come through what is called an "event"—a pastor giving his Sunday morning message, a . . . crusade, or a Friendship Sunday.[3]

Jesus and the Samaritan Woman

> He longs for everyone to embrace his life and return to the full knowledge of the truth. (1 Timothy 2:4 TPT)

Let's listen to Jesus's conversation with the Samaritan woman in John Four. He chose a decisive detour in His schedule to minister to a heathen woman. His encounter flows easily, His words soaking into her waywardness to draw her to truth.

Keep in mind the cultural bias of the day forbids Jesus's interchange with the Samaritan woman. "In their day it would be disreputable and beneath his dignity for a rabbi to speak to a woman in public. But Jesus chose a more inclusive posture than His religious peers."[4] For the Samaritan woman to follow societal rules would be out of character. Instead, she feeds into the conversation. She does not disavow the truths Jesus addresses. The Samaritan woman's personal life includes five failed relationships and, currently, a cohabitating partner. With a past of broken relationships, does she deal with distrust? Now face-to-face with an inquiring Jesus, she chooses to engage. This man, this Jewish stranger, speaks of matters she's never entertained. His words, spoken with gentle authority, wrap around her mind and begin to dismantle that which she's always believed. His words create intrigue and compel the marvel of interplay between the Knower and the known.

Any encounter with Jesus serves truth just as truth serves God's redemptive purposes. As the conversation proceeds, we witness a growing engagement, cognizance that this is no ordinary man. She first addresses Him as a "Jew" (v. 9) then "Sir" (v. 11), then "prophet" (v. 19), before recognizing she has just spoken with the Messiah (v. 29). Incremental revelations are not unlike our clients who move step by conversational step toward a saving knowledge of Christ.

Any encounter with Jesus serves truth just as truth serves God's redemptive purposes.

With compassion and obedience to Father God, Jesus has traveled out of His way to arrive at a common water well in Sychar. Josephus, the historian of the day, "tells us that, although the most direct route was through Samaria, the Jews didn't go that route due to the antipathy between the Jews and the Samaritans. However, our Lord went through Samaria.[5] His foreknowledge revealed that a disreputable woman would be drawing water at the hottest time of day. Ordinarily, women drew water later in the day (see Genesis 24:11), when weather was cooler and they could enjoy pleasantries with one another. But the Samaritan woman's past has not served her well, and it is likely that her intention was to arrive early to avoid wagging tongues.

The Samaritan Woman: Built Up to Witness

> "And so now, I entrust you into God's hands
> and the message of His grace, which is all you
> need to become strong." (Acts 20:32 TPT)

The word *strong* is taken from the Greek root of the word *architect* and means, "to build you up."[6] We are about to observe God's plan unfold in the life of the Samaritan woman as she comes to faith. God has planned destiny in the hearts of those who believe. What is the destiny in store for us and for each of our clients? God has a plan for every life, and His intent is to "build us up" for the mission in store.

The Mission

> But He needed to go through Samaria. (John 4:4 NKJV)

Bible context: "He *needed to go.*" Jesus sends the disciples on an errand. Note that the spiritual mission takes precedence! An important conversation is waiting. The spiritual exchange, though pending, will soon move forward to the applause of heaven.

PRC application: Jesus *needed* to go to Samaria. What is it that *we* need at our centers to follow the Father's will? Is there a sidestep we need to take for God's intended spiritual mission?

He continues to love the sinner. Our prayer is, "Lord, enable me to do no less."

Just as the Samaritan woman has lived in defiance of God, often our clients avoid following God's ways for their lives. As advocates, we, too, have a choice to follow Jesus's example and go out of our way to share the message of the Gospel. God's desire is to address a high-risk lifestyle, which is an affront to God's higher purposes for her life. He is an impartial God, showing no favoritism (Acts 10:34). Neither is He astonished by the sin in people's lives. Yet He calls out sin and, importantly, He continues to love the sinner. Our prayer is, "Lord, enable me to do no less."

The Obstacles

Jesus therefore, being wearied from His journey,
sat thus by the well. (John 4:6 NKJV)

Bible context: Jesus reaches out to the Samaritan woman despite travel weariness. For some, the way we're feeling at a given moment may influence whether we share. But Jesus perseveres. His love and value for the Samaritan woman drive Him to action. The gift of new life must be imparted.

PRC application: As advocates, we must persevere with clients despite weariness or intimidation tempting us to lethargy. Do we feel "brain dead" from too many challenging clients on a given day? Are we tempted to forgo witnessing because we don't feel chemistry with a client? Are we nearing the end of the day, and think, *I'll keep this dialogue abbreviated*? On the other hand, will we, like Jesus, value our client enough to share the transformational message of Jesus? To be consistent, we need our faith strengthened. "Jesus, reboot my spiritual vitality that I may share You with this client in need."

The Conversation

"Give Me a drink." (John 4:7 NKJV)

Bible context: "And at this point His disciples came, and they marveled that He talked with a woman; yet no one said, "What do You seek?" or, "Why are You talking with her? (John 4:27 NKJV). When Jesus asks the Samaritan woman for a drink of water, He counters the customary male response not to engage with women publicly. Not only was there ethnic bias between Jews and Samaritans but, her culturally inferior status as a woman invoked public shunning. The apostle Paul later wrote, "There is neither Jew nor Greek, there is neither slave nor free, there is neither male nor female; for you are all one in Christ Jesus" (Galatians 3:28 NKJV).

PRC application: Jesus led the conversation just as it will be the advocate who speaks first and guides the conversation. Though at times we meet clients who are educated, socially responsive, and well-mannered, other times a client lacks appropriate grooming, speaks foul language, or acts indifferently. Sometimes clients bring young children to their appointments, then fail to discipline them. This invites our humble opportunity to help. Perhaps we arrange to keep her small child entertained while another advocate meets with the mother. The unexpected has a way of challenging our reliance upon Jesus. Living from His Spirit enables us to withhold judgment of clients or, at times, an unruly child. This includes not speaking disparagingly about a client or her child after she departs from the center. "Lord, fill me with your Spirit as we extend Jesus to others."

The Approach

> "How is it that You, being a Jew, ask a drink from me, a Samaritan woman?" (John 4:9 NKJV)

Biblical context: Jesus is treating the woman with uncommon respect. Though it clearly puzzles her, it also wins her attention.

PRC context: The woman's question could have been worded, "Why are you being so nice to me?" Despite the woman's past, Jesus is impartial. Many of our own clients arrive feeling guilty and troubled about the poor decisions they have made. They may also be feeling angry at the boyfriend who abandoned them or angry at themselves for not protecting themselves from pregnancy. They need Jesus's peace. As we treat our clients with respect, trust builds and hearts open to hearing the life-changing Gospel message.

As we treat our clients with respect, trust builds and hearts open to hearing the life-changing Gospel message.

The Gift

> "If you knew the gift of God, and who it is who says to you, 'Give me a drink,' you would have asked Him, and He would have given you living water."(John 4:10 NKJV)

> "But whoever drinks of the water that I shall give him will never thirst. But the water that I shall give him will become in him a fountain of water springing up into everlasting life." (John 4:14 NKJV)

Biblical context: To paraphrase, Jesus is telling the Samaritan woman, "You don't know the gift I have ready and waiting for you!" Jesus is again building intrigue just like the stories of our testimonies. This is illustrated by His words "the gift of God" and "who it is who says to you." He also mentions *living water*. Jesus is continually drawing her interest—slowly, like drawing a bucket of brimming water filled from its well. His words draw revelation from new depths of meaning.

PRC context: At times, clients express pleasant surprise about the spiritual overtones of topics introduced. Initially, they had no expectations of hearing something spiritual—just as the Samaritan woman had no expectations when she arrived at the well for water. Whether a Samaritan woman in the first century or a client today, both have a need—living water to quench their spiritual thirst. Yet there is so much more to offer. Just as our Savior presented an unexpected spiritual message, we follow His example to present new life. We counter Satan's hindrances to sharing Him. "Do not fear, for I have redeemed you; I have summoned you by name; you are mine" (Isaiah 43:1 NIV).

Sometimes His presence in the counseling room is like a divine meandering. It leads us into the client's life in search of the elusive golden thread knotted in spiritual resistance. Truth untangles golden threads to battle vain imaginations, such as, "She won't be interested in the Gospel message."

When we persevere, we often hear our client's voice tendered by new awe of the Savior. "I've never heard these things explained like that."

The strategic moment bursts with potential. A righteous identity through Christ is a prayer away.

The strategic moment bursts with potential. A righteous identity through Christ is a prayer away.

The Need

> "Sir, give me this water, that I may not thirst, nor come here to draw." (John 4:15 NKJV)

Biblical context: The Samaritan woman's spiritual understanding has been limited. Perhaps she wonders if He speaks about the living water in a spiritual way.

PRC context: A little spiritual journey is poised to take place during the client session. As the advocate shares her testimony, the client will hopefully discover her own need for a Savior. A discussion of sin is part of the advocate's testimony. (The BC part of our testimony answers "What are we saved *from*?") An advocate's personal story can initiate the client's thirst for Jesus's living water.

She may conclude, "I want what you have for my life."

The Issue

> "Go call your husband, and come here." The woman answered him, "I have no husband." Jesus said to her, "You are right in saying, 'I have no husband.'" (John 4:16 ESV)

Biblical context: When Jesus suddenly begins talking about husbands, the Samaritan woman must have wondered, *What do husbands have to do with this conversation?* Yet Jesus, as fully man as well as fully God, is led and fed by the Spirit. Having had multiple husbands and currently living with a man not her husband, sin has distanced her from a relationship with the living God. Jesus addressed the issue that would free her to experience genuine, spiritual growth. The Samaritan woman has begun to recognize Jesus as more than she may have initially thought. How puzzling that this man, this stranger, seems to know her —in fact, know everything about her! Yet, unlike others who know about her life, He makes no slurs, nor does He shame her. He *cares*.

PRC context: As the Spirit leads, our conversation with a client can also take a turn as we tread deeper into the territory of a life without God. Asking the right questions or interjecting an unexpected statement can radically move a discussion forward. In the beginning, we, unlike Jesus, don't know much about our client. As we ask God to fill our hearts with love for her, she concludes, "This person *cares* about me." The recognition, reinforced by the advocate's transparent testimony, drives authenticity and inspires the client to get real about her life to include sins, disappointments, desires for change, etc. Our clients sometimes show surprise when they learn God desires a relationship and is pursuing them to "enter in."

Our clients sometimes show surprise when they learn God desires a relationship.

The Conclusion

> "Sir, I perceive that you are a prophet." (John 4:19 ESV)

Biblical context: A true prophet is known as a person who unabashedly declares truth. The situation is puzzling. *How does this stranger know all these things about me?* She concludes, "I perceive that you are a prophet!" This statement is significant because she is not dismissing Jesus's words about her sinful past. When we accept the Savior, we recognize the need to be saved from our sins. The woman from Samaria is drawing closer.

PRC context: The Samaritan woman has begun to attach to Jesus with her growing spiritual understanding. Belief is progressing. When we share our testimonies, the client may readily identify with the advocate's before-Christ segment of testimony. For example, if we were to say to a client, "I used to be puzzled by all the world religions claiming their beliefs were the truth. How can I believe the claims of Christianity are the right beliefs?"

The client may respond, "I agree; how do we know what claims are believable?"

Just as the Samaritan woman becomes engaged in the pursuit of answers, our client may also have questions bubbling up.

The Truth

> "Our fathers worshiped on this mountain, but you say that
> in Jerusalem is the place where one ought to worship."
> Jesus said to her, "Woman, believe me, the hour is
> coming when you will neither on this mountain nor
> in Jerusalem will you worship the Father. You worship

what you do not know; we worship what we know,
for salvation is from the Jews. But the hour is coming
. . . when the true worshipers will worship the Father
in spirit and in truth, for the Father is seeking such
people to worship him." (John 4:20–24 ESV)

Biblical context: The Assyrians, at one time in their history, had besieged Jerusalem. After they conquered the city, they brought some of the Jews back to their country. They also left some behind so that Israel could be absorbed into the conquered Assyrian empire (2 Kings 17:5–6). Thus, the Samaritans' ethnicity was the outcome of eventual intermarriage (2 Kings 17:24–33). The Samaritan people, not considered true Jews, were forbidden to worship in a Jewish temple; the Samaritan people built their own temple on Mt. Gerizim, which the Samaritan woman references.

Jesus tells the Samaritan woman she is not really a true worshiper because she worships what she doesn't know. He speaks about the heart of worship, which is the growing intimacy from a spiritual relationship with God.

PRC context: Although the Samaritan woman doesn't deny Jesus's words, she does give pushback. Like some of our clients, she reasserts her religious background without understanding a more intimate relationship with God. Like the client may say, "I know I should get back to church," and though she is referencing *some* religious background, the statement misses the point. She is speaking about returning to a "church building" and participating in their services without having a worshipful heart to follow and obey Him. Like the Samaritan woman, she is not yet a true worshiper of God. We are *not* speaking of a facility made of bricks and mortar. We are referring to a living church of believers indwelled by God's Spirit.

With God, we become intimate participants in His divinely planned appointment.

We must always keep in mind that God is the seeker, the one who guides her to *where* she will hear His message of salvation. "For the Father is seeking such people to worship Him" (John 4:23). With God, we become intimate participants in His divinely planned appointment.

The Revelation

The woman said to Him, "I know that the Messiah
is coming" (who is called Christ). "When He comes,
He will tell us all things." (John 4:25 NKJV)

Biblical context: The woman is now engaged in spiritual conversation. She is asserting some personal beliefs.

PRC context: The woman does not yet know who Jesus is. This can also be seen in a client at the beginning of our spiritual conversation. That is, the client may first seem resistant when a spiritual topic makes its entry into conversation. Everything warms up quickly when the advocate shares her personal testimony. Our sharing from the heart lowers client's defenses to engage authentically.

The Declaration

Jesus said to her, "I that speak to you
am He." (John 4:26 NKJV)

Our sharing from the heart lowers client's defenses to engage authentically.

Biblical context: Full disclosure has now been made. Jesus asserts He is the One she is seeking. He is the promised Messiah. There is *living* water to be drawn from the wells of salvation!

With joy you will draw water from the wells
of salvation. (Isaiah 12:2–3 ESV)

Hers is an unlikely story. Perhaps it is like our own miracle stories of salvation—love stories all—unworthiness soaking in fountains of grace, and bathed in the righteousness of God. As Jesus's identity more clearly emerges, the glorious discovery of who He is ignites passion. The water jugs at the well are empty, but her heart and soul, are filled with His *living* water. She runs breathlessly through the town, excited to tell others the impact of Jesus on her life.

PRC context: Jesus has spoken plainly. There are occasions in the counseling room when truth comes face-to-face with resistance and should not be mollified. For instance, an advocate looked caringly at her client, saying, "God wants to fill your needs. He is using the hardship you're experiencing to show your need for Him. Do you ever feel that way?"

A statement like this must be accompanied by a gentle tone and genuine compassion. This isn't judging the client but a Spirit-led statement, appropriate and sensitive in the context of right timing.

Often the response is, "I know. You're right." (The kairos moment leads to the Gospel message.)

By sharing one's testimony, it helps the client grow awareness of our interactive God. If the client's interest is piqued, the veil separating the client from the Savior is thinning, and in a timely fashion, the Gospel presentation culminates with "the ask."

"Would you like to invite Christ into your life now?" Or "Do you feel you would like to go deeper with God?" (It is not recommended to ask, "Would you like to become a Christian?" She may, through religious schooling, church attendance, and such already consider herself a Christian.) "Going deeper with God" is not offensive. It creates a sense of adventure in store for her. However, if you sense hesitancy, gently ask, "What is it that's holding you back?")

The Change

> "Come, see a Man who told me all things that I ever did. Could this be the Christ?" Then they went out of the city and came to Him. (John 4:29–30 NKJV)

> "Many of the Samaritans of that city believed in Him because of the word of the woman who testified, "He told me all that I ever did." (John 4:39 NKJV)

Biblical context: The Samaritan woman, forgetful of the water jugs, now runs through the city to tell everyone about her encounter with the Messiah. Truth has been divinely revealed. "However, when He, the Spirit of truth, has come, He will guide you into all the truth" (John 16:13 NKJV). We note that although the Samaritan woman has never received *training* for evangelism, the Spirit is guiding her. She thrills to tell others about meeting Him. Though what we might call a baby believer, she perceives her life with newfound joy and purpose. She is ready to invite others to join His kingdom. "These things I have spoken to you, that My joy may remain in you, and that your joy may be full" (John 15:11 NKJV).

PRC context: Just as the Samaritan woman's story about herself sparks people's interest in the surrounding town, the advocate's testimony is also powerful. It gives credence to the life-changing Gospel. It is God's message coming alive through a changed life. Our Messiah is the embodiment of the Gospel through His life, His death, and resurrection.

Our personal salvation stories are a prelude to the greatest story ever told.

Passion enlivens others' pursuit of God. Our personal salvation stories are a prelude to the greatest story ever told.

The Application

> "Do you not say, 'There are still four months and then comes the harvest'? Behold, I say to you, lift up your eyes and look at the fields, for they are already white for harvest." (John 4:35 NKJV)

Biblical context: Harvest time for crops occurs within a window of time. Jesus speaks of four months—an implication of urgency. It's like saying, "The crop's ready; it is time to go and harvest it!"

PRC context: A bountiful crop of souls is *ready* to harvest. It's time to prayerfully and boldly enter the field waiting for us to harvest. Whether seekers or believers who have wandered from the faith, whether numbed out, shut down, or fearfully stuck, our clients walk through the center's doorway in need of a dose of fresh hope. They need to hear that God personally knows their name (Exodus 33:17). He loves and seeks them personally.

At the center, every appointment is divine, which inspires our expectancy. Just as the Samaritan woman found the living water of salvation, our testimonies offer a sip of living water, inspiring expectancy for all God has to offer. He quenches the thirst for love and forgiveness with the promise of an eternity of knowing Jesus.

The Impact

> And many of the Samaritans of that city believed in Him because of the word of the woman who testified, "He told me all that I ever did." (John 4:39 NKJV)

> And many more believed because of His own word. Then they said to the woman, "Now we believe, not because of what you said, for we ourselves have heard Him and know that this is indeed the Christ, the Savior of the world." (John 4:41–42 NKJV)

Biblical context: Undoubtedly, the men in her town have heard of the Samaritan woman's sordid past. It is heartening to witness how God can use even a sinful life to legitimatize one's transformation. Those who hear her witness respond to the testimony. After she realizes Jesus is her Messiah, her joy is aglow.

PRC context: God desires more than influencing a woman to avoid regrettable choices. As advocates who speak into others' lives, our desire for our client exceeds carrying her baby to term. We desire new life to assure our client's eternity with the Lord. We are also heartened to know a mother's decision for new life greatly impacts sustaining the life of her preborn.

When the Samaritan woman met Jesus, He was a stranger. We, as advocates, also meet each client as a stranger. Just as Jesus took a detour to Samaria from the usual course of travel, we also take a detour to enable our meeting with Jesus. As a stranger, Jesus pursued a young woman sorely in need of salvation. As His advocates, we, too, offer His gift of salvation.

Whenever a client makes a decision to receive the new life of Christ, we encourage her to tell someone about it. Words reinforce the event. "For if you publicly declare with your mouth that Jesus is Lord and believe in your heart that God raised him from the dead, you will experience salvation" (Romans 10:9 TPT). The Samaritan woman excitedly told others. Though the water jugs were never filled at the well, she ran through the countryside spilling the living water of hope into the paths of all whom she met. Indeed, Jesus remains the answer to fulfillment. The One who knows the detail of every life. The One who longs to fill emptiness. The Messiah, a heathen woman, and less than an hour of

Whenever a client makes a decision to receive the new life of Christ, we encourage her to tell someone about it.

conversation brings impact to those "who have ears to hear" (Matthew 13:9 NKJV). A forever impact we lovingly extend to others.

> I will answer your cry for help every time you pray, and you will feel my presence in your time of trouble . . . I will satisfy you with a full life and with all that I do for you. For you will enjoy the fullness of my salvation. (Psalm 91:15–16 TPT)

Once in a while, the client who receives Christ asks the advocate, "Will you share this with my boyfriend? He's in the waiting room." This reflects the assurance she is *experiencing* about the truth she's just heard. Entire families have been known to receive Christ because a newly reborn client witnesses to her family after her conversion. The growing experience of His Spirit propels our faith to share Jesus with others.

Today, it is not unusual for a client who identifies as a Christian to be living with her boyfriend.

Cohabitation Trends

By reading Scripture's account of a disreputable Samaritan woman living with a man who's not her husband, we are reminded that cohabitation is not something new. A 2019 Pew Research study showed that among adults ages eighteen to forty-four, 59 percent have lived with an unmarried partner at some point in their lives."[7] In the biblical era, it may have been a more sensitive topic. Yet Jesus deemed it important to address with the Samaritan woman.

Today, it is not unusual for a client who identifies as a Christian to be living with her boyfriend. We note a sense of detachment from more traditional, moral guidelines. The client's matter-of-fact attitude asserts blithely, "This is the way things are now. When relationships are serious, couples live together." Statistics bear this out. The Pew Research poll shows "Catholics (74%) and white Protestants who do not self-identify as born again or evangelical (76%)" say that it's acceptable for an unmarried couple to live together.[8]

Cohabitation: Male and Female Perspectives

Eighty percent of women who cohabit are more prone to be motivated by "love as a major factor," whereas it's the case for only 63 percent of cohabitating men.[9] The statistics infer that some male partners view living together as an audition for marriage or easy sex with no obligation. Living together for women is viewed as drawing closer to the altar, a reflection of serious intent. Living together has become so culturally entrenched that most cohabitants we see at our centers—irrespective of religious affiliation—display no defensiveness when sharing that she and her boyfriend live together.

Pew Research: Sexual Norms

Based on Pew Research in 2019, today's sexual norms are much more relaxed than in the past. The clientele seen at the pregnancy centers reflect the trend.

> Half of Christians say casual sex—defined in the survey as sex between consenting adults who are not in a committed romantic relationship—is sometimes or always acceptable. Six-in-ten Catholics (62%) take this view, as do 56% of Protestants in the historically Black tradition, 54% of mainline Protestants and 36% of evangelical Protestants. Among those who are religiously unaffiliated, meanwhile, the vast majority (84%) say casual sex is sometimes or always acceptable.[10]

Clients who have received Christ and sincerely desire to follow His guidelines for sex have found it still takes firm belief and resolution to overcome fleshly temptation and cultural pressure. Abstinence requires a continual yielding to Christ and practical approaches to protect oneself from temptation. One former client who had rededicated her life to Christ at the center found that practicing abstinence "definitely narrows the field of men in pursuit." On a positive note, she added that it was also "helpful in determining a man's integrity of intentions."

Abstinence requires a continual yielding to Christ.

Those taking the firm stand for sexual integrity become acutely aware of the cost of following Christ. They also experience rewards that surpass living a compromised life. The following email was received by a former client who received Christ at one center:

> Thank you for starting the whole process of changing my life. My baby daughter is 4 months old. Her father moved away before he ever saw her. I would still make the same decision to have her all over again. I remember you, and thank you for beginning to move me in the right direction. This year has been a life-changing experience for me. I have been abstinent now for over one year. The one date I had recently, I told him my lifestyle was abstinence. I never heard from him again. But that's okay. I have made new friends who share my faith.

Another client shared, "I have told men who ask me out that they should know up front that I'm a Christian committed to saving sex for marriage. The last person who heard those words from me said that he was also a Christian, and that decision was fine with him. We are still dating."

Advocate and Client Exchange on Abstinence

Sexual integrity is discussed with spiritually interested, single clients who arrive at the center for a pregnancy test confirmation. Somewhat rarer are the discussions with married women who have been party to infidelity issues. Whichever the case, our hope is to get them on track with the Lord's plan for their lives.

A Women of Faith resource describes it this way: "Sexual integrity is about living in harmony with God's design for relationships. It leads to healthy, fulfilling relationships and protects us from the physical, emotional, and spiritual consequences of sin. Upholding sexual integrity also helps maintain a clear conscience and deepens your relationship with God" (emphasis removed).[11]

> For you were bought at a price; therefore glorify
> God in your body and in your spirit, which
> are God's. (1 Corinthians 6:20 NKJV)

A common question on a center's intake form is, "What are your living arrangements?" When some clients respond that they are living with a boyfriend, the talk on sexual integrity is delayed until later in the session—after a spiritual discussion in which they have made a commitment or recommitment to Christ.

The motivation for sexual abstinence is ordinarily in the context of a personal relationship with God—wanting to be genuine Christ followers submitted to biblical guidelines or returning to values once lived by. Without a relationship with Christ, a lifestyle of purity has little motivation and lacks meaning.

Without a relationship with Christ, a lifestyle of purity has little motivation and lacks meaning.

For the clients who commit or recommit their lives to Christ, coverage of the abstinence topic should follow. Introduction of the topic could begin by saying, "So many of the women we talk to have said that when they became sexually active, the relationship with their boyfriend was much more focused on the physical rather than emotional intimacy. Do you find that to be true?"

"It's unfortunately true," many agreed.

Once sexually active with a boyfriend, the emotional relationship becomes secondary to the physical.

Rededication: Getting Client Back on Track

When a single client arrived for a pregnancy test, she soon learned it was a Christian center. "Oh, I'm a Christian too!" she exclaimed. Though conducting her dating life loosely as a cultural Christian, she shared she had *once made a sincere commitment to Christ.* She spoke longingly and specifically about the personal relationship with Jesus she once enjoyed.

Advocate: "So it sounds like your relationship with the Lord was stronger earlier in your life. Do you think, with society's acceptance of premarital sex, you were lured into a more secular lifestyle, and that caused distance from God?

Christian Client: "Yes, I'll admit the way I'm living has caused me to distance from God. But, although my boyfriend and I are sleeping together, it's a monogamous relationship, so I don't feel too guilty about it."

Advocate: "It's always a difficult challenge, even for Christians. For years I lived like the cultural Christian also. Yet there's quite a distinction between a cultural Christian and a *follower* of Christ. It's the cultural Christian who's prone to say, 'I believe in you, God, but stay out of my bedroom!'"

Advocate continues: "Do you ever feel that way? Like telling God, 'I believe in You but stay out of my bedroom'?" (This question always prompts good discussion.)

Client: (Chuckles) "That's exactly what I'm doing—telling God to stay out of my bedroom!"

Advocate: "It's not that sex is something bad. After all, God invented sex! Yet He has set specific guidelines, and although the guidelines can feel confining, they're for our benefit. Yet He's not shocked when we desire sex. The heartache we see over unplanned pregnancies reveals the truth of God's guidelines. The unplanned pregnancies cause so much stress and grief. When the situation ends with abortion, at times contrary to values, we see the toll it can take on self-esteem, relationship with a boyfriend, and even with God. We've seen many couples break up after getting an abortion."

Client: "I've never had an abortion, but I hear what you're saying. I have missed feeling close to God like I used to. He feels far away." (A kairos moment.)

Advocate: "It sounds like you desire to draw closer to Him."

If she replies, "Yes, I do," then mention, "It's no accident you came in today. God is pursuing you. He knows you by name!"

It's not that sex is something bad. After all, God invented sex! Yet He has set specific guidelines.

The Rededication Process

If you are convinced the client knows basic Christian doctrine, use the pamphlet *Would You Like to Know God Personally?* to summarize the first four principles in a conversational manner.[12]

"The first spiritual principle of the pamphlet is one we're familiar with. **God loves you and created you to know Him personally**."

Christ took upon Himself all sin of everyone in the world—past, present, and future—at the same time.

(Have the client read John 3:16). Discuss that God is a God of love and sacrificed Himself for us. "In my own life, I knew God loved the whole world, but it was hard to imagine that He personally loved me!"

"The second spiritual principle is, '**We are sinners.**' We know that from time to time we make bad choices. The Bible calls that sin."[13] (Include a Scripture verse.)

"The third spiritual principle is that **Jesus died on the Cross to pay the penalty of sin."**[14] (Read one Scripture verse.) "God is a just God, which means there must be justice for the sins we commit. Jesus chose to sacrifice His life in our place. He was the perfect sacrifice because His life was without sin. Before I was a follower of Christ, I didn't appreciate His sacrifice. I reasoned, *Some people are just more heroic than others.* I hadn't yet considered that Christ took upon Himself *all* sin of everyone in the world—past, present, and future—at the same time. (Have client read at least one verse.) "I cannot imagine the pain and suffering He willingly endured for us on the Cross."

"The fourth principle is key to our salvation. It's the one I wasn't familiar with. *Receiving* Him personally."[15] (Include Scripture verse.) "It is amazing how I finally came to the decision to receive Him. May I share my story with you?" (Advocate shares her salvation testimony)

Advocate: "Before I was a believer, I lived a sinful lifestyle. I thought I was enjoying myself, but I felt emptiness. I often thought, *Is this all there is to life?* There was no sense of peace. Do you ever feel that way?"

Client: "Yes, for a long time."

Advocate: "The good news is these feelings of distance from God don't have to continue!"

Client: "I do miss Him. I need to get back to church."

Advocate: "Church is important, but we're talking about more than church. God wants to draw closer to you. Only He can fill the emptiness and give peace. I wish I'd had a booklet like this to help me understand that God loves me and wants me to invite Him into my life. May I share this with you?"

Client: Nods in agreement as the advocate opens the booklet to share the steps to getting right with God.

Modify Salvation Prayer for Rededication

If the advocate is using the salvation tract with a "backslidden" believer, the salvation tract can still be used with a brief explanation of the sections, but modify the prayer.

NOTE: At times it's difficult to discern if a client is a genuine believer who has grown lax in her faith or whether she has never entered into a genuine relationship with Jesus. If her commitment isn't clear, we need to explain the Gospel message clearly before praying a prayer of commitment to Him. The client can be invited to pray silently in her mind as the advocate reads the prayer phrase by phrase. If desired, the advocate mentions to the client that she'd like to open in prayer first. "Lord, we know you love _____ and are so pleased with her decision to follow You. Enable her and strengthen her as she experiences the joy of following You." Following the opening prayer, the client prays silently or aloud as the advocate reads it. (Advocates find that a few clients prefer to pray the entire prayer aloud, whereas others pray the words, phrase by phrase, as the advocate reads it.)

For a rededication prayer, a few of the words can be adapted from the words of a salvation prayer. For instance:

- Instead of "Lord Jesus, I want to know you," change it to "I want to know you *more deeply* and personally."
- Instead of "I open the door of my life," change the wording to "I *reopen* the door of my life."
- After the client repeats the phrase, "Thank you for forgiving my sins," say, "We're going to pause for you to *silently* confess sins that come to mind. If you think of additional sins later, just confess them to God and ask His forgiveness at that time. We need to keep short accounts of sin daily. When you have finished with the silent confession, just say, 'Okay,' and I'll go on with the prayer." (The prayer ends with, "Make me the kind of person You want me to be.")[16]

We are dependent on the Holy Spirit to bring about the conviction of heart that reveals the client's need for a Savior.

The Salvation Tract

Some have said many salvation tracts are linear and not appealing to millennial or Gen Z clients who generally enjoy meaningful social connection. This need not be a concern. The advocate has warmed up her connection with the client through earlier conversation, especially when sharing her personal testimony with her client.

Also, it's imperative to read the booklet and add comments in a conversational tone. An occasional comment counters a "stony presentation." (But be cautioned against tangential discussions. Essentially, stay on track.)

The booklet, filled with Scripture, is the focus because the Word of God is powerful. We are dependent on the Holy Spirit to bring about the conviction of heart that reveals the client's need for a Savior.

Benefits of Using a Salvation Tract

- The authority of Scripture reinforces each principle. The Word of God "shall not return to Me void, But it shall accomplish what I please, And it shall prosper in the thing for which I sent it" (Isaiah 55:11 NKJV).
- The booklet's illustrations are helpful for grasping spiritual concepts. For example, the illustration of the circles that represent the self-centered life versus Christ-centered life.
- It is adaptable to a conversational presentation. (See note.)
- It emphasizes the authority of the Word of God, not reliance on feelings.
- It includes next steps that need to be taken.
- The client can reread the pamphlet at home.
- On the back of the booklet, you can write the date of her "spiritual birthday."

NOTE: Don't overdo the conversational aspect and detract from the Gospel message. The purpose of conversation is to avoid sounding mechanical.

Gospel Methods: Classic Tract, Bridge Drawing, Bible Roadmap

We will be looking over several different presentations of the Gospel message. All are sound presentations, though you'll find some variations in Scripture and methodology. Methods include:

I. A classic spiritual tract presentation.

II. The Bridge presentation: A rudimentary drawing on a sheet of paper showing how Jesus bridges the gap between man and God.

III. Using the Bible instead of a tract. Evangelist William Fay has a method of presentation that uses Scripture as a roadmap.

Specific Scriptures explaining salvation will be read by the client with the sequential verse for discussion written in the margin of the Bible. A visible "roadmap" creates an easy "GPS" to successive key Gospel verses that follow.

I. Classic Gospel Tract Presentation with Unbeliever

Advocate's Gospel introduction: (to the client) "I'd like to show you a little booklet that's been meaningful to me. It's called, *Would You Like to Know God Personally?* and is set up in four sections." (This is similar to the booklet titled *Have You Heard of the Four Spiritual Laws?* As you go through the booklet, allow only one page to be shown at a time so as not to distract the client and prevent glancing ahead.)

Advocate: "We know that God has physical laws by which He operates. For instance, if I dropped this little booklet on the ground [advocate drops it], it falls to the floor because of the law of gravity. God also has spiritual laws (or principles) He has put in place, and this little booklet describes four of them. I won't be reading the entire booklet. We'll only *highlight* some things from each principle."

Principle One: (Read) "God **loves** you and created you to know Him personally."[17]

I could believe God loved the whole world, but could He love me?

Advocate's conversational comment: "Let's read John 3:16. This is a familiar verse that you've likely heard."

"For God so loved the world that He gave His only begotten Son, that whoever believes in Him shall not perish but have eternal life." (John 3:16 NASB1995)

Advocate's conversational comment: "Frankly, in my own life, I could believe God loved the whole world, but could He love *me*? I couldn't imagine His loving me because, with all the sin in my life, I didn't deserve His love. I still had much to learn! I heard you mention earlier you'd like to feel closer to God. That's good because, as a God of love, He desires a closer relationship with you also."

Principle Two: (Read) "Man is **sinful** and **separated** from God, so we cannot know Him personally and experience His love."[18]

(Read):

For all have sinned and fall short of the glory of God. (Romans 3:23 NIV)

Advocate's conversational comment: "Do you agree we all make wrong choices at times? In the Bible, this is known as sin, and since we commit sins, we're called sinners!"

(Read under principle two): "Man was created to have fellowship with God; but, because of his own stubborn self-will, he chose to go

Nothing we can do can make us fit for God's kingdom.

his own independent way, and fellowship with God was broken. This self-will, characterized by an attitude of active rebellion or passive indifference, is evidence of what the Bible calls sin."

Client: "I've never had an abortion, but I hear what you're saying. I have missed feeling like I used to years ago. God feels so far away now."

Advocate's conversational comment: "I have experienced that void in my life. I had no real fellowship with God. Occasionally, I'd toss up a prayer to Him, but I had a consuming emptiness from not knowing Him."

Diagram: (Read) "'For the wages of sin is death' (Romans 6:23 NIV). Biblically, spiritual death means spiritual separation from God."[19]

Advocate's conversational comment: "In this simple diagram, we see the separation from God illustrated. The arrows show how we keep trying to reach God through our good works. For instance, one arrow might represent prayer, another represents doing something nice for someone, but nothing we can do can make us fit for God's kingdom."

Principle Three: (Read) "Jesus Christ is God's **only** provision for man's sin. Through Him alone we can know God personally and experience God's love."[20]

(Read):

> But God demonstrates His own love toward us, in that while we were yet sinners, Christ died for us." (Romans 5:8 NASB)

Advocate's conversational comment: "Even though we are sinners, Christ died for us. This next verse is what's known as the Gospel, which is the Easter story—Christ died for the forgiveness of sins, was buried, and rose again. There were many eyewitnesses to this event!"

(Read):

> Christ died for our sins . . . he was buried . . . he was raised on the third day according to the Scriptures . . . he appeared to Cephas [Peter], and then to the Twelve. After that, he appeared to more than five hundred. (1 Corinthians 15:3–6 NIV)

Advocate (turns to next page): "The diagram illustrates how Jesus is our bridge to God."

(Read):

> Jesus answered, "I am the way and the truth and the life. No one comes to the Father except through me." (John 14:6 NIV)

Advocate's conversational comment: "Jesus says that getting close to God is only through Him. He is the only way. When you think about it, truth is always exclusive. One and one will always equal two!"

Principle Four: (Read) "We must individually **receive** Jesus Christ as Savior and Lord; then we can know God personally and experience His love."[21]

(Read):

> But as many as received Him, to them He gave
> the right to become children of God, to those
> who believe in his name. (John 1:12 NASB)

Advocate's conversational comment: "I used to think everyone was a child of God. Have you ever thought that? But I discovered that's contrary to the Bible! When we invite Him to come into our lives, only then do we become His child. In fact, before we desire to 'enter in,' the Bible refers to us as 'children of wrath.' This is because God has anger, or wrath, over sin. After we receive the gift of His salvation, Christ's death on the Cross pays the penalty and satisfies the justice required. As believers, we receive His indwelling Spirit, and God's righteousness indwells our Spirit."

Advocate's conversational comment: (Build the client's intrigue.) "Even though I knew the basic Gospel, this next verse takes this biblical doctrine and makes it personal. Principle four is the one I knew nothing about: We must receive Christ personally into our lives by faith. Jesus's death on a cross for us was a gift to mankind. Every gift has a giver and a receiver. I knew about Christ and His paying the penalty of my sins on the Cross, but I had never received Him into my life. (If the advocate has not yet shared her testimony, consider sharing an excerpt here prior to the prayer of commitment to be introduced.)

(Read):

> For by grace you have been saved through faith; and this
> is not of yourselves, it is the gift of God; not as a result of
> works, so that no one may boast. (Ephesians 2:8–9 NASB)

Advocate's conversational comment: "This verse always gave a sense of freedom since I was brought up in a family in which high performance was expected. We were not allowed to use the word *can't* in our family. Notice the verse says, [point to] 'it is the gift of God; not as a result of works.' Also, the verse says gift, not reward, so we are not earning it but receiving a freely given gift. It would have been natural to think I had worked hard to earn the merit for God's acceptance, but this is not what the Scripture says! It's all grace. Jesus died for us. He is the bridge to the Father. And we receive Him personally by inviting Him into our lives.

(Read) Christ speaking:

> "Behold, I stand at the door and knock; if
> anyone hears My voice and opens the door, I
> will come in to him." (Revelation 3:20)

"For by grace you have been saved through faith; and this is not of yourselves, it is the gift of God."

Ephesians 2:8 NASB

Advocate's conversational comment: "The word *behold* means 'Pay attention, I'm going to tell you something important.' Here He wants to tell us that He's standing at the door of our hearts, our lives, and He's knocking to be invited to enter. He desires a personal relationship, and when we open the door, He will come in! It's a promise with a condition: 'If anyone hears My voice.' Are we listening? If we're listening and invite Him into our lives, He promises, 'I will come in to him.'"

Read the next paragraph aloud to the client: "Receiving Christ involves turning to God from self (repentance) and trusting Christ to come into our lives to forgive us of our sins and to make us what He wants us to be. Just to agree intellectually that Jesus Christ is the Son of God and that He died on the Cross for our sins is not enough. Nor is it enough to have an emotional experience. We receive Jesus Christ by faith, as an act of our will."[22]

The Two Circles Illustration: Referring to the circle diagram, point out the location of the S (meaning self) versus the Cross (representing Christ).[23] Both are in the center of the circle. "The circles present a choice: We can live our lives with self on the throne, or we can live our lives with Christ on the throne. He is the one worthy of following."

Advocate's conversational comment: "At one point, I lived my life with self on the throne. Then I began moving toward God, and this brought me to a place *between* the two circles." (With index finger, point to the area between the two circles.) "Finally, I was ready to be 'all in' with the Lord, and I prayed to surrender my life to Him. My life now resembled the right circle, the one with God as the centerpiece of my life."

Advocate continues with a question: "Which circle do you think represents your life?"

Client: "The left circle or somewhere in between the two circles."

Advocate's question: "Which circle would you like to represent your life?" If the circle on the right, ask if she would like to pray a prayer that invites God to be at the throne of her life.[24]

The prayer is on the booklet's next page. Tell the client, "You can pray the prayer aloud if you wish, or I can read it while you silently pray."

Prayer: "Lord Jesus, I want to know You personally. Thank You for dying on the cross for my sins. I open the door of my life and receive You as my Savior and Lord. Thank You for forgiving my sins and giving me eternal life. Take control of the throne of my life. Make me the kind of person You want me to be."[25]

What about clients who are resistant to the salvation prayer? If the client is not ready to pray the prayer of surrendering her life to Christ, explore. "What are your thoughts?" or "What do you think has

If the client is not ready to pray the prayer of surrendering her life to Christ, explore. "What are your thoughts?" or "What do you think has to happen to be ready?"

to happen to be ready?" If her sexual lifestyle or the possibility of abortion is holding back her decision for Christ, ask if she would be willing to ask God to change the desires of her heart. This is the first step.

Prayer after Gospel: Receive Christ or Agnostic's Prayer

The Prayer to Receive Christ

The client has indicated a willingness to receive Christ into her life. At the junction of the desire to enter a relationship with the Savior, turn to the top of the page that says, "You Can Receive Christ Right Now by Faith Through Prayer." Tell her you will first read the prayer because she should know the content before giving consent to pray. After reading the prayer, discuss the last line, "Make me the kind of person You want me to be."[26] This refers to the desire to repent of sins and live differently as a follower of Christ.

Advocate: The way we'll proceed is I will read the prayer aloud, a phrase at a time. You can pray silently in your mind unless you prefer praying aloud. "Which way would be in your comfort zone: silently or aloud?"

After the client indicates her preference, begin the prayer.

As you pray the salvation prayer aloud—phrase by phrase—give the client enough time to repeat after you—especially if she is praying silently.

It's important to pause after reading the sentence that says, "Thank you for forgiving my sins and giving me eternal life." In a quiet tone of voice, tell the client, "Right now, take a moment and silently offer God your confession of sins that come to your mind to clear the decks. You can take your time, and after you're finished with the confession, say 'Okay,' and I'll know to go on with the prayer. Shall we proceed?"

It is also appropriate to ask, after a client has prayed to receive Christ, "What are you feeling right now?"

NOTE: As the one leading the prayer, when you resume the prayer, it's helpful to repeat the sentence: "Thank you for forgiving my sins and giving me eternal life." This is a declaration making clear every sin confessed is forgiven! Then complete the prayer the final two sentences: "Take control of the throne of my life. Make me the kind of person you want me to be."

After the prayer of salvation: If the client is in tears after praying, give her a few moments to recover, then ask, "What was it that touched you?" (It is positive and reaffirming for her new walk with the Lord to articulate the powerful feelings that led to tears. Validate the emotion.)

It is also appropriate to ask, after a client has prayed to receive Christ, "What are you feeling right now?" Many, if not most, will respond, "I feel peace!" If a client were to say, "To tell you the truth, I don't feel any different," bring her assurance. "That's okay, because faith is a fact, not a feeling. By the authority of God's Word, He has responded to you. He came into your life just as He promised He would."

These two tracts have a section entitled, "How to Know That Christ Is in Your Life." This is highly beneficial to review with your client. If time doesn't permit further discussion, point out the section and suggest she read through the material at home. Also helpful is, "Do Not Depend on Feelings." The illustration of the train and caboose graphically emphasize not depending on feelings.[27] If under a time constraint, be sure to tell her she can return to discuss and ask questions.

NOTE: Keep in mind that whether the client prays to receive Him or doesn't pray to receive Him, your witness has been *successful* simply because you have *shared.* You have offered the client an opportunity to meet the Savior. The outcome is in God's realm, not yours.

There is a prayer called the "agnostic's prayer," which isn't an actual commitment, but the prayer invites God to reveal more of Himself.

Non-committal Clients: The Agnostic's Prayer

There is a good middle-ground prayer for noncommittal clients, despite the method of Gospel presentation. To define the agnostic's spiritual belief: The agnostic is "a person who does not have a definite belief about whether God exists or not," or, more broadly, "a person who does not believe or is unsure of something."[28]

The following is an exchange between the advocate and her client introducing the agnostic's prayer.

Advocate: "Since you don't feel quite ready to make a commitment, would you be willing to take a middle step?"

Client: "What do you mean?"

Advocate: "There is a prayer called the 'agnostic's prayer,' which isn't an actual commitment, but the prayer invites God to reveal more of Himself to you. He is a gentleman God who won't violate your free will. It's a way of asking Him to boost your faith. He'll respond if you're willing to ask Him. Are you?"

Client: "That sounds kind of interesting. Sure."

Advocate: "The prayer is: 'God, if you are real, I ask you to reveal more of yourself to me. In Jesus's Name. Amen.'"

Advocate continues: "I'll be silent if you'd like to pray right now and give God permission to reveal more of Himself to you. Then I'd like to pray for you. Is that okay?"

II. Gospel Presentation: Bridge to Life

This Gospel presentation has been around for some time. It remains an effective presentation in the absence of a Gospel tract. (For instance, in a restaurant, the presentation can easily be written on the back of a paper napkin, readily illustrating a visual Gospel.)

Begin by drawing two cliffs opposite one another. (This looks like two L's upside down with space between.) The space separating the cliffs shows the chasm between us and God. Write **Sinful Man** above the left cliff, and write **Holy God** above the right cliff.

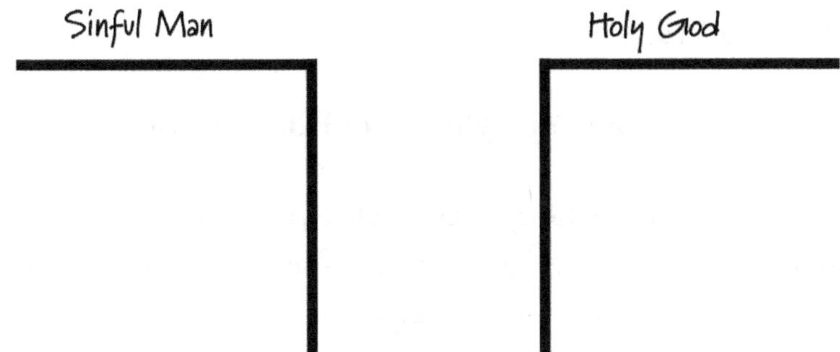

Pose the question to your client: "The Scripture says, 'All fall short of the glory of God.' So how can sinful man draw close to a holy God?" (Point to the chasm between Sinful Man and Holy God.) The answer: Only by Jesus, who has already paid the penalty for our sins.

Draw a cross horizontally connecting the two cliffs like a bridge. Write **Jesus** and **Romans 5:8** above the cross: "But God demonstrates His own love toward us, in that while we were still sinners, Christ died for us" (NKJV). Explain, "When we receive Him into our lives, we have a way to the Father."

Write **John 1:12** beside Holy God. "As many as received Him, to them he gave the right to become children of God, even to those who believe in His name."

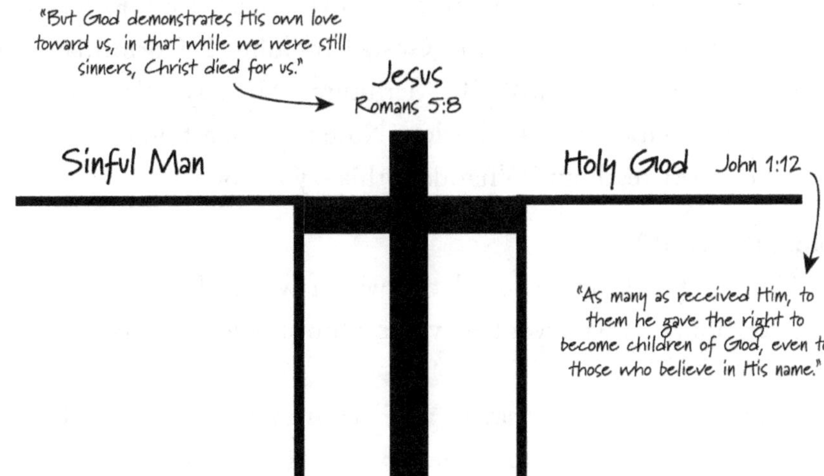

NOTE: : For preparing yourself to master this Gospel approach, go online to find the full illustration with correlating Scripture verses. See the Bridge to Life illustration (with download) at: navlink.org/bridge.[29]

The presentation ends with an invitation to pray a prayer led by the advocate and having the client repeat the prayer in her mind. The prayer thanks God for His forgiveness of sin, dying on the Cross for our sins, enabling us to receive Him and come into our salvation by His guidance in our lives.

III. Evangelist William Fay's Method of Faith Sharing

In his presentation of the Gospel, evangelist William Fay uses the Bible (not a tract) as an effective approach. He uses a method of following Scripture's road to salvation using sequential scriptural prompts written in the margin of his Bible. Each verse he covers has the next verse reference written in his Bible. The person across from him faces the Scripture, and the references he wrote for himself appear upside down to them (right side up for him).

For example, after reading and discussing Romans 3:23, you have written (upside down to the reader) Romans 6:23 in the right margin as the next verse to be read. Then, at the Romans 6:23 page, you've written John 3:3 in the margin, the next verse in the sequence. By writing the verses in the Bible's margin, you don't have to memorize the sequence. You point to highlighted verses and have client read them.[30]

"What does this say to you?"

After each verse is read (by the client), Mr. Fay asks the person, "What does this say to you?"If the meaning is unclear to the client, Mr. Fay simply tells them, "Read it again."[31]

William Fay's roadmap utilizes some verses from Romans but adds other Scriptures from the Gospel of John, 2 Corinthians, and Revelation—all from NKJV. The Scriptures Mr. Fay selected for his Gospel presentation are listed below. Note Fay's question to the person after the verse's reading: "What does this say to you?"

John 3:16 (NKJV)

Client: "For God so loved the whole world, He gave His only begotten Son, that whoever believes in Him should not perish but have everlasting life."

You: "What does this say to you?" (Possible answer: God loves us and sacrificed Jesus's life to atone for our sins to make everlasting life possible with Him.) "Let's turn to Romans 3:23."

Romans 3:23 (NKJV)

Client: "For all have sinned and fall short of the glory of God."

You: "What does this say to you?" (We all sin and, therefore, we are all sinners—separated from God and need reconciliation. He has been reconciled *to* us already and is waiting for us to reconcile *with* us.) (Next verse address is written in the Bible margin.)

Romans 6:23 (NKJV)

Client: "For the wages of sin is death, but the gift of God is eternal life in Jesus Christ our Lord."

You: "What does this say to you?" (You can explain a wage is something we earn; by sinning we are separated from God and "dead in our sins." Therefore, we have earned spiritual death and darkness. This prevents our having a relationship with a holy God.) (See next reference written in your Bible margin.)

1 Corinthians 15:3–4 (NKJV)

Client: "That Christ died for our sins according to the Scriptures, and that He was buried, and that He rose again the third day according to the Scriptures."

You: "What does this say to you?" (Jesus died for our sins, was buried, and rose from the dead.)

John 14:6 (NKJV)

Client: "Jesus said to them, 'I am the way, the truth, and the life. No one comes to the Father except through Me."

You: "What does this say to you?" (Though some say there are many ways to God, Jesus is saying the way is narrow and exclusive. Truth is always narrow in its exclusivity. Look at mathematics; there's only one accurate answer to each problem.)

Revelation 3:20 (NKJV)

Client: "Behold, I stand at the door and knock. If anyone hears My voice and opens the door, I will come in to him and dine with him, and he with Me."

You: "What does this say to you?" (God is pursuing us. He is knocking on the door of our heart. He is bringing us the choice to invite Him in or not invite Him in. He speaks of dining together, which implies sweet fellowship in His presence.) Ask the client if she is ready to go deeper with God by inviting Him into her life. If so, a prayer of salvation follows.[32]

Romans 10:9–11 (NKJV)

Client: "If you confess with your mouth the Lord Jesus and believe in your heart that God has raised Him from the dead, you will be saved.

For with the heart, one believes unto righteousness, and with the mouth confession is made unto salvation."

You: "What does this say to you?" (Confessing Jesus as Lord and believing Jesus is resurrected from the dead is key to our salvation.)

Salvation Prayer

Advocate offers a willing client the salvation prayer. The client will repeat the words, sentence by sentence, as the advocate says the prayer. The following is an example of a salvation prayer. Remember to pause after the sentence saying, "I know I am a sinner, and You have forgiven me of all my sins." Invite the client to silently confess and turn from the sins that come to her mind. Ask her to say, "Okay," when the silent confession of sin ends so you can continue with the prayer by thanking God for paying the penalty.

Example of a salvation prayer:

> Lord Jesus, I want to know You better. I am a sinner and ask You to take control of my life. Thank You for dying on the Cross to pay the penalty for my sins and giving me new life. I receive You into my life and receive Your gift of salvation. Fill me with Your Spirit, Lord, and guide me. I praise You, Lord. In Jesus's Name. Amen.

Gospel by Phone

Especially important is asking God to "warm up your voice" to ensure a friendly and conversational tone.

In our changing world today, with more centers going virtual, we need to anticipate the growing use of the media. Since our objective is to have the caller make an in-person appointment for a pregnancy test, "Gospel by phone" is a rarity. Occasionally an old client calls her advocate, and if she's still an unbeliever, there's always the possibility for a Gospel conversation. Be ready. It's still the same message, but a different mode.

When we meet face-to-face with a client, the primary impact for successful communication is through tone of voice. When we "meet" by phone, the tone of voice is even more important.

A Client and Advocate Exchange by Phone

Sometimes an initial phone conversation, even one about personal matters like pregnancy, can be easier for the client. There's anonymity that goes with the territory. Invite the client to make an appointment so she can access services and experience the intimacy of a face-to-face encounter. If she is calling from far away, in the process of moving or whatever the reason may be for not coming in, take the opportunity to talk. Silently pray and ask God for guidance during the call. Especially important is asking God to "warm up your voice" to ensure a friendly and conversational tone. Despite the limitations of a phone conversation, there's still potential to introduce the spiritual topic by phone.

An advocate told of the following situation: "Last night, I was working after hours to complete a project, and the office phone rang. The caller was a twenty-three-year-old woman who was stressed after self-administering three drugstore pregnancy tests—all of which were positive. She shared basic, pertinent information with me, including the date of her last menstrual period (LMP)."

NOTE: Although it's best to have an appointment face-to-face, the client said it was impossible to come in because she was moving the next morning and was unprepared for the move.

The following is an excerpt from the advocate/client conversation that highlights the spiritual exchange. It exemplifies bringing God into the equation of her decision-making.

Caller: "I've taken three at-home tests, all positive, and am feeling so stressed over being pregnant. Quite honestly, I keep going back and forth between getting an abortion versus keeping 'it.'"

Advocate: "First of all, based on the date of your last menstrual period, you still have plenty of time to make up your mind. You need to slow down. You still have time to think this through to make a good decision you won't regret. Especially with such a life-dominating decision."

(The client seems to quietly acknowledge the point.)

The advocate continues: "I have a question for you. On a scale of zero to ten, if ten would be stating you're definitely getting an abortion, and zero means there's no consideration of abortion, where would you put yourself on the scale?"

Caller: "Maybe a six, but it keeps changing."

Advocate: "Thank you for your honesty. I know it's a huge decision, and I also know it can take adjusting to the idea of being pregnant. It's really the *indecision* that is causing the tension you're dealing with. I'm sorry you're going through this."

Caller: "Thank you. Yes, it's so stressful! Like I said, I've taken three tests. Are tests from a pharmacy as accurate as yours?"

Advocate: "I can't speak for another brand of pregnancy test but can tell you ours are medical grade. (This may provide an incentive to get the client into the center, where further rapport can build and greater support can be offered—like an ultrasound.) Assuming you're pregnant, I can say that abortion is not an easy decision. Even after going through with the procedure, women can suffer for years after aborting their baby—many carry an ongoing burden of guilt. I know it's hard to

"Do you ever find yourself thinking about God?"

The simple question that brings God into the discussion.

think straight when you're feeling overwhelmed by the crisis of it all. Are you aware of the impact abortion can have?"

Caller: "Yes, I've heard. This is all so hard!"

Advocate: "Help me understand more about your situation. What does the father of the baby say about this?"

Caller: "My boyfriend says if I decide to keep 'it,' then it's a decision I have to deal with."

Advocate: "How do you feel having the sole responsibility of the decision-making on yourself? It sounds like a lonely place to be."

Caller: "It is a *very* lonely place to be! He acts like he's had no part in this whole thing."

Advocate: "I want you to know I'd like to be considered part of your support system. Are you sure you can't come to the center this week?"

Caller: "No, it's impossible. I'm in the middle of packing because I'm leaving the area."

(Transition)

Advocate: I can remember a time in my own life when faced with a crisis. Though I didn't expect it, my thoughts began turning to God." (Shares a brief version of her testimony) "Do you ever find yourself thinking about God?" (Notice the simple question that brings God into the discussion.)

Client: "I think about Him a lot. That's why abortion is a hard decision for me."

Advocate: "I understand. He becomes so real when we earnestly turn to Him." (The advocate continues by sharing part of her salvation testimony. She speaks about running from God for years before finally committing her life to Him. "It's often the result of a situation that's overwhelming to us and, God being so merciful, is there when we need Him!")

Caller: "Oh, thank you for sharing that with me. I really needed to hear this . . . I really needed to hear you say that!"

Note: The caller had alluded to being a Christian and although the testimony she heard was encouraging, she stopped short of a rededication prayer, saying she needed "to think through everything" before rededicating her life. Prior to the call ending, the advocate prayed over the phone with her. The prayer asked God to lead the young woman through her difficult circumstance. As the call ended, the advocate could sense tangible peace, though the outcome was unknown.

A Spiritual Decision by FaceTime

Single and pregnant, Mia didn't seem threatened when the conversation took a spiritual detour from the completed intake interview. She shared that her boyfriend was a Christian and added, "Just like I am!"

The advocate and her client began talking about the difference between a cultural Christian and a follower of Christ. A *cultural Christian* is a person who identifies with Christian tradition and values but has not experienced the more personal and transformative relationship with Christ.

NOTE: A committed Christ-follower has the desire to remain in close fellowship with Him and to obey the biblical guidelines that please God. Moral strength is made possible through a continuous yielding to God's will through prayer, personalizing the Word for one's life, and fellowshipping with other like-minded persons.

The advocate spoke of initially being a cultural Christian and explained the meaning. Then she asked the client whether she considered herself a cultural Christian or a follower of Christ.

"A cultural Christian," Mia replied. As a single, Mia said she knew her sexual lifestyle didn't follow Christ's guidelines.

The session continued when, unexpectedly, Mia began to laugh. She informed the puzzled advocate that her boyfriend had been part of the session "the whole time." She next displayed the image of her boyfriend's face on FaceTime. The intrusion had been hidden behind the client's large purse on the couch. The violation, counter to the center's stated policy, had gone unnoticed, and, to say the least, the advocate felt duped.

Mia seemed unphased by the deception she had just pulled off. She smiled mischievously as she showed the boyfriend's grinning face displayed on her cell phone. Exposed, the boyfriend communicated by an overly enthusiastic response.

"Hi!" he blurted loudly.

The advocate made the split-second decision to overlook the infraction so as not to lose momentum. The boyfriend introduced himself by name in a friendly manner. The advocate posed a question to the young man still featured on FaceTime. "Since you have been privy to my conversation with Mia, I'll ask you the same question I posed to her! Do you consider yourself a cultural Christian or a follower of Christ?"

Without hesitation, the boyfriend replied. "I would say I'm a cultural Christian because of the sexual relationship."

His honesty prompted discussion. The advocate spoke of pregnancy-related fears. "Based on what the two of you have said about your spiritual backgrounds growing up, it seems abortion would oppose your basic, core values."

The boyfriend agreed.

A cultural Christian identifies with Christian tradition and values but has not experienced the more personal and transformative relationship with Christ.

As the exchange continued, the advocate introduced the Gospel, and a meaningful conversation followed. She covered the entire Gospel message: God is a God of love, we are sinners, Christ died to pay the penalty of sin for us, and we can receive His gift and enter an eternal relationship with Him. By the end of the session, the boyfriend had become more serious and expressed that he felt convicted of the personal sin in his life. He made the decision to rededicate his life to Christ. Mia joined the renewed spiritual perspective and prayed to rededicate her life.

Afterward, the boyfriend, smiling about his spiritual reset, announced, "I'm going to look up my old youth pastor and tell him what I just did! We were so close at one time, and I'm going to ask him if he'll mentor me!"

Mia wept with joy over their newfound spiritual unity.

Although FaceTime is not recommended for our purposes, this unplanned experience illustrates that God is free to act in any circumstance and despite a mode of communication. Even high tech moves the will of God forward. By trusting Him through unforeseen circumstances, we don't fall prey to what would otherwise hinder the Gospel. In this case, the advocate sensed she needed to move on despite the awkwardness of the FaceTime situation. Faith works wonders in God's kingdom.

"Do you expect that the Lord is going to bless you and save souls every time you open your mouth?"

Charles Spurgeon

A Word from Charles Spurgeon

There is a timeless story involving the famed nineteenth-century preacher, Charles Spurgeon. He has been called the "prince of preachers." Today, his daily devotional is still in print.

Spurgeon tells the story of one of his students coming to him and saying, "I have been preaching now for some months, and I do not think I have had a single conversion."

Spurgeon said to him, "And do you expect that the Lord is going to bless you and save souls every time you open your mouth?"

"No, sir," the student replied.

"Well, then," Spurgeon said, "that is why you do not get souls saved. If you had believed, the Lord would have given the blessing!"[33]

> "According to your faith let it be to you." (Matthew 9:29 NKJV)

We deliver God's Gospel message with the same power that accomplished His resurrection. It is "the immeasurable greatness of God's power made available to you through faith. Then your lives will be an advertisement of this immense power as it works through you" (Ephesians 1:19 TPT).

Chapter Eight

Practicum: Client and Advocate Conversations

Lord Jesus, as we step into the practical outworking of sharing our faith with clients, we yield to Your mentoring and hold fast to Your promise: "I will instruct you and teach you in the way you should go; I will counsel you with my eye upon you."

(Prayer based on Psalm 32:8 ESV)

By definition, a practicum gives those in training "supervised practical application of previously studied theory."[1] The purpose of the practicum is to expand information learned in a formal training and add a simulated, hands-on experience. Information transitions to knowledge when the advocate in training gains skill and insight from application.

You'll find learning to be enhanced by role-playing with seasoned advocates and/or joining their sessions as an observer (referred to as *shadowing*). Shadowing is a silent role unless the trainee is asked a specific question by the advocate or invited to share her testimony. After meeting with the client, a debriefing follows between the trainee and her supervising advocate. The Q and A that follows the appointment is necessary preparation to hone the trainee's readiness.

Roleplay set-ups are based on real-life exchanges common to the clients. A client appointment includes addressing the immediate situation of possible pregnancy as well as the interplay of her spiritual, emotional, and practical issues.

Through the client's desert of crisis, God charts His course in her life by smoothing the road ahead.

Willingness to share one's faith with clients recognizes two things: First, a client's *most* significant need is to know and follow Christ. Second, when God calls an individual to be a part of a faith-sharing ministry, He will equip her.

The client's perspective of her pregnancy, not the pregnancy itself, is what affects attitude, vision for the future, and ultimate decision-making. An advocate speaking into her life becomes a voice of influence who makes "straight in the desert a highway for our God" (Isaiah 40:3 NIV).

Through the client's desert of crisis, God charts His course in her life by smoothing the road ahead to "straight and level, so that [we] will know where to walk" (Psalm 5:8 TPT). God's Spirit enables us to guide her along the "highway" leading to the Savior. With a diverse clientele at the resource center, we encounter a variety of spiritual backgrounds and differing perspectives. God's Spirit is an active participant who enables us to minister.

Part One

Listening for Distorted Versus Biblical Beliefs

The objective of this section is to prepare the trainees for an interactive discussion with the client. Each of the three client cases cited includes an example of advocate/client dialogue. Note the timely insertion of the advocate's testimony and sampling of purposeful questions.

As a preface to engaging in spiritual discussion, advocates ask God to direct them with discernment and grant spiritual favor to receive truth. The advocate hopes to glean what a client *thinks* are realistic issues surrounding a pregnancy.

Example One

An abortion-vulnerable client says, "My sister is the black sheep of the family, and my parents think I'm the good daughter. If they find out I'm pregnant, I will disappoint my parents."

Client's distorted belief: During the appointment, the client expresses the necessity to sustain her intact image as the "good daughter." "If I don't get an abortion, my parents will find out I'm not who they think I am." She is entertaining the coverup of the pregnancy while contending with self- disappointment. Estranged from the Lord and void of peace, the sin issue of fornication is expanding to thoughts of abortion.

Biblical belief: The authentic core issue is the need for the client to get right with God. This entails recognition of her sin, confession, and prayer—inviting Christ to take control of her life. New harmony with God will bring her the peace she desperately seeks. Her truest image is "image bearer" of Christ. If she humbles herself and turns to Him, she will find unity with God and healing through His forgiveness.

Example Two

A client says, "God feels so far away. I should get back to church."

Client's distorted belief: The client's statement may be one of religious legalism, believing the "good work" of church attendance earns God's acceptance. Defined, legalism is "adherence to moral law rather than to personal religious faith. Stress obedience apart from faith and you produce legalism."[2]

Biblical belief: Acceptance by God cannot be earned. It's freely given and available. The atonement made for sins on the Cross is Christ's gift to us and must be received. If the client's return to church is a heartfelt desire to seek God in a personal way, this expresses an intrinsic motivation rather than a legalism tied to adherence to religious law. One motivational psychologist wrote:

> True motivation must come from within—it must be intrinsic. Prizes or awards (extrinsic) may bribe someone into performing a certain action but compliance is not motivation. . . . An intrinsic motivational environment (the group) can actually change a person's perceived perceptions of self and guide them into changing their behavior.[3]

Legalism is "adherence to moral law rather than to personal religious faith."

Three Client Cases: Adapting Spiritual Responses

Case One: Appointment with a Post-abortive Client

Background: A nineteen-year-old client arrives for a pregnancy confirmation appointment. Early in the session, she learns it is a Christian center and claims, "I'm an atheist, but I'm exploring religion."

NOTE: Declaring herself an atheist yet saying she is "exploring religion" reflects that the client is more of a *seeker* and possibly an agnostic (who doubts that God can be known), rather than an atheist (who doesn't believe God exists). When she says, "I'm exploring religion," the advocate may pause here and ask, "How are you going about exploring religion?" (Consider diverting to one's testimony.)

Advocate: (Progressing through the intake form) "Have you ever experienced abortion?"

Client: "Yes. This past year."

Advocate: "Do you recall which month that was?"

Client: "August. This past summer."

A client's feelings stem from what she is thinking. Ask her about it.

Advocate: "How far along in the pregnancy were you?"

Client: "Around two months. Right on the line for getting an abortion."

Advocate: "Many persons find counseling helpful after the procedure. Did you ever receive counseling after the procedure?"

Client: "Yes, I went to a professional counselor afterward."

Advocate: "Was that helpful for you?"

Client: "Yes, it did help. I'm not having any problems now about the abortion. Ever since that time though, I have felt a lack of purpose in my life."

Advocate: (She notes that the "lack of purpose" could be revealing the numbness or emotional flatness that can occur after an abortion.) "Are you dealing with anxiety or guilt about the abortion now?"

Client: "No, because of my abusive circumstance with my former boyfriend, the counselor told me I had made the right decision. She said I needed to get on with my life and just forget it." (Note: She does not answer the question regarding guilt.)

Advocate: "She told you, 'Get on with your life and forget about the abortion?'"

Client: "Yes."

Advocate: "Have you been able to do that—forget it and move on with your life?"

Client: "Well, no. I haven't forgotten. I really wanted to have that baby. I couldn't because my boyfriend began to change." (Tears begin.) "He was angry about the pregnancy and started hitting me. It brought back the past abuse I'd had from my family. I told myself, 'I can't do this!' After I left him, I had the abortion."

NOTE: The client, previously stoic, is beginning to get in touch with her emotions. When there are tears, never miss the opportunity of pausing to have the client express what she is feeling—even when you think you know. A client's feelings stem from what she is thinking. Ask her about it. For instance, "It seems that really makes you sad. Tell me more about that."

Advocate: "It sounds like you were disappointed about the way things worked out. You really wanted to have the baby." (Recapping her previous statements is important.)

Client: (Nods) "Yes, it's hard to believe everything that's happened."

Advocate: "It's difficult, but it's also healthy when you can address things like a past abortion before attempting to put everything behind you. Otherwise, the memory is buried alive. It's hard to find peace that way."

Client: "Yeah, I can see that."

Advocate: "The abortion is past, and you'd like to move on, but unless you deal with the issue, the memory can haunt you."

Client: "Especially since I know abortion is wrong." (Kairos moment.)

Advocate: "What makes you say that?" (Notice the advocate doesn't simply agree with her statement. She uses the opportunity to draw out the client's beliefs.)

Client: "I know God thinks it's wrong." (This has officially moved her to the category of agnosticism rather than atheism's belief that there is no God. Refrain from pointing out.)

Advocate: "You're right. The Bible calls it a sin to 'shed innocent blood,' yet the Bible also tells us God will forgive and not condemn us when we come to Him and confess our sins. (If not done prior, this may offer the timing to insert personal testimony. The advocate speaks of "running away from God" because of His disapproval of choices she was making. The advocate's testimony concludes with submission to Christ.) "Through Him, I found peace and purpose in my life."

Client: "You did?"

Advocate: "Yes. In fact, I know now that God has a plan for every life. In your life too! You described earlier feeling a lack of purpose in your life. Isn't that uncomfortable to feel unsettled?"

(The question invites the emotional aspect, and the client agrees it's uncomfortable.)

Advocate continues: "It seems this is related to the lack of peace in your life."

(Client nods.)

Advocate: "Would you like to have a sense of peace that only God can give you?"

Client: "Actually, I've started to look into religion."

Advocate: "That's good, yet what I'm talking about is not religion, per se. I say that because the word *religion* is based on trying to earn favor from God by doing certain things to win His approval. What I'm speaking to is so much deeper than that.

"May I share a meaningful little booklet with you? It's a booklet I wish I had had when I accepted Christ into my life because it adds understanding about the personal relationship with God." (Advocate shows her the spiritual tract.)

Client: "Sure."

The word "religion" is based on trying to earn favor from God by doing certain things to win His approval.

NOTE: Sharing the spiritual tract led to the client's decision to invite Christ into her life. She was also given the opportunity to enroll in our post-abortion Bible study.

Case Two: Session with a Client Seeking Abortion

Purpose: This dialogue is included to illustrate how to lead a mildly resistant person into spiritual discourse.

Background: A client came to the center complaining of her *bad experience* at another pregnancy center. "They made me feel so guilty!"

NOTE: If the client says something disparaging to you about another center (or an individual), remain neutral. Simply listen. At the other center she's referencing, her guilt may have been triggered by a question on the intake, and the client is now blame-shifting. Also, she may have mistakenly thought your center was an abortion clinic, and she's seeking commiseration and speaking disparagingly about "this other center."

When the client is contemplating abortion, any life-sustaining options given to her could be interpreted as coercion or an attempt to "guilt her" out of the decision. Instead, advocates encourage clients with respect, compassion, and truth rather than manipulating them to avoid an abortion decision. At the right timing, it is both direct and appropriate to say, "Abortion, as a solution, is not God's best for you. That's because abortion can't serve your physical, emotional, or even spiritual well-being." Our hope is that the Spirit will use our conversation to lead the client with grace and the knowledge that God's ways are transformative and lead to contentment.

Allow her to experience the choice she's considering. The truth encounter points her to the need for Jesus.

Client: "Those people told me I was killing my baby! They made me feel so guilty!"

Advocate: "What exactly do you think makes you feel guilty?" (It's important to clarify, not moralize.)

NOTE: Questioning serves the purpose of leading your client to truth. The advocate may understand why a client asserts a particular statement, but she still asks a connecting question to enlarge awareness.

Client: "I don't know. I guess it's taking a life. Murdering my baby. I get that."

NOTE: The advocate listens. The client is expressing that she understands abortion to be wrong. Her strained emotions likely align with this truth. An abortion procedure will bring her sin's condemnation and anguish. Allow her to experience the choice she's considering. The truth encounter points her to the need for Jesus. Acknowledging the sin of abortion places her on the path to meet her Savior.

"On the one hand, you see abortion as a solution, but, on the other hand, it doesn't line up with your beliefs."

Advocate: "Are you saying what they told you at the other center agrees or disagrees with your personal moral compass? Or was the issue upsetting to you tied more to *how* they expressed themselves?"

Client: "I hated what they said to me!" (Notice she doesn't answer directly.)

Advocate: "What is it that makes you feel so strongly?"

Client: "The guilt associated with it."

Advocate: "Tell me more." (A productive statement, taking conversation to the next level.)

Client: "If I'm really honest with myself, I don't believe abortion is right."

Advocate: "Your honesty is a good thing. Yet it sounds like you're feeling conflicted."

(Client nods)

Advocate: "On the one hand, you see abortion as a solution, but, on the other hand, it doesn't line up with your beliefs."

Client: "That's right. But I also know God will forgive me." (Kairos moment.)

Advocate: "It sounds like you're thinking this through."

Client: "Yes, I do believe there's a God. As a child, I always went to church with my grandma." (Breakthrough.)

Advocate: "So you know Jesus died on a cross to pay the penalty for our sins—all sins. Then as we confess our sins, we experience His restoration. Forgiveness offers us peace. In my own life, I'd spent many years pushing God out." (The advocate, if she's given her salvation testimony, may give a brief topical testimony about how God came through for her during a difficult period in her life.)

Advocate continues: "Do you know what really brings pleasure to God?"

Client: "What?"

Advocate: "When we welcome Him to take control of our lives and trust Him with our lives and challenging situations. He loves us. He helps us avoid choices we would regret. Like, in your case, you don't believe abortion is the right thing to do. Jesus knows you're hurting and wants to walk through this with you. I'd like to be here for you also."

NOTE: If the client is receptive to your words and gesture of support, consider presenting the Gospel message.

Case Three: Session with a Muslim Client

Purpose: The following exchange between advocate and client illustrates spiritual dialogue with a client from another faith background.

Background: A woman wearing a hijab has walked into the waiting room. Perhaps it helps to think of the head covering as a *veil* over her mind. It keeps her faithful to Allah and insulates her from the truth of the Savior Jesus. The Muslim woman had called for an appointment earlier in the week to seek resources for medical help for her pregnancy, and we scheduled an intake appointment for pregnancy confirmation and an overall assessment of her needs.

The following is an excerpt of the client/advocate conversation:

Client: "Things are difficult financially right now."

Advocate: (After discussion) "I'm sorry you're having such a difficult time."

Client: (Nods her head. Eye contact is made.)

Advocate: "You mentioned attending a mosque in the area. Are they aware of the help you need?"

Client: "Yes, I tried to get help from them, but the mosque won't help in these situations."

Advocate: "We will be happy to help wherever we can." The advocate smiles and adds, "We are a Christian organization, as you may know, but we love serving people from different faith backgrounds too. Jesus loves all people, and we do too!"

Client: (Returns the smile) "Yes, I know about Jesus." (To a Muslim, He is a prophet, not regarded as Savior. A Muslim's hope for atonement of sin and "paradise" depends upon their good works outweighing the bad works in their lives.)

Advocate: "Tell me more. What are your thoughts about Jesus?" (Kairos moment.)

As you can see, the spiritual conversation is off and running. It's caught in the flow of easy conversation.

Inserting the testimony: The advocate introduces her personal testimony by saying, "It may be hard to believe, but in some ways my beliefs were like a Muslim's beliefs. I too had once concluded Jesus was a prophet and an enlightened man. The advocate proceeds to the powerful apologetic regarding Jesus being either a liar, or a lunatic, or He was who He said He was—God. Mention that even Jesus's enemies didn't think of him as a liar or lunatic.

Though your personal testimony may not easily relate to your Muslim client, the longing to fill spiritual emptiness is common ground.

Though your personal testimony may not easily relate to your Muslim client, the longing to fill spiritual emptiness is common ground.

Avoid being intimidated. Though a client may have a non-Christian faith background, you can prompt discussion by asking if she has ever had a Christian friend. Or have you ever attended a Christian church? Look for discussion entries:

Client: "My children attend Sunday school with a Christian neighbor's children."

Advocate: "Do you ever become curious about what they're learning?"

Client: "I grew up Muslim, but I don't attend mosque."

Advocate : "Tell me more. Does that reflect your feeling distant from God?"

Part Two

Practicum: Testimony Sharing

The objective of this section is to provide advocates with testimony training and practice for use in client sessions. The material is versatile as one-on-one training or as a group exercise for special training events such as continuing education in-services. The section includes pertinent questions for the client with transitions to sharing one's testimony.

Sharing Your Testimony During Intake

Begin Part Two by dividing into pairs when the occasion is an in-service event. (This can also be a one-on-one training by a seasoned advocate.) Attendees have printed a hard copy of their three-minute testimony beforehand. The training begins by sharing the testimony contents with a partner. (See chapter 5 on testimony writing.) The two training partners conversationally recite their testimonies, role-playing as an advocate sharing with a client.

After each partner completes her testimony, the other partner gives an evaluation of performance. If the group is small, this can work as a classroom. Those assessing will note when the testimony was interjected during the "mock intake." The debriefing session that follows may include ideas about various places the testimony would have fit into the conversation. Or if a topic testimony could have been shared about "God coming through for me when _____," which can also lead to the Gospel presentation.

When practicing the testimony with the general intake form, a handout of varying client statements can be used. (See appendix C, "Advocate In-Service on Testimony Practice.") As the two trainees practice taking turns with various client statements. The "client" reads one of the client statements, which initiates a response by the "advocate."Trainees should familiarize themselves with helpful follow-up questions. The practicum helps fine-tune appropriate responses to the client.

Because the advocate is privy to the possibility of pregnancy, her questions, rather than being threatening, build a caring connection.

Engaging Your Client with Good Questions

In his classic book entitled *How to Win Friends and Influence People,* the late Dale Carnegie advised, "Ask questions the other person will enjoy answering."[4] Though an unplanned pregnancy may not be the context for an enjoyable conversation, the advocate can still create a comfortable rapport by friendly, neutral questions. "How did you hear about us?" Or "Did you bring anyone with you today?" If the client looks fearful, even tearful, learn to be comfortable with seeing tears. Let her hear concern when you ask, "How are things going for you? Today, let's just take a step at a time, slow down a bit, and find out what we're dealing with." The advocate's empathy sets the tone for trust and rapport.

Because the advocate is privy to the possibility of pregnancy, her questions, rather than being threatening, build a caring connection. After the pregnancy is confirmed by a test, ask, "Who do you consider your best support person for the pregnancy?" If the client responds, "I don't have any support," the advocate's low-key response could include: "You can consider me one of your cheerleaders. You simply don't have to figure everything out yourself."

The Influence of Questions

As you go through the intake with the client, consider asking a few questions at a time before entering notes. Though the advocate takes the lead, the added eye contact and relational tone of the interview avoids the posture of mechanical formality. The rapport that is building sets the stage for openness based on feeling acceptance. A study by Harvard Business School concluded, "People interacting with a partner who asks lots of follow-up questions tend to feel respected and heard."[5]

A Tip for the Advocate Trainee

During the intake process with the client, some advocates feel uncomfortable asking intrusive questions, so they preface with, "I'm sorry to ask you this but . . ." Or "I have to ask you some personal questions now." More effective is gentle assertiveness. Don't preface or be apologetic. The client fully *expects* to be asked personal questions in the process of pregnancy confirmation! Think of it this way: Would you want your obstetrician or gynecologist to act embarrassed or apologetic when asking *you* a personal question? Wear the hat of authority comfortably, especially during times of crisis.

Setting the Stage: Testimony Sharing

In general, sharing one's testimony is encouraged whenever the client interview leads to an opening (kairos) for spiritual discussion. When the advocate is sharing her testimony about the BC (before Christ) days of her life, a candid testimonial story is an icebreaker. It is a prelude to the deeper conversation to follow. Though an advocate's sharing from her life may not align with a secular counseling model (which refrains from personal disclosure), selective disclosure brings tangible benefits. A client's initial defensiveness often dissolves into greater openness.

Wear the hat of authority comfortably, especially during times of crisis.

Research reveals what promotes transparency between people. One's vulnerability is correlated with the perceived transparency of the group. For instance, one study involved a group of participants who had been told that "most others in the study were willing to reveal stigmatizing answers or that they were unwilling to do so." A 27 percent higher transparency occurred within the group who was told others were willing. But when the other group was told that their group was likely to withhold sensitive information, there was *less* likelihood of transparency.[6]

The same principle of transparency can be seen at the pregnancy center. When the client hears transparent disclosures from her advocate's testimony, she's likely to be vulnerable.

Testimony Transitions

This segment involves real-life client statements that flow naturally into testimony sharing. A productive, spiritual discussion hopefully leads to the Gospel message with an invitation to pray and receive Christ. Be attentive to client statements that lead to good follow-up questions. The warmth and openness of a personal story of redemption paves the way for a deeper exchange and the Gospel message. Pray for God's timing regarding *when* to turn the corner for more in-depth spiritual sharing.

Guiding the Client to Truth: Scenarios

1. Client Statement: "I want to know God better, but I don't know how!"

Advocate: "To begin with, God is so pleased by your desire to know Him better." (Authentically affirming your client sets the tone for her openness.)

Examples of follow-up questions by advocate:

- "What do you think is motivating your seeking greater closeness with God?" (Affirm the peace and strength that God provides even in times of challenges.).
- "We can be comforted by knowing there are people in the Bible who wanted to know God better but didn't know how. Have you ever heard of Nicodemus? He was an intellectual, a scholar, yet completely baffled by spiritual things!" (Open the Bible to John 3.)

Authentically affirming your client sets the tone for her openness.

An example of the advocate transitioning to testimony:

- "I experienced how unsettled life feels without a personal relationship with God. I remember periods of seeking God, but I was puzzled by all the different world religions that claimed to know the truth. Some mainstream religions respect Christ as a prophet or enlightened person. When I was searching for truth, I had begun thinking of Christ as a great prophet. Then I read the C.S. Lewis apologetic known as 'liar, lunatic, or Lord,' meaning He is who He says He is. This became pivotal in believing Christ was more than a prophet."[7]
- "The more personal relationship came when . . ." (Share your testimony as a prelude to the Gospel message and an opportunity to receive Him.)

2. Client Statement: "This baby isn't planned, and I'm a planner! Everything is happening too fast."

Background: The client is pregnant and abortion vulnerable. She shares, "My parents live in the Middle East. My boyfriend is American, and they wouldn't approve of marrying a non-Muslim like my boyfriend. So I've never mentioned I have a boyfriend to my parents.

Advocate: "Thank you for sharing that—cultural backgrounds can have strong influence. Since the situation you're facing is complicated by family relationships, your circumstance must feel so out of control."

Client: (Agrees.) "When he proposed last year, I didn't accept because of my parents. Now everything is worse! In my country, it's a terrible thing to be pregnant outside of marriage."

Examples of follow-up questions by advocate:

- "Without question, your situation is challenging." (This may be a good time to share a topical testimony of leaning on God during dire circumstances.) This can be followed by further discussion. Ask her, "Is there anything at all you view as positive in your situation?" (Examples: The love between the client and the father of her baby, the boyfriend's desire to marry, and her parents, who live outside the United States, which limits excessive parental pressure and encourages more freedom of thought.)
- "What are your thoughts regarding possible solutions?"
- "How would you foresee your parents responding if they became aware of your pregnancy? (One client replied, "They would be so angry with me, there's a good chance they'd cut ties with me, and I'd never see them again.")

(The advocate followed up with the next cited question.)

- "Have you ever considered quietly getting married prior to disclosing the marriage, then, at some point, announcing the marriage, and later, the pregnancy?"

- "Do you think aborting your first-born child with someone you're in love would set you up for emotional trauma?"

Advocate transitions to testimony:

- "I remember a time in my life when things seemed to be spinning out of control. One day I received a book in the mail from a relative. It was a spiritual book entitled *Something More* by Catherine Marshall. Because I hadn't considered the spiritual aspect of life as key to helping my situation, the book became an unexpected blessing. I spent hour after hour digesting the contents. The author's words encouraged me to 'enter in'—referring to entering into a personal relationship with God because He loves me. Peace was exactly what I needed. Before I had read the book, I had never thought about surrendering my life to God. When I did, it was like I could rest in the peace He offered."

3. Client: "With two abortions, I deserve hell." (Do, Value, I am)

NOTE: Before the appointment ends, the client should be asked if she'd like to attend a post-abortion healing Bible study to deal with abortion's aftermath of guilt and condemnation.

Examples of follow up questions by advocate:

- "When you say, 'I deserve hell,' this implies a strong, moral standard. Do you come from a faith background?" The client's words have potential for leading into the Gospel. A lead-in is: "We all deserve hell. Do you know why?"

- "Do you believe heaven is something we have to earn?" If the client says, "Yes," ask, "Did you know there is no way we can earn a place in heaven?" Turn to Ephesians 2:8–9, which refers to "works." Ask, "What are these verses saying to you?"

- "If you could be free of your heavy sense of condemnation, would you want to know how?"

- Depending on circumstances, the advocate could proceed to the Gospel or show her the charts below, contrasting the difference between legalism versus grace. The falsehood is that good works earn us a place in heaven (legalism) versus a Savior's grace of death on a cross paying the penalty of sin through forgiveness.

Advocate transitions to the concept that "who we are" isn't necessarily determined by what we do. "That's the world's way, but I found that God wants to give us a new identity based on the new life He gives us. For instance,

- "In my own life, I made many sinful choices. I believed if I started over, divorced, and wiped the slate clean, I could reset my life. What I didn't realize was the slate had been wiped clean by Jesus over 2000 years ago. I had only to receive the gift of God paying the penalty for my sins." (Finish telling testimony emphasizing God views us through our relationship with Christ and our sin burden gone.)

Legalism, A Secular Worldview Versus Biblical View of Grace

To quote theologian John Piper: "Legalism is the conviction that law-keeping is now, after the fall, the ground of our acceptance with God."[8] One's performance becomes ever important. Law-keeping may be important in the secular world, but biblically, a person's sins are never justified by doubling up effort to improve performance. "For by works of the law no human being will be justified in his sight, since through the law comes knowledge of sin" (Romans 3:28 ESV).

The secular world's belief system tells me that what I do determines my value and defines who I am (my identity).

Clients often measure their "spiritual selves" by what they are *doing*. "I know I should get back to church," while not understanding the personal relationship with Christ, is a prime example of legalistic thinking. The secular world's belief system tells me that what I *do* determines my value and defines who I am (my identity). Many societies define personal value through one's education, wealth, and position. These are considered foundational to establishing "who I am" (my identity). The Bible refutes this. (See Ephesians 2:8–9.)

Do, Value, Be

Advocate: "In our society, we *do* things and win *acceptance*. We forge our identity in various ways. Higher education, wealth, and position are often paths that lead to acceptance in our society. Let's select one of these, like higher education, to illustrate the two approaches: secular versus biblical."

The advocate writes the title SECULAR WORLDVIEW on a piece of paper. Underneath the title, she makes three columns on one line: DO, VALUE, I AM (Be)[9]

The advocate fills in talking points under each heading progressively for the client as she explains each section. For example:

SECULAR WORLDVIEW

DO	VALUE	I AM (Be)
PhD	Society values me	I am accepted by peers

Example of advocate's explanation for the Secular Worldview section:

Do: "According to the world's way, accomplishment enhances our self-identity. Let's say we earn our PhD." (Advocate writes the word under the DO column.) The advocate's caveat to her client is, "We're not saying earning a higher degree is negative. However, this illustrates the antithesis to God's way of acceptance versus the world's way of acceptance."

Value: The advocate proceeds by mentioning, then writing in, "Society values me." Since higher education is highly respected, higher value esteems the educational accomplishment.

I am: The advocate fills in the outcome: "I am accepted by peers."

The advocate continues, "Even Christians can operate by a performance system. For instance, some believe DOing good works for God earns our salvation. More good deeds, they falsely believe, creates increased value to God. This is flesh (self-life). The worldly way to determine significance. In truth, Christ alone establishes worthiness through our identity as God's child and family.

Even Christians can operate by a performance system. For instance, some believe DOing good works for God earns our salvation.

"Grace says it's not what we ourselves have done but what Jesus has done for us. From the point of salvation, God made every believer 'accepted in the Beloved' (see Ephesians 1:6 NIV). Jesus's good work on the Cross must be received to come into our new identity—one heart, one mind, one Spirit (Philippians 2:2). Jesus's gift of salvation brings assurance of God's acceptance.

Be, Value, Do

The advocate writes the title, BIBLICAL WORLDVIEW on a piece of paper. Underneath the title, she makes three columns on one line: I AM (Be), VALUE, DO.[10]

The advocate fills in talking points under each heading progressively for the client as she explains each section.

BIBLICAL WORLDVIEW

I AM (Be)	VALUE	DO
I am His child	I'm valued by Him!	As Spirit leads

Example of explanation for the Biblical Worldview section:

I am: "When we turn from our sins and invite Him to take control of our lives, we are *receiving* Jesus's sacrifice on the Cross for us. Our new identity is instantly established. That is, I *am* His child, a new person with a new heart to follow Him."

Value: "He loves us. We are *valued* by Him—so much so that He sacrificed His life to pay the penalty for our sins. When we receive His gift, He fills us with His Spirit of righteousness."

Do: "We conduct our lives with reliance on His Spirit. With a transformed heart to do His will, He will lead us to the good work He has prepared." Have client read:

> Ephesians 2:10: For we are His workmanship created in Christ Jesus for good works, which God prepared beforehand that we should walk in them. (NKJV)

Even our good works are ordered by our sovereign God.

Even our good works are ordered by our sovereign God. He has prepared them, and we accomplish them as He leads us. Watchman Nee, famed man of God, author, pastor and prisoner for many years in China understood this. Nee wrote, "For Christianity begins not with a big DO, but with a big DONE. Point out how Ephesians opens with the statement that God has 'blessed us with every spiritual blessing in the heavenly places in Christ' (1:3) and we are invited at the very outset to sit down and enjoy what God has done for us; not to set out to try and attain it for ourselves."[11]

4. "I'm a Christian. I was confirmed when I was twelve.

Note: Among denominations with confirmation are Catholic, Methodist, Lutheran, Episcopal. Confirmation is a sacrament in the Catholic Church. It is a public affirmation of committed faith. "Confirmation completes the grace we receive at baptism, since we receive a 'special strength of the Holy Spirit.'"[12]

Confirmation and its prior academic and spiritual preparation are intended to reflect a young parishioner's deepening walk of faith and devotion to Christ. Other denominations view confirmation as a doctrine, ordinance, or (sacramental) rite. Across the board, there can be differences in specifics. But despite any variance, confirmation is intended as a spiritually nourishing event.

A.W. Tozer once said, "For it is not mere words that nourish the soul, but God Himself, and unless the hearers find God in personal experience, they are not the better for having heard the truth."[13]

If a client's faith background includes confirmation, explore where her heart for the Lord is. Be sure confirmation didn't merely satisfy what she was supposed to do. Many clients have said they attended confirmation. Confirmation day felt celebratory, and although they had been strengthened in prior biblical study, many did not grasp the significance intended. The following exchange between advocate and client illustrates an opportunity for the client to revisit her faith walk.

Advocate: "So you were confirmed! How old were you?"

(Clients' answers vary.)

Advocate: "I have had clients who shared with me that they participated in confirmation because their parents expected them to. Or they say, 'All my friends were being confirmed at the time, so I didn't give it much thought.' Would either be true for you?"

Client: "Yes, my parents completely expected me to go through confirmation."

Advocate: "Despite their expectation, did you think of the occasion as a decision to draw closer to Christ?"

Client: "No, not at all."

Advocate: "Do you feel that *now* you would be ready to go deeper with God?"

Client: "I feel much more ready now."

The statements reveal an incompletion from the real intent of confirmation. Yet God's character perseveres toward completion. "He who began a good work in you will carry it on to completion until the day of Christ Jesus" (Philippians 1:6 NIV). Perhaps the client will find her earlier "incompletion" fulfilled through a genuine commitment to Christ at the center.

Example of a follow-up question by advocate:

- The client's admission leads to a further question. The advocate asks, "Would you like to go deeper with God *now*?" (If yes, present the Gospel message and prayer to receive Him.)

As an advocate, keep in mind: If a client identifies as a Christian and has made an appointment for a pregnancy test, it would be timely to challenge her to a reset of her spiritual life or invite a commitment to a first-time decision. Both entail a relationship with the Lord and a desire to *follow* Him.

If a client identifies as a Christian and has made an appointment for a pregnancy test, it would be timely to challenge her to a reset of her spiritual life.

5. Client: "I'm a Christian but haven't been living it. Now I might be dealing with a pregnancy!"

Advocate: "I'm sorry you're going through this turmoil. You mentioned not living like a Christian, which reflects your sensitivity to a high moral standard. Would that be true?" (Wait for her response.)

"Do you feel you have to *earn* God's acceptance?" Discussion leads to, "Can I show you a little booklet?" (If using *Have You Heard of the Four Spiritual Laws?* or *Would You Like to Know God Personally?* the fourth law speaks to salvation being the result of God's grace. "When we personally receive His gift of sacrifice on the Cross, we are drawn into a relationship with Him." (Reinforced by Ephesians 2:8–9.)

Examples of follow-up questions by advocate:

- "Do you recall a time in your life when you yielded your life to Him?" (This scenario could also warrant the Do, Value, Be discussion. Refer to charts.)

- "It sounds like you're feeling uncomfortable about your lifestyle. If you could have a fresh start, would you take it?"

- "Do you have certainty Jesus is still in your life despite wandering from Him?" (Discuss how a believer can quench the Spirit, yet God will never leave nor forsake His child (Hebrews 13:5).

- "Do you recall the time when you received Christ into your life?" If so, ask her, "What was that like for you?"

- How would you describe the difference between God's approval versus His acceptance of you?"

Advocate transitions to topic testimony: (God's acceptance versus God's approval). This brings to life the worldly perspective of, "Do, Value, I Am" versus the biblical perspective of, "I Am, Value, Do.

- "Let's talk about the difference between *acceptance* and *approval.* How do you think they differ from one another?" (Discuss that God completely *accepts* the child of His salvation, though He may not always *approve* of behavior. It is like the parent who *accepts* her child but doesn't always *approve* of her child's behavior.)

NOTE: The chart has been effectively used with clients to counter legalistic views especially those that believe the Christian life is dependent on good works instead of Christ's sacrificial *good work.*

---

6. Client: "I know I've messed up! I feel so far from God. I need to get back to church!"

Advocate: "It sounds like you're wanting to draw closer to God in your life. Do you recall a time when you felt close to Him?" (Wait for response.) "He forgives us when we have distanced from Him, but He's joyful when we return."

Examples of follow-up questions by advocate:

- "How do you think God views you?" the advocate says. "Very negatively," the client replies.

- "What makes you draw that conclusion?" (Skip countering her words and explore her thoughts. Rather than saying, "God doesn't view you negatively. He loves you," say, "What makes you think God views you very negatively?") Possible responses: "Because I'm sleeping with my boyfriend," or "I've had an abortion," etc.

- "It sounds like you're feeling bad about it. Are you?" (As mentioned previously Romans 8:1 is foundational to a discussion about "no condemnation in Christ." Add, "This applies to those who are believers.")

- "Would you like to be free from the burden of condemnation?" If so, the advocate proceeds with her testimony and Gospel message.

- "Let's read from Ephesians 1:4 to answer the question about how God views you: 'Just as He chose us in Him before the foundation of the world, that we should be holy and without blame before Him in love.' How do you think He views those who are His children?"

- "You seem to feel bad about 'messing up,' as you describe it. The guilt reveals sensitivity to God's ways. God always leaves the door open to restore our relationship with Him. (Discuss acknowledging sin, thanking Him for His forgiveness, and, with the help of the Spirit, becoming a true *follower* of Christ. Are you ready to get back on track with Him?")

Advocate transitions to testimony:

- "In my own life, I went through a period of feeling distant from God. I wasn't sure I could live like a Christian at the time, but since then I've learned it's the Spirit who enables it." (Follow up with the Gospel and prayer of commitment to Him.)

A personal God will always desire a personal relationship.

7. Client: "I used to attend church growing up, but my life has gotten busy. I don't attend anymore."

Advocate: "More than even church attendance, God wants us to be in a relationship with Him. He loves us and wants to guide us. Do you believe in a personal God?" (Client acknowledges.) "A *personal* God will always desire a *personal* relationship." (Follow with a brief testimony and the Gospel message.) "Our God wants us to know and experience Him."

Examples of follow-up questions by advocate:

- "You mentioned church attendance growing up. Do you ever miss Him?"

- "When you attended church, what was that like for you?"
- "Do you think God has the desire to walk through your situation with you?"

(Be alert to whether you should share your testimony.)

8. Client: "I'm a Buddhist. We believe in karma."

Actions and consequences are linked, but rather than paying a penalty for our sins, our faith is based on forgiveness and redemption.

Karma has been defined as a "source of supernatural justice through which actions lead to morally congruent outcomes, within and across lifetimes."[14] Essentially, cause and effect are at work. Our actions produce consequences. One guru said, "Positive karma is wholesome or virtuous." It "comes from desirable actions," but "negative karma is unwholesome or non-virtuous." It "comes from undesirable actions."[15] Buddhists believe wrongdoings produce "karmic debt."

Christianity believes actions and consequences are linked, but rather than paying a penalty for our sins, our faith is based on forgiveness and redemption, not cycles of reincarnation to enforce certain consequences. (Karmic debt determines the form of reincarnation experienced in the next life.)

Examples of follow-up questions by advocate:

- "How would you describe karma?" (Even if you know karma's meaning, ask. It will provide understanding of her spiritual perspectives.) In a general sense beyond Hinduism and Buddhism, karma is "the cosmic principle according to which each person is rewarded or punished in one incarnation according to that person's deeds in the previous incarnation.[16]
- "Do you know how a Christian deals with 'bad karma?'" Tell her Christians believe actions have consequences too. Bad actions are called sins. Negative behavior leads to consequences—what you would call 'bad karma.'" (This opens the gate to add, "We are a faith of forgiveness and redemption, etc.")
- Discussion: "God provided the solution, which was having sinless Jesus pay for the penalty of our sin by dying on a cross. It's as though someone, in your place, offers to pay for the bad karma you accumulated. Jesus's death eradicates our wrongdoing to enable His gift of eternity with Him. We also are given a new heart to follow Him.
- "Who do you believe Jesus is?" (Client replies, "A prophet.") Advocate responds, "I used to believe Jesus was a prophet too, but after reading the Bible, I realized an enlightened prophet wouldn't lie. Jesus made a claim to be God. You may know that

neither Buddha nor Mohammad claimed to be God. What are your thoughts?"

Advocate transitions to testimony:

- "In my own life, I've made wrong choices. Wrongdoing builds 'bad karma' and becomes 'karmic debt.' In Christianity, sin can be accumulated, but when we receive Christ as Savior, His forgiveness covers our sins. Confession of future sins committed, though forgiven at the Cross, must be confessed to keep our relationship with the Lord close. Otherwise, it's difficult to experience Him when we distance because of sin. This interferes with experiencing His peace.

9. Client: "I am a Buddhist." (The client asserts her faith in response to the advocate saying, "We're a Christian ministry.")

Examples of follow-up questions by advocate:

- "Are you familiar with Buddhist teachings? The Dalai Lama's perspective of Jesus is that He exemplifies a 'spiritually mature, good, and warm hearted person.'"[17]

- "As someone who is 'spiritually mature, good, and warm hearted,' do you think Jesus taught truth?" (Client will likely agree.) Next share Jesus's claim to be God. When she agrees that an enlightened person would teach truth, share that Jesus claimed to be God, so as a "fully enlightened being," He would teach truth and not lie.

- "We have seen many persons of the Buddhist faith here at the center. What do you enjoy about being a Buddhist?" (She may answer, like many Buddhists do, that she is a Buddhist because it is her family tradition. (She bypasses the "enjoyment" aspect of the question.) "Christians believe we don't inherit God as part of a family tradition. It is a decision we must make for ourselves. Otherwise, we'd be like robots obeying a command rather than having a heart to follow Him." (If the client seems interested, consider reading Psalm 139:7–10 to her, which speaks of God's relentless pursuit.)

It is a decision we must make for ourselves.

Advocate transitions to testimony:

- "For a long time, I resisted following God, but what I now enjoy about being a Christian is the assurance that Jesus completely accepts me." (Can refer to Ephesians 1:6 about being "accepted in the Beloved.")

10. Client: "I believe there are many paths to God."

Examples of follow-up questions by advocate:

- "Have you personally found a pathway to God?"
- "Do you believe truth is exclusive?

Advocate transitions to testimony:

- "Truth is exacting. Look at mathematics. Its truth is precise! There's only one answer! Regarding the spiritual realm, biblical truth narrows. There is only one way to the Father. Jesus says, 'I am the way and the truth and the life. No one comes to the Father except through me' (John 14:6 NIV). Do you see how exclusive Jesus's claim is? Jesus made other exclusive claims as well. He is the only prophet among the world's mainstream religions who claims He forgives our sins and promises eternal life when we accept His gift." (Share testimony.)

11. Client: "I believe in Jesus too." (Client's response to learning the center was Christian.)

Examples of follow-up questions by advocate:

- "How would you describe your belief in Jesus? (Do not assume client is a follower of Christ.)
- "Who would you say that He is?" (If she says, "Son of God," ask if she also believes He is God.) It may be appropriate to point out "just a belief in the historical Jesus dying for your sins is not enough. Do you believe He is more than a historical person who once lived on earth?"
- "Do you believe Jesus is God, died, was buried for our sins, and was resurrected from the dead?"
- "Are you familiar with Scripture that confirms Jesus is God?" (See Colossians 1:15.) "The verse tells us Jesus is the image of the invisible God and His exact representation.

Advocate transitions to testimony:

- "In my own life, I accepted that Jesus died for my sins and rose from the dead, but I didn't know He wanted a personal relationship with me, and I needed to yield my life and personally receive Him." (Share testimony.)

What is most important is Jesus, the Christian God, who gives absolute assurance my sins are forgiven.

12. Client: "I am a Muslim. We believe a lot like you do."

Advocate: "It's true there are some similarities. Christians are also called to tithe, to pray, even to fast, but what is most important is Jesus, the Christian God, who gives absolute assurance my sins are forgiven—past, present, and future. From His Holy Book, the Bible, I know I'll spend eternity with Him when I accept His gift of dying on the Cross for my sins. I never have to be concerned whether good deeds outweigh the bad deeds to spend eternity with Him." (In the discussion that follows, share your personal testimony.)

I never have to be concerned whether good deeds outweigh the bad deeds to spend eternity with Him.

NOTE: If the client says we worship the same God, ask: "If we worshipped the same God, wouldn't it be true that expectations of Allah would be the same as Jehovah God? Does that make sense to you?" (Pause for her answer.) "With Allah, no provision has been made for the sin problem everyone must deal with. In Islam, there's hope for the good deeds to outweigh the bad deeds. But the Christian God I worship is a God of love; He's made the provision to pay the penalty for our sins through Jesus's sacrifice on the Cross.

Examples of follow-up questions by advocate:

- "Do you feel assured, as a Muslim, that your good works outweigh your bad works?" (Pause for answer.) Follow-up question: "Do you have the assurance you are going to heaven?"
- "What do you know about Jesus?" (Can insert into the discussion: Jesus has already paid the entire penalty for sins as a gift to us. Even though you aren't a Christian, He died for you because He loves you. But, like any gift, we must individually receive it for the transaction to be complete.)
- "Do you believe Allah loves you and knows you personally by name?" (Share and discuss Revelation 2:17.) "This verse regards God's special name reserved for each of us. A name that reflects Jesus uniquely knows us."

Advocate transitions to testimony:

- "My God is a God of love, He pursues us. In the past, I believed Jesus to be a God of love but thought His love was conditioned upon my good behavior. I didn't know how to approach Him when I sinned. Instead of confessing my sins, I distanced." (Share testimony.)

13. Client: "I am a Muslim."

Advocate: "When you say you are a Muslim, does that mean you were born into a Muslim family?" (Wait for acknowledgement.) "In the Christian faith, if we can be born into a family where the parents are

Christian, our God values us with the freedom to decide if we want to follow Him. He is a humble God."

Examples of follow-up questions by advocate:

- "Are you a practicing Muslim who follows the principles of the faith, or a cultural Muslim, who accepts the faith because of family tradition?
- Follow the question with: "I used to be a cultural Christian. I understood the central points of the faith, but I wasn't actively practicing Christianity by reading my Holy Book, the Bible, attending church services, or caring to seek God to know Him in a deeper way." (Discussion)
- Have you ever had a Christian friend? (If yes, ask if the friend has ever spoken about Jesus. Ask her what thoughts she has about Him. Offer personal testimony to her.)

Advocate transitions to testimony:

- "I was brought up as a Christian. I knew about Christian doctrine but didn't know God personally. I was searching to know Him." (Share testimony.)

14. Client: "Jesus is the Son of God, but He is not God."

Advocate: "When I was younger, it was confusing to hear Jesus referred to as the 'Son of God.' Now I understand this means Jesus's earthly role as a distinct member of the Trinity: God the Father, God the Son, God the Holy Spirit. They share the same nature." This may initiate more questions. If more questions arise, address them.

Example of follow-up questions by advocate:

- "Are you a sister? A daughter? A mother? The Trinity is challenging to explain. It resembles my saying, 'I am a sister, a daughter, and a mother, yet I am one person with the same human nature.' The Trinity refers to one God eternally existing in three persons—Father, Son, and Holy Spirit. All are divine, share the same 'God nature,' but have different roles.

I am a sister, a daughter, and a mother, yet I am one person with the same human nature.

15. Client (Muslim): "I believe that all of us pray to the same God."

Advocate: "To determine if we pray to the same God, we must look at the holy books of our two faiths. The Bible portrays the Christian God to Allah as being distinctly different." (The advocate focuses on explaining Jesus, not denigrating Allah.) "For instance, Jesus wants a loving, personal relationship with us. Sin hinders, and until we receive His sacrifice, we cannot draw close. Sin is a dividing wall separating us, but Jesus's death atoned for our sins. We receive the gift of Jesus's sacrifice individually."

Examples of follow-up questions by advocate:

- "Do you ever wish you could know God personally?" (Discuss.)
- "What is the most outstanding feature about God for the Muslim?"
- "How does your God bring you comfort? The story about the God of the Bible is quite different from the Muslim's concept of God. The biblical God is a God of love who tells us to love our enemies. This is so contrary to the way a human being thinks! It shows me my God supremely loves. He chose us" (Ephesians 1:4).
- "Did you know the Quran recognizes the Bible as a Holy Book? The Bible tells us something important about the gift of salvation: God, in His great love, has paid the penalty for sin that allows us to spend eternity with Him."

The biblical God is a God of love who tells us to love our enemies.

Advocate transitions to testimony:

- "The Quran says Allah demands that people earn paradise by performing good deeds, yet people never know if they qualify for paradise by doing enough. My Holy Book tells me my God, in His love, did it all! He died on the Cross for me—for you too—so that we can receive the life of His Spirit. But we must choose to receive." (Shares testimony.)

Kamal Saleem's Conversion

Muslims enjoy hearing a good story! Kamal Saleem is a former Muslim who authored a book entitled *The Blood of the Lamb.* "Have you heard of the astonishing story about a Muslim man named Kamal Saleem. Can I share it with you?"

From childhood, Kamal's Muslim mother had told him Allah would be honored by Kamal dying as a martyr. As a young man, he was in a terrible accident, and when released from the hospital to recover, he accepted the invitation to convalesce with his Christian physician—a household of notable kindness. When Kamal recovered and returned to his home, he began questioning his faith. Feeling he had betrayed Islam by his weakened allegiance, he contemplated suicide, but at the last moment, he cried out "with every fiber within me." Crying out to God, he said:

> "God, the Father Abraham, if you are real, would You speak to me? I want to know You." Well, God of Father Abraham came to the room. He filled the room with His glory. . . . Kamal said, "My Lord, I will live and die for you!" He said, "Do not die for me. I died for you so that you may live."[18]

Instead of taking his life that day, Kamal gave it to Jesus.

Advocate transitions to testimony:

- "I can relate to Kamal's need for God. My life before Christ was like death—sinful, despairing, and purposeless. After choosing to follow the Lord, I felt so overjoyed to have found God and the peace I found that I wanted to tell everyone about Him. I knew beyond a doubt Jesus was the answer to my deepest longings." (Share testimony.)

Jesus's death was a perversion of justice, but it was a redemptive perversion of justice for the sake of humanity.

16. Client: "I have heard the Bible has contradictions."

Examples of follow-up questions by the advocate:

- (To client's saying there are contradictions in the Bible.) "What contradictions are you referring to?" (Wait for response) Depending on the client's response, mentioning many contradictions can be cleared up through researching answers. For instance, John's Gospel states Jesus was crucified and died during the sixth hour. In Mark's Gospel, it states Jesus was crucified and died on the third hour. The third hour would have been 9:00 a.m. on the Jewish clock. Although John, on the Roman clock, said it was the sixth hour, or 6:00 a.m., he also said the trial was "about this time" and that "later Jesus was handed over to be crucified." This would harmonize with Mark's account.[19]

Advocate transitions to testimony:

- "I, too, was willing to believe there were contradictions in the Bible before I studied the Bible for myself. Believing it had contradictions, I had an excuse not to follow God." (Share testimony.)

17. Client: "For me, it seems like a perversion of justice when God had Jesus die for other people. I could never let my child die!"

The client is passing judgment on God because He allowed Jesus's death on the Cross. *How terrible that God would do that to His Son!* Yet, it was Jesus who *chose* to live and die by God's will for the sake of paying the penalty of sin for you and me. "Not My will, but Yours, be done" (Luke 22:42 NKJV).

Advocate: "You are right. Jesus's death was a perversion of justice, but it was a *redemptive perversion* of justice for the sake of humanity. It was motivated by the greatest love in the world. You are right by saying it was a perversion because it wasn't fair." (Agree with client if you can agree with authenticity.)

Questions for deeper discussion on purpose of the Cross:

- "Do you believe a noble purpose can justify a choice? If so, this can shed light on the question: 'How could God condemn His own son Jesus to death?' For the sake of discussion, let's say you are the mother of one child. Let's add that five thousand people could be saved from a certain and unjust death by an evil tyrant if you were willing to sacrifice your one child in exchange for freeing five thousand people from death."

- "If the one sacrifice meant five thousand people could live, would you do it?" The client replies, "No, I couldn't. I'd never be able to allow my child to die! How could a loving God let His Son die!" The advocate responds, "As a parent, I agree it would be heart-wrenching to allow one's child to die, regardless of how many others would escape death. That's why we aren't God!"
- (Questions continue) "By giving up the life of your one child so (let's say) five thousand people could live—even if you couldn't personally bring *yourself* to that choice—do you consider this a noble choice, or would you condemn a person who made the decision?" Without hesitation, the client replies. "Yes, I can say the choice was noble."
- The advocate continues, "God allowed Jesus, who lived in consent to His Father's will, to pay the sin penalty of death on a cross. The sacrifice enabled millions of people to receive salvation and be assured of spending eternity with Him. Do you see the great love this act reflected? It cost God dearly to take on the burden of sin for all people, yet His love *enabled* the sacrifice." (Discuss and share testimony: "In my own life, I did not regard the gift of the Cross until I was in my thirties, etc.")

Question for deeper discussion on God's justice:

- "Do you believe God's 'law of justice' and God's law of love are harmonious? When Jesus was asked, 'Teacher, which is the greatest commandment in the Law?' Jesus replied: 'Love the Lord your God with all your heart and with all your soul and with all your mind' (Matthew 22:36–37 NIV). He also said He did not 'come to abolish the Law' (Matthew 5:17). We see the connection between law and grace. God met the law of justice (His requirement for a perfect atonement for sin) by His law of love that *enabled* it."

God met the law of justice by His law of love that enabled it.

After discussion, the advocate transitions to her testimony:

- "I'm thankful for God's love that permitted Jesus to meet the requirement of justice. The exchange of His sinless life for ours qualified for the perfect atonement to pay the penalty of sin." (Share testimony: "In my life, God's pursuit of me was from His great love. My life was out of control and . . ."

We can never fully understand the mysteries of God. However, He has given each of us a "measure of faith" enabling us to yield our lives to Him.

18. Client (Muslim): "Christians believe in more than one God. Isn't that right?"

Advocate: "I know that many Muslims believe Christians worship multiple Gods, but this is not our Christian belief. Allow me to illustrate. As Christians, we believe in three persons in one God. Sometimes the metaphor of ice, steam, and water are used as an illustration because all three are made of the same substance. All three share H2O. They have the same 'nature,' but they present differently. They have different roles, you might say."

Follow-up question:

- "Christians believe God is three persons in one. It can be proven mathematically. As you know, mathematics is precise. May I show you by a simple, mathematical equation the truth about God's nature?" (Client nods.) The advocate writes on a sheet of paper: 1 + 1 + 1=____. She asks the client, "What is the answer to this equation?" The client replies, "Three." "Correct," says the advocate and fills in the blank with the digit three. Beneath the equation, a second equation is written: 1 x 1 x 1=____. "What do you think the answer is?" When the client replies, "One," the advocate fills in the answer, then explains.
- "Each 'one' is a whole number, just as God the Father is a whole person; Jesus the Son is a whole person, and the Holy Spirit is a whole person. God is three persons in one—all three have the same God nature. Does this make sense to you?" (See Resources for additional reading regarding Muslim beliefs.) Pastor J. Jeffrey Smead sums it up with a common illustration in discussion of Trinitarian theology: "What happens when you multiply 1 x 1 x 1? It equals One! So even numerically God is 1."[20]

Advocate transitions to testimony:

- "We can never fully understand the mysteries of God. However, He has given each of us a 'measure of faith' enabling us to yield our lives to Him. We can adopt a new mindset of 'letting God be God' by an ongoing yielding to His care. Ephesians 1:4 says God *chose us!*" (Share testimony.)

Two Role-Plays: Teaching Client Crisis Management

Role-play One: Abortion-Vulnerable Client Breaks the News to a Parent

Kerry was a senior in college. She had lived with her boyfriend for several years, and they were the parents of two young children. The positive pregnancy test meant her third baby would be delivered in the spring.

Kerry said, "At the time. I felt overwhelmed. How could I finish school with three children under four years old?" She and her boyfriend agreed to abort. "I went online several weeks ago and ordered herbs that would supposedly cause the abortion. But it didn't work."

The pregnancy test at the center confirmed her pregnancy had continued. Kerry mentioned her mother would rage if she knew she was pregnant a third time. She recalled how livid her mother was about her second pregnancy. She had yelled, "Why do you let yourself get pregnant while trying to get through school?" (The mother had acted exasperated because she helped with babysitting the previous two babies.)

Kerry was conflicted. When the herbal abortifacient failed, it made Kerry reconsider. At the same time, avoiding another tongue-lashing and ongoing criticism from her mother made abortion tempting. This, and possible damage from the herbal abortifacient, weighed heavily on her mind. Her advocate detected a hint of sadness when Kerry spoke of terminating the pregnancy. "I just wish I knew if the baby would be healthy and if my mom would come through to help me finish school. I don't know how to break the news to her."

"Kerry, you have a mom who cares about your completing school, and that is a good thing. However, you're also an adult, and you have your own decisions to make. Why don't we do a little practice role-play, which may help you to handle your mom by drawing boundaries, yet respecting her. Would you like to do that?"

Kerry agreed.

"Kerry, I'll play the part of you and, since you know how your mother would respond, you play the part of your mother."

As the client engaged in the role-play, her voice became shrill as she imitated the mother's previous response to her pregnancies.

Client (as the mother): "You're crazy to let yourself get pregnant again!"

Advocate (as the client): "Mother, I know this is upsetting to you. It's upsetting to me too! I'm sorry. You've always been so supportive of me and, right now, I need your support more than ever."

Client (as the mother): "You're taking advantage of my supporting you! I can't keep rescuing you!"

Advocate (as the client): I know I've made mistakes, yet you've always come through for me—no matter what. The pregnancy news is a shock. It was for me too, but I don't want to argue. For now, I'm going to head home, and, after you've had some time to think about it, please call me, and we'll get together to talk."

The role-play enhanced Kerry's skill level to deal with her mother. Encouraged, she said she felt better equipped to deal with her mother's response.

NOTE: In summary, remember the role-play setup is the advocate playing the part of the *client,* because it's the client's part that needs to be modeled.

Outcome: Kerry's fears about the baby's health were reassessed after speaking with the center's medical affiliate, the on-call physician. "The placenta," he explained, nourishes the baby. It begins to form at eight days. "The placenta isn't fully developed until the eighteenth to twentieth week of pregnancy. This likely means the herbs taken won't *necessarily* pose a problem that adversely affects the baby." (An encouragement with no promises.) When Kerry learned of the time frame for a placenta's formation, she felt she'd been given a reprieve.

As Kerry expressed how thankful she felt that the herbs were not likely to cause damage to the baby, a new optimism filled the room. The advocate sensed the right timing (kairos) to present the Gospel message. "God is truly a God of 'second chances!'" the advocate exclaimed. Heartened and with deepened trust in God, Kerry repented of her sins (silent confession) and received Christ into her life.

In the week that followed, Kerry told her mother the news of her third pregnancy. She withstood her mother's disdain while breaking the news. She went on to complete her senior year at college. The advocate helped devise a practical plan for the semester's final examinations prior to receiving her degree. Kerry arranged early finals with her professors. After successfully completing the requirements for her Bachelor of Science degree, she gave birth to her third child, a healthy baby boy. Her forbearing mother helped with childcare.

Role-play Two: A Pregnant Client Prepares to Break the News to Her Parent

Parental support can be key to a client's choice of life for her baby. Preparation for disclosing pregnancy news to a parent is highly beneficial. Clients have said the preparation builds their confidence, makes them feel more confident. A supportive parent interplays well with a client's decision about the pregnancy. But if the parent believes abortion to be the best choice, this bends the client's conversation with the parent to the need to stand up to the challenge. The prior discussion with her advocate has prepared her with a constructive plan for keeping her baby. If the client is willing to explore going deeper with God, a decision for Christ provides her with His strength to see her through. If the client decides to continue the pregnancy, the parent often comes around after the baby is born and soon becomes a doting grandparent.

As part of the advocate/client discussion:

- Pray with your client regarding the right timing for disclosing her pregnancy to her parent(s). (Non-believers often welcome the prayers of an advocate. If the client is a believer, encourage her to pray for right timing.)
- Advise the client to share the news with the more sympathetic parent first. It helps to have support from an ally.
- Have the client decide whether disclosure will work by herself or with a supportive person accompanying her. Consider the boyfriend (if parents are fond of him) or a family member whom the client and her parents trust, for example, an older sibling, an aunt, a close friend of the family.

Pray with your client regarding the right timing for disclosing her pregnancy to her parent(s).

As previously discussed, for the role-play of client with parent, the advocate takes the client's part, and the client takes the part of the parent because she's familiar with the responses. The following role-plays demonstrate how to initiate the discussion and some of the topics that are helpful to talk about.

Advocate (as client): "Mom, please sit down with me in the living room. I have something very important to share and need your input." After both are seated, the daughter begins.

Advocate (as client): "Mom, I'm pregnant. I'm sorry because this isn't how everything's supposed to be. But I've had a pregnancy test, and it's certain." (Tell the client she needs to pause after the announcement to give the parent time to respond.) Questions inevitably will come, like asking who the father is and his response to the pregnancy, discussion of the due date, questions about school or housing, etc.

Advocate (as client) continues: "Mom, before we get into a big discussion, I want you to know I've spent a lot of time thinking through this situation. I've put a plan together, and I'd love your input." Describing a *plan* sends the message of the adult child's willingness to take responsibility. In addition, it inserts a measure of comfort and stability to the unexpected news.

The conversation now heads into more details of our client's plan. This includes details of pregnancy not discussed earlier (due date, situation with the father of the baby, etc.) If initially this has been discussed, then other topics might include housing plans, employment, medical coverage availability, or adjustments needed for educational matters.

Pregnant College Student and Future Academic Plans

NOTE: If the client is a college student, talk through educational plans to be considered:

- Research the scholarship availability for pregnant or parenting (single) mothers within a specified income.
- Taking a gap year from college.
- Continuing with school and exploring available options such as a continuing education program online or at night school.
- To be addressed in context of the due date: Can she complete the semester, or will special accommodation have to be made with her professors for early examinations?

"My flesh and my heart fail; But God is the strength of my heart"

Psalm 23:6 NKJV

If the advocate has not yet shared her faith with the client, she could say, "Telling a parent about the pregnancy is one of the more difficult challenges. Quite honestly, I can't think of a time when God's wisdom is needed more than right now! I remember a time in my life that also felt troubling. . ." (Share the topic testimony.) Wherever the conversation leads, close with a comforting Scripture. A relatable Scripture serves as a reminder of how much God understands our stressful situations. For instance, "My flesh and my heart fail; But God is the strength of my heart" (Psalm 23:6 NKJV). Ask the client, "Would you like to have the assurance of God's strength in your life?"

Chapter Nine

Overview: How It All Works

Father, "Let gentleness be seen in every relationship, for our Lord is ever near."

(Prayer based on Philippians 4:5 TPT)

As we extend attitudes of love and acceptance to our clients, we are *laying the foundation* to present the Gospel message. A woman experiencing a crisis pregnancy is in a state of vulnerability, yet we are there to love the seeker.

The following reflection by a front-desk office administrator captures the spirit-filled attitude of serving our clients well.

The Girl at the Front Desk

Dear (client/patient),

When you called on the phone and tripped over every answer with an apology, I was not annoyed. When you told me your age, I didn't judge. When I thanked you for calling, I meant it.

When I smiled at you as you entered our center, I was happy to see you had come in. When you went back to meet with your advocate and nurse, I prayed for you.

When your pregnancy was confirmed, I rejoiced at the miracle while feeling sorrow for your circumstance, which you had described as "too dark for (you), let alone for a baby."

When I chaperoned your ultrasound, I felt honored to be a part of your moment. When you saw the flicker of your baby's heartbeat, I was not examining your reaction. I hoped to give your head and heart the time to meet without distraction.

When you spoke of being conflicted, I was proud that you were so honest.

Often centers retain a vacant block of time kept available for the abortion-minded caller with an opportunity to book an ultrasound.

When I noticed your face change as you learned of the help and love available to you here, I was glad. When you let out a deep breath, I exhaled with you. When you began to cry, I focused on holding in my own tears. When you chose life for your baby, I silently thanked God.

When you arrived for your parenting class weeks later, I was excited to see you again, and when you left, I prayed for you, feeling that even if you had made a different choice, I would love you. I longed for you to know that.

In Christ,

Annie Jeschke[1]

Client Process at the Center

When the prospective client calls the pregnancy center to make an appointment, information gathering is underway! Name, last date of her menstrual cycle, pregnancy intentions, etc. are logged into the scheduling calendar. This limited information is ready for further development through the intake process, followed by the ultrasound—if appropriate. The appointment to confirm the client's pregnancy is now matched with an available advocate.

Often centers retain a vacant block of time kept available for the abortion-minded caller with an opportunity to book an ultrasound following the intake (if the LMP is at least six weeks). Booking sooner rather than later is important for the abortion-minded client. The intending-to-carry clients require a less critical time frame.

The decision point for the life or death of the baby is confounded by all the moving parts of the client's life that enter her final decision-making. It is ordinarily within her right to request that the free ultrasound imagery be transferred to a specified abortion clinic. (Check your state regulations.) If a woman calls because she thinks we are an abortion clinic, we give her the respect of being heard and simply reply, "We are not an abortion clinic, but many women thinking about abortion make us their first stop. We also offer free ultrasounds."

Synchronizing Medical and Non-Medical Components

Our first-time client arrives at the center, and the medical component goes into action. The nurse administers and confirms the outcome of the pregnancy test. The sequence of intake, timing of the pregnancy test, and disclosure of outcome varies by center.

Often the pregnancy test is administered upon the client's arrival. Depending on the policy at the center, the pregnancy test results sometimes follow immediately. Some have the policy of reporting the pregnancy results later, after the intake is underway, to give the nurse time to complete client information after a brief medical interview with her.

The advocate's initial part of the client intake could begin with a more general collection of information (marital status, number of children, etc.) while waiting for the nurse's test results. When the nurse knocks at the counseling door, the advocate transitions by saying to the client, "Let's put a bookmark on our discussion, and we'll complete the intake after the nurse shares results and other information." After the nurse discloses the pregnancy test outcome, a short medical briefing follows in which she addresses miscarriage and ectopic pregnancy precautions.

If the client has been identified as abortion-minded during the initial call to the center, and if her last menstrual period has been six weeks ago, she would be eligible for an ultrasound.

On each day's schedule, many centers find it helpful to reserve one two-hour block of time daily for abortion-minded callers. This ensures availability. On the other hand, when a client is "intending to carry" (ITC), the ultrasound appointment has more flexibility. Some centers arrange for their ITCs to wait eight weeks after the last LMP. Others redirect the client to a private obstetrician. (Physician resources are given when needed.) With the abortion-vulnerable clients, an attempt is made to schedule the ultrasound with more expediency than clients intending to carry.

Beginning the Intake Process

Greet your client warmly, then begin the intake session with a friendly opening statement, such as, "Let's begin with your sharing what brought you in today!" This is preferable to an immediate jump into the intake questions, which can be too mechanical and uncaring. Though intake time is limited, the client must recognize we care about her by establishing an emotional connection. Though at first, we may glean she feels uptight—posture visibly rigid, etc.—we often observe her relaxing in a few minutes when she senses the advocate's sincerity.

If the client initially omits how she feels about a possible pregnancy, be sure to ask, "If your test confirms you are pregnant, is that going to be good news, bad news, or uncertain news for you to deal with?" Early during the intake, a good question to pinpoint the client's thinking is: "On a scale of zero to ten, how abortion-minded are you?"

In the beginning, the client may view her pregnancy as causing her unwelcome repercussions, such as terminating school plans, struggling with finances, dealing with a boyfriend's abandonment, contending with angry parents, or needing housing when "my parents kick me out of the house."

Whatever the reasoning for a client's consideration of abortion, the advocate listens well to that which is said and that which is left unsaid. Pertinent questions could be: "In the midst of this difficult situation, if you are pregnant, what do you consider your biggest challenge?" (Client responds.) A follow-up question: "If this challenge could be resolved, does that mean you'd consider a different option rather than abortion?" (Discuss.)

The intake involves discussion of personal issues as well as practical issues, such as medical insurance to cover prenatal care. (Is she abortion-vulnerable because she doesn't think she has medical coverage?) If the client qualifies for the state's low-income insurance, she can be directed to apply for Medicaid. Be familiar with your state's policies for Medicaid coverage for pregnancy. This information can make the difference between a client choosing an abortion versus choosing life for her baby.

NOTE: One scenario that comes up is the client who has been rejected for Medicaid coverage because her and her husband's combined income was too high to qualify for the previous year. (Medical coverage through the state is available if combined income is beneath a certain amount. The number of children is considered for a family's eligibility. Eligibility is determined by the couple's combined earnings and considers the number of children in the family.) If she and her husband didn't qualify for Medicaid the year before, they may now qualify currently because of the pregnancy. That is, adding one more child. Her in-utero baby *is counted* as an additional child in the family *as if already born*. For example, if last year she didn't qualify for Medicaid as a family of four—husband, two children, and herself—she may now qualify. The life of her preborn brings the number of family members to five, *even if* the combined income has remained the same.

Length of Client Appointments

Your center may be flexible about the time allotted for a client's appointment—some designate one hour, others one and a half hours, and still others remain flexible according to any given day's schedule. *God orchestrates faith sharing to the available time!*

When the medical component of ultrasound is introduced at a center, client scheduling is revisited. Sometimes it necessitates experimenting with different options before finalizing decisions. One center, for instance, limited each appointment to a one-hour time frame (for pregnancy test and intake). The staff's opinions varied. Some of the staff questioned whether everything—except for the ultrasound procedure—could be accomplished within this time span to adequately discuss two life-dominating issues: the life of the preborn and the offer of the Gospel message.

Advocates quickly become aware of their dependence on the Holy Spirit as they encourage new life in Christ for the mother of the baby and continuing life for the preborn.

During a typical one-hour session, the agenda items for client discussion with the client seem to conflict with the appointment's required agenda and limited time. For instance:

- The nurse must collect pertinent medical information through a medical interview and then make computer entries.
- The nurse performs and confirms a pregnancy test. A positive test is followed by forms of miscarriage and ectopic precautions signed by personnel and client.
- An advocate collects pertinent information by asking pertinent questions and listening to the client's concerns. This leads to an assessment for a plan to help her.
- The advocate presents testimony excerpts and/or Gospel message to the client.
- If a client is receptive to a spiritual discussion, the opportunity is offered to receive Christ.
- If a client commits or recommits her life to Christ, before leaving the appointment, she will be gifted with a Bible and will be connected with a list of area churches while encouraging her to take steps to grow in her faith. (See appendix C, "Now What?")

Regarding the length of appointments, remember God is in the equation. If the center's policy has time restrictions on each appointment, we can count on God to "show up" within that time span, enabling a fruitful appointment. The Savior's touch is tangible in finding favor and rapport, as well as enough time to clarify needs and extend encouragement. We need not be surprised when time isn't a problem for God!

Beyond Time Limitations: The Holy Spirit

Because for every matter there is a time and judgment. (Ecclesiastes 8:6 NKJV)

Advocates quickly become aware of their dependence on the Holy Spirit as they encourage new life in Christ for the mother of the baby and continuing life for the preborn. Spiritual interest from a boyfriend who accompanied the client to the center needs to be explored. Most assuredly, it is not a rarity for the boyfriend to make a life-changing decision for Christ.

One advocate said, "I recall meeting a twenty-year-old young man in the waiting room while his nineteen-year-old girlfriend was meeting with an advocate. As I walked past him toward the center's kitchen area, I distinctly felt the nudge of the Holy Spirit to stop and talk with him. It was an opportune time since the waiting room was empty. Engrossed with cell phone messages, he abruptly looked up when I greeted him. We both smiled, and the conversation began in short order."

....

Advocate: "Are you waiting for someone who's being seen here?"

Young man: "Yes, my girlfriend. She and I are pretty sure she's pregnant."

Advocate: "So, if the test confirms she's pregnant, will that be good news, bad news, or unsure news for you?"

Young man: "Kinda good news. An upcoming court case could complicate things. The problem involves my drinking while taking prescription drugs. Sometimes the combination causes me to have blackouts or drive unsafely. My driving was what caused me to be pulled over and ticketed recently.'"

Advocate: "Would you like to come back to my office and talk?

Young man: 'Sure!"

When they retreated to the office, the two re-engaged.

The kairos moment showed up like a light in the darkness.

Advocate: "You mentioned combining drugs and alcohol recently. May I ask, what pain in your life are you trying to medicate?"

Young Man: (Without hesitation) "My parents' divorce!"

The kairos moment showed up like a light in the darkness. This led to discussing the pain of his mom and dad's divorce. "That's a tough situation—even when children are grown up, it doesn't modify the pain. Despite that, the Cross of Jesus Christ is like a stake driven in the ground that divides your parents' divorce from the plan God has for *your* life!" The intensity in his eyes locked into her words. After sharing her testimony, she followed with the Gospel message.

Unknown to them, the young man's girlfriend in the next room was also hearing the Gospel message. Later he discovered, just before her appointed ended, she prayed to commit her life to Christ. The Holy Spirit had divinely orchestrated the timing. In less than an hour, both he and his girlfriend entrusted their lives to God's plan. Shortly afterward, the couple left the center with much to celebrate. As parents, united in Christ, they are prepared to bless the life of their baby.

Partnering with the Holy Spirit to Serve Others

For what man knows the things of a man except the spirit of the man which is in him? Even so, no one knows the things of God except the Spirit of God. Now we have received not the spirit of the world, but the Spirit who is from God, that we might know the things that have been freely given to us by God." (1 Corinthians 2:11–12 NKJV)

A Seasoned Advocate Shares Wisdom with Future Advocates

It is love that urges us to just "go there," and Jesus will carry us through.

Dear volunteers:

Praying before a client's appointment is essential. We become attuned to the Holy Spirit, who identifies areas of similarity between the client and me. He nudges me about when to share a part of my testimony, and He creates an opening for the Gospel.

After training and observation of client sessions, I began mentoring clients on my own, and I found the hardest part was sharing the Gospel. It seemed like such a personal thing to ask if someone wants to let God "take the wheel" of her life. I was also nervous about the quick timing of it all. There was a big learning curve to figure out that included pertinent information exchanged and how to connect during the allotted time frame. God managed my getting up to speed, and with the help of the person coaching me, I adapted to a timely and productive dialogue.

Connecting pregnant clients with community resources is valuable, but I've also grown knowledgeable with helping the client in a far greater way. Advocates can minister the peace that comes directly from our Lord, the Prince of Peace. It was Jesus's peace that brought me through my life's hardest times, and He continues to do so. Why would I hesitate to take the step to let someone else in on this? What was holding me back?

I once thought, prior to being a Christian, that Christians were pushy with their agenda. Now I realize it is a great act of love to share Christ's love—to reach out, to risk embarrassment or rejection, to take a chance because of a potentially transformed life. It is love that urges us to just "go there," and Jesus will carry us through. Be encouraged, God will show you the open doors. It may take getting used to, but you'll see!

Wishing you God's blessings!

Chapter Ten

Prayer: Seeking Truth, Receiving Guidance

Father, at the very moment I called out to You, You answered me. You strengthened me deep within my soul and breathed fresh courage into me.

(Prayer inspired by Psalm 138:3)

We are His intercessors, and God hears the prayers of His servants on behalf of our clients. In a verse spoken to Job, God presented a special directive for him to pray for others. Job obediently responded.

As you personalize God's challenge by praying for clients who come to the pregnancy center, listen for His mercy—especially for those living outside of His will.

As an advocate working with clients who may not know Christ as their Savior, insert your first name (twice) into the following passage and read aloud to *hear* God's personal encouragement.

"My servant______________ will pray for you, and I will accept (her) prayer and not deal with you according to your folly . . . and the Lord *accepted* ______________'s prayer."[1]

Prayer is our lifeline to God and is crucial.

Prayer: Ushering God's Grace into the Appointment

Morning prayers open the center; ongoing prayer sustains it. Prayer is our lifeline to God and is crucial—advocates praying alone and advocates praying together. God's presence, so near, His grace ushered swiftly by the wings of prayer. God hears the cry of our hearts. Early prayers shining through the day, the "huddle of two" prayers offered for sudden concerns, and collective prayers gathered with the spontaneity of a flash mob—instant assembly for immediate needs. Many centers also have a prayer line for volunteer prayer warriors. The warriors are instantly alerted by text to pray for those especially vulnerable to abortion.

Like manna, prayer is a staple—the bread of life, nourishing favor with our Sovereign God. Prayer utterances silently settle through conversations with the client. Silent prayers offered during the session enable kairos moments and guide us along the way.

We choose to believe that God's Spirit has orchestrated His plan for an ordinary life to encounter the King of kings.

A client advocate recalls the time her session with the client got underway. As she is praying silently asking God for a spiritual opportunity, a spiritual opening comes with a simple statement. "Did you know Jesus understands what you are going through? He loves you and wants you to invite Him in your life. Let Him draw you close."

The young client looks pensive as she shares, "My grandma used to talk to me about Jesus." The recollection visibly relaxes her into the moment. "Grandma always took me to church with her when I was growing up."

The advocate smiles. "Do you miss that time in your life?"

A blush pinkens the client's cheeks. The distant memory brings a nod of the head. Kairos has arrived.

Kairos Initiates Unity with Christ

We know that all things work together for good
to those that love God, to those who are the called
according to his purpose. (Romans 8:28 NKJV)

At God's delegated time, He brings all things "together for good." As advocates, we're appointed to serve others spiritually. As we step out in faith, we choose to *believe* that God's Spirit has orchestrated His plan for an ordinary life to encounter the King of kings.

Prompting and Releasing Christ's Intercessory Work

For there is one God and one mediator between God and
mankind, the man Christ Jesus. (1 Timothy 2:5 NIV)

Jesus is the One qualified to mediate, to bridge a heavenly realm with an earthly realm. He bridges "the gap," and believers are to prayerfully "stand in the gap" as intercessors. This is God's heart becoming our heart. In Ezekiel 22:30, God said, "So I sought for a man among them who would make a wall, and stand in the gap before Me on behalf of the land, that I should not destroy it; but I found no one" (NKJV). He is lamenting that Jerusalem did not have to fall if only there had been someone to stand in the gap. Let us be willing to stand in the gap with Him to invigorate the connection between earth and heaven.

Meaning of Standing in the Gap

Christ's work on the Cross brought reconciliation between God and man. We are fit prayer *partners* with the work of intercession. To stand in the gap is to "release, extend, and apply" the Savior's intercessory work at the Cross.[2] Through prayers of intercession, the believer joins Christ's act of reconciliation through prayer. We are to be "praying always with all prayer and supplication in the Spirit" (Ephesians 6:18 NKJV). Prayers bring God's will into action to continue His redemptive work.

Prayers bring God's will into action to continue His redemptive work.

Distributing Loaves and Fishes

Author Dutch Sheets teaches that "prayers of intercession are an extension" of God's work with a marked difference between *distributing* versus *producing*. "We don't have to *produce* anything," he says, not reconciliation, not deliverance, and not victory— "but rather we *distribute*, as the disciples did with the loaves and fishes." God produced the fishes, and we are to dispense His bountiful provision. Our specific calling and function do not replace God but release Him.[3]

Time for a Truth Encounter with God

> Create in me a clean heart, O God, And renew a steadfast spirit within me. Do not cast me away from Your presence, And do not take Your Holy Spirit from me. Restore me to the joy of Your salvation, And uphold me by your generous Spirit. Then, I will teach transgressors Your ways, And sinners shall be converted to You. (Psalm 51:10–13 NKJV)

Behind the adulterous tale of a king named David is a memorable love story. Not the story of a man and his mistress, but the story of a loving God and an imperfect man who loved Him. A God so loving, He refused to let go of the one He would later call "a man after [His] own heart." Despite David's wanderings and flaws of unbridled sin, God arranged the prophet Nathan to confront David's arrogance of sin. In the life of a king, when the kairos moment came, truth went to war with deception. David's prayer of confession started a renewal in his soul. It prompted a humble request: "Create in me a clean heart, O God."

With King David's restoration came the joy of his salvation. We can still hear revival in his words, "I will teach transgressors Your ways, And sinners shall be converted."

The psalmist's message is surely for us all. Confessed. Renewed. Restored. When we embrace freedom from our personal shame of sin, we open the God-given capacity to serve in the way He calls. When God brings renaissance into our souls, we share His heart to "teach transgressors" and to "convert sinners."

Keeping Short Accounts with God

At the pregnancy resource center, Christian workers must sidestep disunity and turn to God to restore our peace. Disagreements that occasionally arise will need mending. (Even coming to work with unresolved conflict with a spouse can be managed by arranging a mutually agreeable time for resolution.) Having made our attempt at resolution, our hearts are "right before God." Pray for the other person and your reconciliation. To keep the windows of the soul clean allows the "Sonshine" to filter through our outreach to others.

Welcoming the Spirit of Truth

"However, when He, the Spirit of truth, has come, He will guide you into all truth." (John 16:13 NKJV)

Do you believe truth is worthy to be shared? Jesus did. He knew setting people *free* from the burden of sin must begin with a *truth encounter.* Just as in David's life, this remains our hope. We are participants with Jesus in a client's encounter with truth.

Prayer: The Desires of Your Heart

"And whatever you ask in My name, that I will do, that the Father may be glorified in the Son. If you ask anything in My name, I will do it." (John 14:13–14 NKJV)

Truth uproots distorted thinking and realigns us with God's will.

Truth uproots distorted thinking and realigns us with God's will. A truth encounter was an advocate's earnest prayer for Cassie.

In her mid-twenties, Cassie had enrolled for a master's program with a full-ride scholarship. One week away from moving into campus housing, a positive pregnancy test threatened her plans. Though she was conflicted, abortion seemed a viable option. An option favored by her boyfriend. He was already supporting two children from a previous relationship. Abortion avoided adding another child to the mix.

When Cassie met with her advocate at the center, the complexities of her situation were discussed. An unexpected spiritual perspective was introduced by the advocate. God's peace was the very peace Cassie craved. The advocate also shared her salvation testimony, but Cassie was not ready to turn to God. "I'd feel like such a phony if I received God and then I had an abortion."

Abortion-vulnerable, seven weeks pregnant, and leaving for school in one week prompted the urgency of an ultrasound appointment the following day. The boyfriend came with her, and together they witnessed their new reality on the screen.

The nurse suddenly spoke. "What have we here?" She directed their attention to two baby sacs. As the nurse spoke of the finding, the boyfriend peered at the screen glumly. Twin babies doubled the need for abortion.

But Cassie was transfixed. *Twins. How special,* thoughts whispered. The earlier thoughts of abortion were crumbling, and she left the center troubled. According to plans, Cassie moved the next week into campus housing two hours away. When the advocate contacted her, she said she hadn't made up her mind what to do. She added that she had told her mother about the pregnancy and said, "My mother wants me to keep the pregnancy."

Disclosure to a parent is a good sign. Parental support is even better. When Cassie phoned the advocate, she expressed how painful it would be to drop out of the graduate program. The advocate agreed it would be difficult to *postpone* school for a while. But she was also quick to highlight the importance of her mother's support. "Cassie, you will never regret giving birth to these babies—especially a gift of twins. Your mother also would receive this special blessing. This is so exceptional that if you choose to abort, you will always wonder about them—what gender they were, what they would look like, what they would *be* like, and what you might have done differently! These thoughts will haunt you after an abortion."

....

In the coming weeks and months, the advocate was unable to contact Cassie. Could it be she had aborted and didn't want to talk about it? Despite the lack of contact, prayers continued. When her due date came up, a final call was attempted, but no one answered. Cassie's file was closed.

Eighteen months later, a woman called the center to make an appointment with her previous advocate. She wanted to drop by to say thank you for the encouragement when she was pregnant with twins. It was Cassie. Staff and volunteers who prayed for her were joyful to hear the outcome.

When Cassie met with the advocate, there was much to share. So much had changed. Months before, the twins had been born—a boy and a girl. Single, she had ended the relationship with the father of the babies and now had a new boyfriend. "This man adores these babies—can't spend enough time with them!" she said happily. She also shared she had begun coursework for a new master's degree program.

"So much has happened," she chattered. "Last year, I also became a Christian!"

Cassie's choices had released God's plan rather than her suffering the consequences of a false solution. Just as His Word says, "Delight yourself also in the Lord, And He shall give you the desires of your heart" (Psalm 37:4 NKJV).

Grace is the relational aspect of God's character.

Grace-Filled Truth

Wise input and testimonies shared by advocates are a continuing avenue of grace-filled truth. Clinical psychologist and author Dr. Henry Cloud has aptly said, "Truth without grace is judgment." Conversely, "grace without truth should be named License."[4] Taste the significance of these words: Truth without grace is painful and stark. When truth is spoken with the grace of compassion, defenses are lowered, and the window of the soul opens wider to receive. On the contrary, pure grace without truth becomes a "sloppy kindness" that serves no one well. In sum, grace, when infused with truth, becomes "a healing combination because they deal with the main barrier to all growth: guilt."[5]

When God imparts grace, He bestows "the first ingredient" for growing up in the image of God. His grace is unbroken, uninterrupted, unearned, and accepting. Grace is the *relational* aspect of God's character. It shows itself in His unconditional connection to us. Truth is the second ingredient necessary for growing up in the image of God. Truth is what is real, how things really are, the structural aspect of His character, the skeleton life hangs upon.[6]

Because we often meet with clients indulging in high-risk sexual behavior and other self-destructive lifestyles, the restorative process begins with a relationship with Jesus Christ. Speaking truth into others' lives requires boldness, and boldness, rightly flavored with grace, necessitates prayer to flavor our words.

Lottie's Story: Leaving a Cult and Finding Jesus

Some of our Christian clients have wandered from the faith and bought into Satan's deceptions. Strongholds of the Enemy's deception become fortified by learned cultural values rather than the biblical guidelines God has provided. Satan is committed to keeping truth estranged from the battlefield of the mind.

The story comes to mind of a thirty-year-old woman named Lottie, who arrived at the center with Missy, her precocious seven-year-old. Lottie tested negative for pregnancy. A soft-spoken woman, she was elegantly dressed in an African sari colorfully splashed with red and gold print with a luxurious sheen. Yet Lottie was not a foreigner. Born on the East Coast, she spoke of the productive, "normal" life she once lived, which included earning a master's degree. "It was a credential required by my position." Suddenly, she looked embarrassed. "I know it sounds crazy that my life has come to *this!*"

Prompted by a marriage dissolved in divorce, she had moved several states away to a big city where she became deeply involved in a relationship. She became pregnant and gave birth to her daughter, Missy. As the interview continued, Lottie was asked about her current marital status. At first, when asked if she was married, she replied, "Yes," then quietly added, "but African style." (She added, "That means it's not legally recognized in the United States.")

Lottie said that her "husband" was extremely wealthy, but his income source was questionable. Though strangely limited in her knowledge of him, she said, "All I know is that his work involves making international contacts during middle-of-the-night phone calls." She was speaking more freely now, and she shared that their household included four other wives and multiple children her "husband" had fathered. Apparently, there wasn't any backlash in their upscale neighborhood about the household's bizarre lifestyle. Within a home of many bedrooms, everyone in the household was comfortably accommodated. By restricting contact with people outside the home, their secrets were contained.

It soon became evident Lottie was dealing with much fear and shame. The fear of being pursued when *they* discovered she and her daughter had run away, and shame for the years she had allowed the situation. She felt imprisoned—as well, she was—and despite getting along with the other "wives," she said she could no longer live in the closely monitored environment.

As the intake process proceeded, the advocate mentioned, "We are a Christian center." Smiling, Lottie replied that she had attended a Christian church as a child. However, it seemed clear Lottie didn't understand the personal relationship with Christ, the advocate assured her God's love for her had never changed.

The spiritual discussion progressed as the advocate shared her salvation testimony with Lottie and her little daughter. She, too, had been in *her* mid-thirties when God won her attention. When the Gospel tract was shared, a deeper understanding of the faith led Lottie to commit her life to Christ. The advocate asked Missy if she would like to invite Jesus into her life, and, with childlike eagerness, she nodded her head excitedly as her delighted mother observed. After sharing a children's cartoon copy of the Gospel message, the invitation extended to receive Him. Missy enthusiastically responded.

> He stooped down to lift me out of danger from the desolate pit I was in . . . A new song for a new day rises up in me. (Psalm 40:2–3 TPT)

Though the advocate recognized that swaths of information could have been concealed when Lottie spoke of her strange household—drugs, sex trafficking, or even a prostitution ring—the process to provide help for her had begun appropriately. God was the first stop, and great blessings were poised to follow.

With the intake completed, the advocate, in agreement with her client, arranged a county safe house interview over the phone. Her

"He stooped down to lift me out of danger from the desolate pit I was in."

Psalm 40:2 TPT

acceptance into one of the county's residences for women and their children was quickly approved. The protected environment eased fears of repercussion when Lottie and her child would be discovered to be absent from the home. (When the county agrees a safe house is in order, transportation is arranged to their new housing. Clothing and food provisions are part of the support package, as well as professional counseling.)

After settling into their new environment, several weeks passed. Lottie and her daughter timidly ventured out to worship at a small, Bible-believing church within walking distance. In God's providence, the church was about to become a strong support system inclusive of biblical counseling and discipleship.

> Then we cried out, "Lord, help us! Rescue us!" And He did! He led us out by the right way until we reached a suitable city to dwell in. (Psalm 107:6–7 TPT)

As Lottie grew spiritually, she became deeply aware of her identity as God's child and assumed rightful "authority" over entrenched Enemy strongholds in her life. (A spiritual stronghold is a habitual pattern of thinking built into a person's life.)

Lottie was learning that the only power Satan wields over the believer is when desires find *agreement* with him as opposed to God's truth. Scripture tells us to "put on the new man" in Christ Jesus and walk as the new creations we are! When mindsets have been renewed through a relationship with Christ, we are freed from the Enemy territory to live according to God's truth.

> Tell the world how he broke through and delivered you from the power of darkness . . . He has set us free to be his very own! (Psalm 107:2 TPT)

Lottie was ready to exchange Satan's strongholds in her life for the healing Christ offered. She was learning to trust Jesus as her new Source of life. Though Lottie had entered the *process* of being conformed to Christ, she had already been freed to live by the Spirit and follow truth rather than the earlier emotional programming. "For the law of the Spirit who gives life has set you free from the law of sin and of death" (Romans 8:2 NIV). Having chosen Jesus as her salvation, she was equipped to make godly choices and embrace His Word with assurance.

She had already been freed to live by the Spirit and follow truth rather than the earlier emotional programming.

> My shield and the horn of my salvation, my stronghold. I will call upon the Lord, who is worthy to be praised; So shall I be saved from my enemies. (Psalm 18:2–3 NKJV)

The outcome of Lottie's restoration: Months after Lottie and Missy joined the church, mother and daughter experienced the joy of bearing witness to their faith by a public baptism. One year later, Lottie called her advocate to excitedly share her good news. "I wanted you to know I have met a 'child of God,' and he and I have become engaged!" She also added that they were currently attending premarital counseling together. After announcing the date of their upcoming wedding, she said, "I hope you will attend!"

The day of the wedding arrived—a celebration of matrimony enhanced by celebrating the transformative love of a God who overcame the plans of the Enemy. Lottie had been freed to live as an ardent follower of Christ. This God-honoring day was exhilarating. Lottie's matron of honor described the couple's devoted commitment to God. She gloriously concluded, "Not only has a marriage begun, but a ministry to others."

> And when we are fully restored, you will rejoice
> and take delight in every offering of our lives
> as we bring our sacrifices of righteousness
> before you in love. (Psalm 51:19 TPT)

We Serve a Soul-Winning Father!

> Now when they saw the boldness of Peter and
> John, and perceived that they were uneducated and
> untrained men, they marveled. And they realized
> that they had been with Jesus. (Acts 4:13 NKJV)

Peter and John had been boldly sharing their faith. They were ordinary men with no religious training.

Peter and John had been boldly sharing their faith. They were ordinary men with no religious training. Most importantly, when the respected elders and leaders of the people heard them, the observers embraced the extraordinary, knowing Peter and John *had been with Jesus*. As advocates interact with clients, we pray our clients will glean that we, too, are different as followers of Jesus.

When Peter and John continued speaking of the Messiah, there was a man standing nearby, whom the council knew had been healed. Despite the supernatural healing, council members shunned his belief in the Christ. As they conferred among themselves, they pondered what they "should do with" Peter and John. They said, "Everyone in Jerusalem can clearly see that they've performed a notable sign and wonder—we can't deny that. But to keep this propaganda from spreading any further among the people, let's threaten them severely and warn them to never speak to anyone in this name again" (Acts 4:16–17 TPT).

The council brought Peter and John back into the room and ordered them to stop teaching. The men responded, "Whether it is right in the

"For we cannot but speak the things which we have seen and heard."

Acts 4:20 NKJV

sight of God to listen to you more than to God, you judge. For we cannot but speak the things which we have seen and heard" (Acts 4:19–20 NKJV). May we, as advocates and participants in God's mission, act no differently. We have seen and heard much since our conversion. Let us openly speak of these things as the Spirit leads. We, too, can expect that some will believe and some will not: "They worshipped Him; but some doubted" (Matthew 28:17 NKJV). Despite the merits of a strong witness, to include the miracle of healing, there will always be those who reject the truth.

Like Peter and John, we, too, have been tasked as vessels of the Holy Spirit to touch the hearts of the unsaved. Not alone in this endeavor, we find unity with our Lord, who "came to seek and to save the lost" (Luke 19:10 ESV). Timidity loses its power when faith is our powerhouse. As Corrie Ten Boom once said, "Trying to do the Lord's work in your own strength is the most confusing, exhausting, and tedious of all work. But when you are filled with the Holy Spirit, then the ministry of Jesus just flows out of you."[7]

In partnership with God, we enter the spiritual battlefield, "casting down arguments and every high thing that exalts itself against the knowledge of God, bringing every thought into captivity to the obedience of Christ" (2 Corinthians 10:5 NKJV). Despite the discouraging thought bombs Satan throws at us, such as "This person has no interest in spiritual things," we can choose to walk by faith and share Christ. Though we are a part of the harvesting team, it is God who saves souls. "Behold," He says, "all souls are Mine; The soul of the father as well as the soul of the son is Mine" (Ezekiel 18:4 NKJV). He already knows the unbelievers who will be "caught" for salvation. What a privilege to be part of the process.

Divine Intervention in the Counseling Room

Sadly, there will be clients with no interest in entering a deeper relationship with Christ. Yet staff and volunteers feel comfortable, knowing God continues to seek them long after they depart from the center. God continues to honor our desires to make Him known, and we remain amazed at each intervention. God bends discussions into intersections of supernatural insights and brings His sense of joy and adventure at the least expected times. You'll see!

One day an East Indian couple arrived at the center. The husband appeared much older than his wife—a dark-eyed beauty whose tiny frame was draped in a colorful sari. On her forehead was a dot, the featured *bindi,* believed to be the place where the body's energy is retained, and, being seen as a third eye, is believed to focus "inward toward God . . . and signifies piety."[8]

Seating themselves, the husband readily asserted he would be the one answering questions. "My wife's English is not good." Perhaps the decision reflected their cultural bearings as well. The wife submitted to his lead, pleasantly silent as he responded to the intake questions. At times the demure wife nodded agreement to his answers revealing she understood English. Once the pregnancy was confirmed, the husband clarified intentions for their child's life. "My wife will be getting an abortion."

The session proceeded. A growing intensity became apparent especially when various emotional risks of an abortion procedure were discussed. The outspoken husband looked resolute as his pace of speech accelerated. "My wife needs to get an abortion since she must complete her PhD at the university." Despite the advocate's amiable attempts to explore a different option, the issue was closed. The husband's mind was clearly made up, and his wife was compliant. The battle for their child was over.

With the session ending, the advocate rose from her chair in sync with the couple rising from the couch facing her. As they rose, the husband's eyes locked with the eyes of the advocate, the intense stare between them triggered unfiltered words. She heard her voice saying with unmistakable authority, "This may be the only son you will ever have!" The stunning statement met with silence and the couple left.

Particularly sensitive to abortion-minded clients, numerous staff prayers were offered for the abortion-minded couple. Later, after the due date of the lovely Indian student had come and gone, it was time to finalize the official outcome and close the file. The advocate made the last follow-up call to the home. When the husband answered, a baby's cry could be heard in the background. In disbelief, the advocate asked, "Do I hear a baby crying?"

"Yes!" came the reply.

"Oh, what did you have?" she stammered.

"A son!" he replied proudly.

God bends discussions into intersections of supernatural insights and brings His sense of joy and adventure at the least expected times.

Prayer: A "Drinking In" of His Spirit

Eat, O friends! Drink, yes, drink deeply, O beloved ones! (Song of Solomon 5:1 NKJV)

We, who serve the clients, feel the daily need for a Savior's refreshment. The need for deeply "drinking in" His Spirit settles us into His peace before the "pouring out" of His Spirit. Upon hearing our sighs of "I thirst," Jesus comes to fill us once again with living water. "All you thirsty ones, come to me! Come to me and drink!" (John 7:37 TPT). The streams of living water, like a fountain of refreshment, anoint us.

His Spirit settles us into His peace before the "pouring out" of His Spirit.

An advocate shared about the time she had been heavily booked with clients in an unusually challenging afternoon. Near closing time, she felt emotionally drained and was looking forward to the end of the working day. The last appointment slot was vacant. But, at the last minute, a walk-in client appeared and was assigned to her.

"Believe in Me so that rivers of living water will burst out from within you, flowing from your innermost being." (John 7:38 TPT)

At the beginning of the session, the advocate felt tempted to keep the spiritual dialogue short. Instead, she asked God to help her. During the client interaction, the advocate began to feel increasingly refreshed and took the appropriate time with the woman. After sharing her testimony, the advocate presented the Gospel message. The young woman, responsive to a fresh start in her life, left the center a newly committed believer. The Lord is with us as we "come boldly to the throne of grace, so that we may obtain mercy and find grace to help in time of need" (Hebrews 4:16 NKJV).

How To Keep His Flame Ablaze

Never restrain or put out the fire of the Holy Spirit. (1 Thessalonians 5:19 TPT)

Do not quench the Spirit. (1 Thessalonians 5:19 NKJV)

Quenching the Spirit in the Greek language makes spiritual reference to quenching "things on fire," like smothering the spark. It is when "the impulses of the flesh might usurp the place of the energy of the Spirit."[9] Walking in the Spirit means believers, all of whom have permanently received His Holy Spirit, choose to live their lives freshly confessed of sin and with a personal integrity empowered by His Spirit. This is important in the counseling room so that the *fullness of His Spirit* can guide a supernatural path tailored to our client.

If we can be *filled up* with the Spirit, sin can cause us to "leak." That is, unconfessed sin is so contrary to yielding to His lordship that it smothers the flame of passion. It quenches it. This means that when we sin, we need to confess the sin, thank Him for forgiving us, and ask Him to refill us with the fullness of His Spirit. This has been called "walking in the Spirit."

If we can be filled up with the Spirit, sin can cause us to "leak."

Is the Christian Life Impossible to Live?

There are multiple ways to enter a spiritual discussion. For instance, an advocate says to her client who just learned we were a Christian ministry, "In my own life, I didn't know the Christian life is impossible to live!" It seizes attention, and the client will wonder, *Is this a trick statement?* A moment later the advocate adds, "I've learned it's impossible for me to try to live in a pleasing way to God without my relying on Him. I can't muster it up!" Expect good discussions to follow!

At first the client may not understand and may talk about putting more effort into her "religious life," like going to church or trying harder to be a better person. (The Do, Value, Be chart on pages 186–188 fits well into this discussion.) Instead, we point to the need to shrink self-effort and depend on His leading and enablement.

When the client hears about living from God's Spirit indwelling us, this is not "pipe theology"—as if the life of His Spirit flows through our being like a pipeline. Rather, as we allow God to take the reins of our life and we live in a partnered covenant with Him, He will lighten our burden, just as Jesus has promised. "For my yoke is easy and My burden is light (Matthew 11:30 NKJV).

"For my yoke is easy and My burden is light."

Matthew 11:30 NKJV

From the Old-World culture, we have likely seen pictures of a team of harnessed oxen pulling a wooden-wheeled cart. The two animals appear to be equally yoked as they pull the cart's load, but one ox is the lead—the alpha. In our relationship with Christ, believers are yoked in covenant with the Savior. He is our leader. He is the Alpha. As believers, we can enhance our unity with Him by reading His Word, worshipping, fellowshipping with like-minded people, choosing to avoid sin, and stepping out in faith to witness to others. He also walks with us into the counseling room and imparts His guidance with our clients.

God's Answered Prayer for Morgan

Morgan was engaged to be married and admitted she felt hesitant to abort her pregnancy. In the beginning, her reasoning was more self-focused. "I'm afraid if I had this second abortion, my depression would return, and I don't want to go through that again."

Yet, whenever she expressed her thoughts to her fiancé, he became angry. "It's not the right timing for a pregnancy!" His frustration was pressuring her into an abortion decision.

She spoke of how much she loved him and admitted to the fear of losing him if she didn't abort. She said she was a Christian; she didn't believe in abortion, but she was also feeling conflicted.

A further discussion about faith highlighted the importance of *courage.* "Courage," the advocate said, "is a quality of character that too frequently is limited to the likes of war heroes rather than the fortitude needed to 'walk out one's beliefs in difficult circumstances.'" Recognizing the power of God's Word, the advocate turned to Joshua 1:9 and asked the client to read the passage:

> "Have I not commanded you? Be strong and of good courage; do not be afraid, nor be dismayed for the LORD your God is with you wherever you go." (Joshua 1:9 NKJV)

Morgan nodded agreeably after she read the Scripture. A discussion followed that included the advocate's testimony. The client, inspired by hearing how God tenderly pursues us, decided to rededicate her life to Christ.

After praying the rededication prayer, the advocate asked the client if she could also pray for her fiancé.

"Oh yes, please!"

The prayer asked God's intervention on behalf of the unborn child. She prayed Morgan would have the courage to stand strong in her faith. The advocate also prayed for the fiancé's change of heart toward his unborn baby. She ended the prayer with a daring request. "Lord, touch his heart even if it's through a dream."

Three days later, Morgan returned to the center for an ultrasound. This time her countenance was unmistakably joyful. It was such a contrast from the client's last appointment, her advocate exclaimed, "What has happened with you, Morgan? You look so happy!"

The exuberant client exclaimed, "Yes, everything has changed! The day you prayed for my fiancé, he was unable to sleep that night. He tossed and turned all night in his sleep. The next morning, he told me about his dream and how God had appeared to him. [A kairos moment.] He said, 'When I woke up this morning, I immediately knew you should keep this pregnancy.' He even apologized to me for being selfish about the pregnancy. Today, we came together to view the ultrasound," Morgan said.

God Hears the Prayers of the Righteous

> But, without faith, it is impossible to please Him,
> for he who comes to God must believe that
> He is, and that He is a rewarder of those who
> diligently seek Him. (Hebrews 11:6 NKJV)

A married couple arrived at the center. Anna was in her late thirties. Her husband, Horace, a former economics professor in his country, was nearly twenty years older. A trim, distinguished-looking man, he seemed exceptionally attentive toward his wife. It soon grew apparent Horace was a high-control person and assumed decision-making for the two of them. She deferred.

Anna was dealing with a severe condition associated with pregnancy. Though she was in her second trimester, nausea caused her to throw up day and night. Despite her suffering, she wanted to continue the pregnancy, whereas Horace, worried about his wife, insisted she abort. "Your health is at stake! You're sick all the time and hardly able to eat!"

The advocate asked her client if she had a faith background. Anna replied she had received Christ into her life years ago. "I was led to the Lord by my older brother. He is a well-known evangelist in my country."

When the Gospel message was later brought up, Horace piped in, "I am a Catholic!"

The advocate assured Horace that "trusting Jesus as Lord and Savior" is not a denominational issue. Whether Catholic or Protestant, we bring pleasure to God and ourselves when we yield control and "go deeper" into our experience of Him. After more discussion, Horace listened carefully, ultimately deciding to yield his life to Jesus. Before leaving that day, a final prayer closed the appointment, and the couple left with doctor referrals in hand. No decision had been made regarding the baby.

A few weeks later, Anna and Horace returned to the center with a story to tell! Anna said she had awakened one night with her usual retching nausea. This time, after throwing up, she reclined on the living room couch to avoid disturbing Horace. Not only did she feel physically sick, but she also felt sick with worry as she contemplated the abortion appointment her husband had scheduled for the end of the week. She said she was sobbing and clasping her stomach, pleading with the Lord, begging Him to help her. Over and again, she pleaded, "Jesus, I want my baby. I want my baby. Please help me."

Eventually Anna fell asleep and miraculously *remained* asleep until morning. When she awakened, she felt refreshed with a new sense of wellness. No early morning sickness greeted her; no waves of nausea; no lingering malaise; no hint of a single symptom remained. God had answered her prayer! Horace, hearing his wife's exuberance with God's healing, was so taken aback by the return of her happy disposition, he immediately canceled the abortion appointment. Indeed, she was healed. Anna's pregnancy continued to term without a single incident of sickness.

His loving parents named him Matthew, a name that means, "gift from God."

A few months later, they welcomed a baby boy into the world. His loving parents named him Matthew, a name that means, "gift from God."

Prayers for God's Co-Laborers

> "He who abides in Me, and I in him, bears much fruit." (John 15:5 NKJV)

We co-labor in prayer to bring what God has already ordained, a plentiful harvest.

> Then He said to His disciples, "The harvest truly is plentiful, but the laborers are few; Therefore pray the Lord of the harvest to send out laborers into His harvest." (Matthew 9:37–38 NKJV)

Believers tend to pray for more souls to respond to the Gospel, yet Jesus's emphasis is having enough co-laborers.

We have heard this familiar verse so often that we mute its powerful message. Believers tend to pray for *more souls* to respond to the Gospel, yet Jesus's emphasis is having enough *co-laborers*. As the Great Commission arrives at our centers daily, the *harvest* comes from the *laborers*. "The laborers are few," He says. Plentiful are the numbers of those who would be ready to receive, but the laborers are missing. WE are missing! Will we believe what Jesus is saying to us? Will we take our Lord at His word? Will we respond?

Bill Bright, founder of Campus Crusade for Christ (now known as Cru), often asked Christians two questions:

1. "What is the most important experience of your life?"
2. "What is the most important thing that you can do to help another person?"

Throughout years of ministry, Mr. Bright said that to the first question, persons said, "Knowing Christ as my Savior is absolutely the most important experience in my life." To the second question, they answered: "Help [the person] to know Christ!"[10]

How would you respond to these two questions? If you agree that "coming to know Jesus as my Savior" is the most important personal experience of your life and that helping a person to know Christ is the next most important thing we can do, then you understand the significance of a transformed life. A decision to follow Christ by depending on the Holy Spirit changes the course of a life and transforms a person from the inside out. Worldly perspectives meld into a biblical worldview that includes an eternity spent with God.

Prayers of Weeping and Seeking

Those who sow in tears shall reap in joy. (Psalm 126:5)

Charles Spurgeon felt that those who shared the Gospel should be "weeping" and "reaping."[11] This refers to experiencing heartfelt sorrow for those without Christ. It involves the knowledge that without Him, they will miss a magnificent inheritance—an eternal kingdom filled with the love of a Savior and revelations beyond what we can ask or imagine. Compassion for our clients brings the motivation to stand in the gap between the unbeliever and a Savior to offer, as special conciliator, the "keys" to His kingdom. Prayers we silently offer during the counseling session continue to break down Enemy strongholds to bring spiritual impact.

For the love of Christ compels us, because . . . if One died for all, then all died; and He died for all, that those who live should live no longer for themselves, but for Him who died for them and rose again. (2 Corinthians 5:14–15 NKJV)

The love of Christ compels us to the protective grip of the God who loves us. *Compels* in the Greek language (*sunecho*) refers to a "sense of constraint, a tight grip that prevents an escape. The love of Christ leaves us no choice except to live our lives for Him."[12] By seeking Him fervently in prayer, He equips us to woo lost souls into His kingdom.

> With passion I pursue and cling to you. Because I feel Your grip on my life, I keep my soul close to your heart. (Psalm 63:8 TPT)

Prayers to Share God's Burden for the Lost

> How shall they believe in Him of whom they have not heard? And how shall they hear without a preacher? And how shall they preach unless they are sent? As it is written, "How beautiful are the feet of those who preach the gospel of peace, Who bring glad tidings of good things." (Romans 10:14–15 NKJV)

> And don't allow yourselves to be weary or disheartened in planting good seeds, for the season of reaping the wonderful harvest you've planted is coming! Take advantage of every opportunity to be a blessing to others. (Galatians 6:9–10 TPT)

Do you feel *compelled* by your desire to share Jesus with others? If you are one to reply with an honest "No," then dare to ask Him to give you a burden for the lost—even a *heavy* burden for the lost. Essentially this is like asking the Lord for a prayer assignment in sync with the heart of His will.

A mission of life represents all that God loves and Satan hates.

A believer once shared that at times when a friend asked her to pray for someone that she had never met, she would forget to continue praying for the need of "some stranger." Guilt would predictably settle in because of her desire to follow through with the prayer request. She began to ask God to "give me a burden to faithfully pray." He responded. At times He awakened her at odd hours of the night—the prayer request weighing heavily on her mind. She found, after prayers were faithfully offered, she fell gently back to sleep.

Warring in Prayer

The pregnancy resource center is a spiritual war zone. This becomes understandable when we consider the mission and the devotion needed to fulfill it. A mission of *life* represents all that God loves and Satan hates. The Enemy despises what we do—New life in Christ and life in the womb expound the antithesis of Satan's culture of death.

The Enemy of Our Souls wields an onslaught of deception, lies, defeating thoughts, and confusion. Yet this Enemy has already been defeated at the Cross. Satan lost power when the Father "delivered us from the power of darkness and conveyed us into the kingdom of the Son of His love, in whom we have redemption through His blood, the forgiveness of sins" (Colossians 1:13–14 NKJV).

There are times when Satan militantly stirs things up. Though he is already defeated, by faith, believers *enforce* this defeat by truth, by believing we are delivered from the Enemy's authority over us. We stand firm, asking God's help to deal with disparaging situations. Though Satan's power was cut off by the triumph of the Cross, we must confront and exercise the rightful authority given us. "In the name of Jesus, I command you to depart to where God is directing you to go." The power of sin and death defeated by the Cross is an exaltation of the resurrected Christ, "far above all principality and power and might and dominion" (Ephesians 1:21 NKJV).

As believers, we walk by faith, still celebrating the victory of our King Jesus.

Historical Background for Parading the Enemy

Jesus made a show of victory over the world's dark powers, leading them through the heavenlies in a procession of triumph. "And having disarmed the powers and authorities, he made a public spectacle of them, triumphing over them by the cross" (Colossians 2:15 NIV). This envisions the ancient custom of defeated kings in battle. In biblical times, when a king and his kingdom were defeated, the thumbs and large toes of the king and his men were amputated (Judges 1:7). This "hampered effective use of a weapon" since footing was now "unreliable in battle." Satan and his demonic realm also experienced defeat at the Cross. As believers, we walk by faith, still celebrating the victory of our King Jesus.[13]

We who follow Christ enjoy God's protection that withstands the kingdom of darkness. Under God's rightful authority, we are anchored in the knowledge that Satan's rule over sin and death was decimated at the Cross. We live in eternal triumph of new life. For the believer, "the weapons of our warfare are not carnal but mighty in God for pulling down strongholds, casting down arguments and every high thing that exalts itself against the knowledge of God, bringing every thought into captivity to the obedience of Christ" (2 Corinthians 10:4–5 NKJV). This is the hope of the Gospel we offer to our struggling clients.

Great Power Available to the Believer

God's "power is the same as the mighty strength he exerted when he raised Christ from the dead and seated him at his right hand in the heavenly realms" (Ephesians 1:19–20 NIV).

We rejoice as believers, knowing we are conquerors with Jesus. He has given us the power to love our client and offer her *living* hope, encouragement, and growth in faith. We pray the words of Paul for her that she may "know Him and the power of His resurrection" (Philippians 3:10 NKJV).

J. Vernon McGee amplifies the significance of this verse by pointing to the original language:

> What is the exceeding (intense) greatness of His power (*dunameos*—dynamite power) to usward who believe, according to the working (*energeian*—energizing) strength of His might. How great is that dynamite power that's energizing strength? . . . It is power enough to raise Christ from the dead. . . . Think of the power it takes to lift a missile off its base and take it out into space . . . power in the physical realm. The power that took Christ to the right hand of God is the same power that is available to believers today.[14]

When disruptions occur, they become manageable through our willingness to join the Lord's peace.

Spiritual Warfare at the Center

"I love coming here," the client said. "I feel something special. It is peaceful." Though words like this might bring deep satisfaction, we also know a center's peace is an easy casualty if ministering from our flesh, not from His Spirit.

Maintaining peace, even at a *Christian ministry*, requires discipline and choice and God's love, as well as consistent surrender to His will. With the different personalities serving at our centers and the high stress that comes with the territory, misunderstandings and judgments can flare too easily. Dissention must be addressed biblically to avoid injury to the ministry and those who serve there.

A Prescription for Restoring Peace at Your Center

Every Christian center needs to follow sound biblical policy in the event of conflict. When disruptions occur, they become manageable through our willingness to *join the Lord's peace.*

For believers, Matthew 18:15–17 is the Bible's prescription for restoration from conflict between believers.

> "Moreover, if your brother sins against you, go and tell him his fault between you and him alone. If he hears you, you have gained your brother." (Matthew 18:15 NKJV)

The burden of resolution is upon the believer who was injured by another person's sin. The person sinned *against* initiates meeting with the other party. Just as Jesus approached us in our sin, we must go "incarnately" to the other person.

If the perpetrator will not hear the grievance, return to her with one or two more persons, "that 'by the mouth of two or three witnesses every word may be established'" (Matthew 18:16 NKJV).

And if there's refusal "to hear them, tell it to the church. But if he refuses even to hear the church, let him be to you like a heathen and a tax collector" (Matthew 18:17 NKJV).

If the perpetrator still refuses to accept responsibility despite additional witnesses, the matter proceeds progressively to higher levels of authority—center director, then the CEO, and ultimately the board.

NOTE: If the perpetrator circumvents the appropriate authority for resolution, it is incumbent upon the person in authority to redirect to the appropriate authority according to the precepts of Matthew 18.

Anyone not seeking resolution and who refuses Mathew 18 as a biblical mandate for resolution exposes a questionable heart attitude. It is a precursor for ramping up the Enemy's warfare through disobedience. Because unresolved conflict causes destruction, escalating tension causes divisiveness, and the Enemy of Our Souls gains a strategic foothold for the center's demise.

Abortion decisions center around wants. But God's desire is caring for needs.

Satan Caters to Our Wants, not Needs

What would drive someone's preference for choosing abortion rather than preserving life? Satan's appeal to the flesh is by answering "wants." Abortion decisions center around *wants.* "I want to finish school on schedule." "I want to be free, not tied to an unwanted child." "I want to build my savings." But God's desire is caring for *needs.* As mortal beings, our most authentic need is personally knowing Jesus, following Him with obedience to align with His purposes.

God's plan for us can be mysterious. Through the chaos of an unplanned pregnancy, the client, floundering for emotional survival, finds herself discovering how ill-equipped she is to handle the situation. Introducing her need for Christ deepens perspectives. Accepting Christ often changes the outcome for a preborn. Many times a former abortion-vulnerable client returns to the center after her baby is born and says, "I can't imagine life without my baby!"

Prayer Relief: Godly Versus Ungodly

Sometimes we ask a client, "Do you know what emotion a woman feels after an abortion?" She learns it is relief—relief that the abortion procedure is over, and she can return to the status quo. At least, *that* is what she believes. We then ask the client, "Do you know what a woman feels after making a decision to *keep* her baby?" And she learns that it is relief. No longer is she burdened by teetering between two choices. And, in her heart, the choice of life settles contentedly.

The woman who chooses an abortion procedure soon discovers her initial relief has a short life. Her misguided decision to end her baby's life pops up repeatedly. One woman confided, "After my abortion, I married and had two children. When someone asked, 'How many children do you have?' I felt uncomfortable answering, 'Two.' Would I always feel haunted by the erasure of my child?" (She later was freed from her guilt by the center's post-abortion Bible study.) Restoration is part of God's plan. Advocates continue offering post-abortion clients the opportunity for healing.

The woman who chooses an abortion procedure soon discovers her initial relief has a short life.

The Battle Between the Flesh and the Spirit

"I Call the Shots"

Bonnie was a thirty-year-old client. A non-believer who took pride in her independence. Past disappointments had been exchanged for a penchant to be in control. "I call the shots in my life!" She, the self-appointed authority over her life, made decisions independently. Her four abortions proved it! With a fifth pregnancy now confirmed, she announced, "I plan to carry this one."

At many centers, a common question on the intake is, "Do you have a faith background?"

Bonnie's response was, "I'm not involved in religion. I make decisions on my own terms."

(The advocate perceived a kairos moment.) "Bonnie, it can be a good thing to reach decisions on your own if you're protecting yourself from poor influences."

Bonnie proudly responded, "I've always been independent-minded."

The advocate said, "It's a good thing to think for yourself. In fact, spiritual decisions are exceptionally personal. It's not legitimate decision-making when someone gets 'roped into the decision.' I, too, had prided myself on making independent decisions."

(Advocate began to share her story.) "In the past, I insisted on calling all the shots in my life. But I admit it didn't always turn out well!"

(Bonnie was *really* listening now.)

"I took my time in coming to terms with God, but I regret that delay. The advocate went on to share details of her testimony with the client, which led to discussion. The conversation culminated in sharing the Gospel tract retrieved from a nearby table.

Pausing after describing the prayer of salvation, the advocate stressed inviting Christ to take control of one's life "is an independent decision. This decision belongs only to you, with no coercion. What are your thoughts about doing this?"

Bonnie's defenses were disarmed. She chose to yield her life to the Savior. With this life-transforming decision, Bonnie's faith was released to grow.

A Couple Enters the Spiritual Battleground

Satan revels in keeping people blinded or indifferent to the life of an unborn baby.

The Enemy would like to foil the spiritual outreach of a pregnancy resource center. Satan revels in keeping people blinded or indifferent to the life of an unborn baby. The male partners of our clients remain the strongest influence between the life and death of the baby. Generally, it is the women in the crosshairs of crisis, but sometimes a male partner is also thrown into crisis over a girlfriend's intention to abort. Such was the case of a young man who fought hard to save his preborn baby's life.

> All who seek you will see God do this for them, and they'll overflow with gladness. Let this revive your hearts, all you lovers of God. (Psalm 69:32 TPT)

"I want to be the kind of father I never had." Rod was adamant about preserving his baby's life. "My father rejected me all my life. He also never married my mother." Now, given the chance, he was determined to fix the past and do better for his child.

When Rod and his girlfriend, April, came to the center together, it signaled a new start for righting the wrongs of his primary family. At the close of the session, he joined April in the counseling room, shared his life of the past, and received Christ as his Lord and Savior. April witnessed the surrender but was not ready to do the same. Despite Rod's new commitment, the life of his unborn baby was endangered.

After leaving the center, April remained undecided about the pregnancy. That week Rod joined her for the ultrasound procedure. The advocate took a few minutes with the couple prior to the ultrasound. She spoke of God's desire to walk through the situation with her. This time, the client listened intently and trusted Christ as her Savior. Her attitude toward keeping her pregnancy improved, but after several weeks, Rod called to say she was again talking about abortion.

Prayers resurged by the staff—intercessions asking God for her change of heart. The center's nurse called the client to offer her a second ultrasound. (Follow-up ultrasounds, though not routine for all clients, can be helpful for an abortion-minded client.)

Life and death decisions are often made during an ultrasound procedure. Today was no different. As April and Rod, the advocate, and nurse gathered into the small room, voices silenced, and the room grew heavy with anticipation. The life of a preborn teetered in delicate balance. Suddenly the screen featured a tiny, animated life—floating, moving, *living*.

As the client's eyes peered at the screen, abrupt words banished indecision. "I will keep my baby for sure!" Like a light flipped on, the room quickened to the triumph of life's victory over death. April would not change her mind again.

Two months after their baby son was born, the young parents dropped by the center to introduce him. God's peace was a triumph. It could be seen in the eyes of a new mother, the gentle cooing of a baby, and the proud posture of a committed father.

In response to prayers, the Spirit of the Lord weaves through the conversation and guides us to the moment of witness.

Progressive Prayer

Through our prayers, we silence the voice of the Enemy insisting, "This person will never be interested in spiritual topics! She's never going to choose keeping her baby."

Advocates find strength by equipping themselves prior to meeting with a client. "Lord, you know everything about this young woman. Please grant me Your words to speak into her heart. Enable her ability to receive truth."

As the session progresses, the advocate's silent prayer petitions Him again. "Lord, direct me to Your kairos moment for sharing You." In response to prayers, the Spirit of the Lord weaves through the conversation and guides us to the moment of witness. It *can* happen. It *does* happen. It *will continue* to happen in every center across our nation and beyond.

A Grandmother's Prayer Team

> We fasten our hopes on him to continue to deliver us from death yet again, as you labor together with us through prayer. Because there are so many interceding for us, our deliverance will cause even more people to give thanks to God. What a gracious gift of mercy surrounds you because of your prayers. (2 Corinthians 1:10–11 TPT)

Although the center staff and volunteers pray consistently for clients, we recognize others who enter the *throne room* with us—warriors all, storming past enemy lines to enter the throne room of King Jesus.

In this case, the client's mother has a prayer team of friends to pray regularly for her endangered grandchild. The grown daughter has already shared her intent to abort the baby, and the heartsick grandmother has invited her prayer warrior friends into the spiritual

Their battle cry was storming the heavenlies to spare the life of a tiny preborn scheduled for destruction the next morning.

battleground. Scripture records an earlier time in history when God found no one to stand in the gap to pray against destruction. "I looked for someone among them who would build up the wall and stand before me in the gap on behalf of the land so I would not have to destroy it, but I found no one" (Ezekiel 22:30 NIV).

The night prior to the scheduled abortion, the prayer warriors gathered for battle. By faith, they willingly stood in the gap as a prayer assault to abortion's looming destruction.

Throughout the night, they fervently prayed. Their battle cry was storming the heavenlies to spare the life of a tiny preborn scheduled for destruction the next morning.

Tanya, the daughter, was a woman in her late twenties. She and her steady boyfriend were both employed, yet she had told her advocate, "Jason and I aren't financially ready to bring a child into the world." As she detailed her defense, the volume grew with her anger, and soon her exasperation seemed to spit from her mouth. "My father was an alcoholic," she cried. "My poor mother was forced to earn the income to feed our large family. Sometimes we had nothing but potatoes to eat. Just to survive!" She wiped away tears before yelling, "I refuse to feed my child potatoes for dinner!" Without question, Tanya was determined to end the pregnancy.

Following up with each client is routine, but the advocate was unable to connect. When the client's due date came and went, the file needed to be closed. One more call, if answered, could take the guesswork out of the outcome. To the advocate's surprise, Tanya answered. Her voice was pleasant, even relaxed, when she said she'd given birth to a baby girl. "Tell me more," said the stunned advocate. "What changed your mind?"

"The night before my abortion, I was so stressed I couldn't sleep. Through the entire night, whenever I began to doze, I'd suddenly awaken thinking about the abortion appointment later that morning. It sickened me to think about it. I tried to shake it off, but the feelings wouldn't go away. Finally, at dawn, I'm still awake and I knew I couldn't go through with it. I called the abortion clinic and canceled. Later my mother told me she and her prayer group had spent the entire night praying!"

By intervention through prayer, the grandmotherly prayer warriors imparted "the riches of the Spirit of wisdom and the Spirit of revelation" to this life-threatening situation (Ephesians 1:17 TPT). As they stormed God's throne room with petitions, God availed Himself. His Spirit moved upon wings of prayer to bring an encounter with truth. For Tanya, God tipped the scales. And for her baby, His destiny was delivered.

Succinctly Spoken

Prayer wires us to God, an incalculable gift from the Father who promises to always hear and always answer. *Neglect not* the prayers that God welcomes.

Jim Cymbala, author of *Fresh Wind, Fresh Fire,* captures the importance of prayer:

> If we call upon the Lord, he has promised in his Word to answer, to bring the unsaved to himself, to pour out his Spirit among us. If we don't call upon the Lord, he has promised nothing—nothing at all! It's as simple as that. No matter what . . . , the future will depend upon our times of prayer.[15]

Neglect not the prayers that God welcomes.

Prayer Encouragement

As believers, we all know we *should* pray. But sometimes prayer is deterred by thinking that good praying is lengthy praying—especially when hearing our "prayer warrior" friend speak of spending endless hours praying. Certainly, we can be thankful for the fervent prayer warrior willing to stand in the gap between heaven and earth. However, we can also be assured that God values shorter prayers as well!

The disciplined morning gathering for prayers at our centers are spiritually positive events. Yet we can still feel good about shorter prayers offered throughout the day. The constant desire to communicate with our Lord must bring Him great pleasure.

A woman in crisis confided feeling so overwhelmed she could only pray three short prayers for months. "Help me, Lord." "Thank you, Lord." "I love you, Lord." We recall Peter walking on rough seawaters, frightened by the menacing size of the waves. "Save me, Lord!" he cried. And with only three words uttered, "Jesus immediately stretched out His hand and lifted him up" (Matthew 14:30–31 TPT).

Peter's three-word *prayer shout* to Jesus, "Save me, Lord," touches our hearts when we think about Jesus waiting for one of our clients to turn to Him in their need. Her fright over an unplanned pregnancy has her world narrowing to crisis mode, with emotions frantically attempting to sort it all out. We've seen desperation in vacuous eyes and trembling young fingers clutch together. A crisis knows how to rough things up. Centuries ago, Peter could have drowned, but his hope turned to Jesus. Today, our client's hope is still Jesus.

A distraught young woman is nervously seated across from her advocate in the small but cozy counseling room. How will she respond to the jarring news of a positive pregnancy test? Perhaps she will open her life to all Jesus offers her. God's gift of redemption readies its offer. And our hope shapes into a prayer of salvation.

Take Heart! Jesus Is Praying!

"So with deep love, I pray for my disciples. I'm not asking on behalf of the unbelieving world, but for those who belong to you, those you have given me. . . . and my glory is revealed through their surrendered lives." (John 17:9–10 TPT)

Prayer is like exercising our spirit.

We are thankful to receive Jesus's prayers filtering through the years to bring His glory to our clients.

Prayers That Avail Much

The effective, fervent prayer of a righteous man avails much. (James 5:16 NKJV)

"It is the Spirit who gives life; the flesh profits nothing. The words that I speak to you are spirit, and they are life." (John 6:63 NKJV)

Prayer is like exercising our spirit. It joins us to God's life, *applies* His life to that for which we're praying. Prayer is God's *system of operation* for bringing His will to earth. Yet why does He tell us to pray for *everything,* even "the certain things," the things that were "going to happen anyway." Author Dutch Sheets puts it this way:

> Didn't He tell us to ask for our daily bread? (See Matt. 6:11.)
>
> And yet He knows our needs before we even ask.
>
> Didn't He tell us to ask that laborers be sent into the harvest? (See Matt. 9:38.) But doesn't the Lord of the harvest want that more than we do?
>
> Didn't Paul say, "Pray for us that the word of the Lord may spread rapidly and be glorified" (2 Thess. 3:1)? Wasn't God already planning to do this?
>
> Are not these things God's will? Why, then, am I supposed to ask Him for something He already wants to do if it's not that my asking somehow releases Him to do it?[16]

God's giving is inseparably connected with our asking.

Andrew Murray succinctly speaks of our need to connect with God. "God's giving is inseparably connected with our asking . . . Only by intercession can that power be brought down from heaven which will enable the Church to conquer the world."[17]

Prayer: Walking in Truth

Lord, thank you that You enable me to walk in discernment and truth that allows recognition between evil things in the guise of good and good things in the guise of evil. When we encounter Enemy strongholds, You, the Stronghold of every believer's life (Psalm 18:2), are greater. You alone can demolish Enemy strongholds; truth cuts "the bait" of the Enemy! Thank You that, as a mentor, I do not have to be intimidated by life's occurrences. You have given the ability to guide others into truth with Your Holy Spirit faithfully leading. In Jesus's name. Amen.

Prayer: For Boldness in Witnessing

Lord, "the righteous are as bold as a lion" (Proverbs 28:1). In You, I have boldness and confidently come into Your presence by faith (Ephesians 3:12). As Your child, I boldly enter holy ground and by the blood of Jesus (Hebrews 10:19) and the word of my testimony (Revelation 12:11), I enact Your power. Thank you, Jesus, for inviting me to approach Your throne of grace boldly, where mercy and grace are found in time of need (Hebrews 4:16). In His name. Amen.

"You are our helper, and we will not fear."

Hebrews 13:6

Prayer: Seeking God's Help

Father, enable me to confidently say, "You are our helper, and we will not fear" (Hebrews 13:6). Thank you for the gifts you have distributed according to Your grace; empower me to operate my life in the fullness of the Spirit. Your Word says the Son can do "nothing by Himself" (John 5:19). How much more do I recognize that without You, I can do nothing. Lord, through You, Your children can bear much fruit—I pray for an abundance of fruit, soul-winning fruit, to shine Your glory! In Jesus's name. Amen.

Prayer: Drinking in the Fullness of His Spirit

Lord, I long to drink deeply from You to feel the streams of pleasure flowing from Your presence. For I know You will break through for me in the mission You have assigned to me. Your faithfulness brings plentiful reasons for praising You all over again! In Jesus's name. Amen. (Based on Psalm 42:1, 11 TPT.)

Prayer: Pouring Out His Spirit

Lord, with the gifts You give to Your own, empower us with Your Spirit, filling us with the desire to abound in every good work! Let us serve one another in love and live worthily of the calling You have given. We ask that grace abound so that in all things, at all times, we will abound in every good work. In Jesus's name. Amen.

Prayer: Restoring One's In-filling of His Spirit

Lord, thank You that You always hear my prayers, that You are "faithful and just and will forgive us our sins and purify us from all unrighteousness" (1 John 1:9 NIV). You are a worthy God, and I love You. I confess my sins of______________ that I have committed against You. Holy Spirit, please help me recall other sins I have committed. (Pause.) Thank You for Your forgiveness and Your redemption in my life. I ask, Lord Jesus, that You fill me again with the fullness of Your Spirit and lead me into Your ways. In Jesus's name. Amen.

Prayer: Co-Laboring with Him

Lord, You have called me to be your co-laborer. According to Luke 8:15, You say, "The seed on good soil stands for those with a noble and good heart, who hear the word, retain it, and by persevering produce a crop" (NIV). God, I join Your purposes. I ask You to use me so that others will come into a knowledge of truth. Thank you, Your life in me brings the bearing of much fruit! In Jesus's name, Amen.

Lord, grant to me a burden for the lost so that many may turn to righteousness.

Prayer: Serving Others with Compassion

Lord, You are holding me snugly with Your love. You alone exchange the natural compunctions of my flesh and exchange them with love and compassion for the lost. Strengthen me for living Your words through the life of Your Spirit. You call me to the continual harvest of souls. It is plentiful, yet there is work to be done! Bring the co-laborers, other advocates who desire to know You and walk in Your will. Fill me with Your Holy Spirit—an abundance of Your ability within me to nurture "fields of souls" awaiting salvation's harvest. I invite You to pour into my life Your passion for the lost. Fill me with supernatural love to reach those in need. In Jesus's name. Amen.

Prayer: Carrying God's Burden for the Lost

Lord, grant to me a burden for the lost so that many may turn to righteousness (Daniel 12:3). Enable me to feel Your compassion for those who don't know You, seeing them as "sheep without a Shepherd" (Matthew 9:36). Anoint me, Lord, to desire proclaiming the "Good News to the poor" (Luke 4:18). "Continually revitalize" me according to Philippians 2:13. Grant to me Your passion for those without a God. May I continue "holding fast to the word of life, so that I may rejoice in the day of Christ that I have not run in vain or labored in vain" (Philippians 2:16 NKJV). I ask You would flourish in my life to bring the fruit of Your ministry. Thank you, Jesus. Amen.

As we pursue peace, help us to stand in one Spirit and with one mind

Prayer: Unity and Peace at the Center

Father, I pray that there would be no divisions among us, and You will be joined together in the minds of Your followers (1 Corinthians 1:10). As we pursue peace, help us to stand in one Spirit and with one mind, striving together for the living faith of the Gospel. Help us to be motivated to follow Your ways of resolution day by day as we seek to serve You. Father, enable us to act as true followers who have Your heart of compassion, loving one another and finding common ground to unify us in Your will. Thank you, Lord. Amen.

Prayer: Breaking Down Fleshly Strongholds

Lord, though we walk in the flesh, we do not war according to the flesh. "For the weapons of our warfare are not carnal but mighty in God for pulling down strongholds, casting down arguments and every high thing that exalts itself against the knowledge of God, bringing every thought into captivity to the obedience of Christ (2 Corinthians 10:4–6 NKJV). In Jesus's name. Amen.

Prayer: Uplifting Gratitude to God

Thank You, Father, for inspiring an outpouring of gratitude. I praise You for knowing my need for Your presence every moment of my life. Thank You for the gift of salvation. Thank You for not giving up on me until You won my attention. Regarding clients, Father, thank You for giving them Your God-inspired conscience to feel remorseful over sin, leading to repentance and victory through You (2 Corinthians 7:10). Thank You that I can continue to depend upon You to awaken the holy longing in our clients and a passion for You. Lord, I continue to thank You, for this is Your ministry, the result of Your amazing gift of Jesus (2 Corinthians 9:15). King Jesus reigns as the King of kings in our hearts and in our centers! Thank You for the triumph of the Gospel as we share the Good News of Your kingdom. In Jesus's name. Amen.

Epilogue

Appointed for His Glory has been written in the context of the pregnancy resource center, yet there's wide application in other venues of Christian ministry. Its preparation for Gospel sharing may be approached in various ways to include a retreat format or a ten-week program of study—group or one-on-one.

Just as lacking the special gift of mercy doesn't mean believers forego merciful responses to others, lacking the special gift of evangelism doesn't mean believers forego sharing their faith and the Gospel message with others.

The content of this handbook is designed to equip Christian advocates to overcome the fear of witnessing and competently present the Gospel to the unbeliever or backslidden believer. Those willing to step out in faith and go deeper with God have experienced powerful outcomes for the kingdom. Every advocate would do well to have a God-expectation for each client walking through the doorway. *Lord, what are you about to do here?* Those responding to God's call to share their faith find excitement and deep contentment as they interface with the heart of God. As we live in harmony with God's Spirit, we're consumed by wanting His best for others as we give voice to the Good News that no one "should perish" (2 Peter 3:9 ESV).

Afterword

Is the Gospel a Spiritual Antidote Against Burnout?

A volunteer advocate expressed, "I've heard a lot about high burnout rates of those who work at pregnancy centers. Personally, if I could not share *real* hope with clients, I know I wouldn't last long either."

As advocates who hear daily crisis stories, we are not deterred. Despite advocates' exceptional ability to empathize, rather than fueling burnout, we ignite the power of the Gospel to stir in our hearts and summon the unbeliever from darkness. To bring forth the new life of the Gospel is to experience God's glory filling the room.

On a continuing basis, staff, volunteers, board members, and donors happily grasp depth of spiritual purpose God ordains for every center. His Spirit fills us with the joy of living the adventure of a Savior's love. *I wonder what God is up to* with regard to a client appointment. Scripture says, "Everyone will say, 'Come and see the incredible things God has done; it will take your breath away! He multiplies miracles for his people!'" (Psalm 66:5 TPT).

Just as God loves and serves our clients, He loves and serves us. A staff advocate said, "To share Christ with persons in crisis is a great honor and absolutely puts a spring in my step every week." The Good News of His redemption need not fall to idle lips but those giving voice to His promises.

> The LORD your God is in your midst, A Warrior who saves. He will rejoice over you with joy; He will be quiet in His love [making no mention of your past sins], He will rejoice over you with shouts of joy." (Zephaniah 3:17 AMP)

Acknowledgments

I am so grateful to the many individuals I've enjoyed a professional and personal relationship with who encouraged and inspired the writing of *Appointed for His Glory.*

Kelley Wesley, the former CEO of Sanctity of Life Ministries, is currently a ministry advisor. Ever since Kelley hired me at SLM, we've enjoyed a depth of friendship woven with the desire to share Jesus with clients. Kelley's passion for Christ resounded in her leadership as she promoted a strong prayer foundation at the center and fostered equipping staff and volunteers to share their faith. We strongly featured evangelism at our centers because we knew it would impact both the mother and her baby's life. Kelley has an unceasing desire to see others come to a saving relationship with Jesus Christ and live transformed lives by the power of the Gospel.

The Sanctity of Life Ministries (SLM) Board and Margery Williams, the CEO of Sanctity of Life Ministries after Kelley's departure, are appreciated for permitting selective evangelism material, developed at the center, to be used for this advocate training handbook.

Stacey Boyd, a volunteer advocate, was the first to prompt writing *Appointed for His Glory.* She said, "Every appointment with a new client, I think of the stories shared about lives being changed. Why don't you write a book?" Stacey was recalling the impact of client salvation stories shared during training. She became faithful to share the Gospel with clients, which led many to salvation.

Mary Sawyer, former Sanctity of Life Ministries advocate, ardently believes Jesus is exactly who the clients need in their lives. Though her faith background was not evangelistic, she reached a pivotal point of choosing to go deeper in her personal relationship with Jesus. Mary's letter of encouragement to advocate trainees is included in the handbook.

Michelle Russell, a volunteer advocate before joining SLM's staff, initially had qualms about sharing the Gospel. She didn't want to be viewed as pushy. Being open-minded, she took to heart the input of a gifted trainer, Gail Johnsen, who convinced her that inroads to the Gospel can be made in a conversational manner—without being aggressive. Michelle said, "I finally realized that just as I had badly needed Christ in my life, my clients *also* needed Christ." She faithfully began sharing her testimony, and many of her clients made the life-changing decision to follow Christ in a deeper, more personal way.

Gail Johnsen, former SLM advocate trainer, a spirit-filled, exceptional teacher who encourages advocate trainees to depend upon God's leading in the counseling room. She knows firsthand that sharing one's testimony breaks down barriers for the Gospel message. She proceeds in a nonintrusive, caring, but purposeful manner. Gail has inspired many lives of advocates and clients alike by her joy in sharing and the joy of seeing lives changed for the kingdom.

Mai Bean, former SLM statistician, a godly woman who assisted me with statistic-related material.

Kip Gardner, my dear husband, has been exceptionally helpful—providing office space to write with no distractions. He's also my go-to "800 number" for computer anomalies. I am so thankful for his technical expertise and encouragement he brought while writing *Appointed for His Glory.*

I am thankful for all others who had a part in praying: Alice Moore, Liz Sanders, Stephanie Fisher, Jill Harper, Hope Cinquegrano, Cati Robinson, Monica and Domenic Sanza, Lynne Farrell, Denise Napoli, Lanie James, Niki Mattson, Valarie and Jim Elwell, Janet Totsch, Janey Clark, Margan and Joe Meadows, Kelley and Paul Wesley, and additional prayer warriors like my husband, Kip, his prayer group and many others who believed in this project to enhance spiritual impact at our centers. Lanie James, Director of Client Services at Mosaic-Virginia, used excerpts of the material for training Mosaic's advocates while the book was still in manuscript form! To all of you and others unnamed, thank you for united hearts to spread the Gospel!

APPENDICES

Appendix A: Q and A – Sharing Your Faith at the Center

1. Question by center staff members: Isn't it "mission drift" to include sharing the Gospel with clients? Our pregnancy resource center is medically equipped for ultrasounds. Our focus is on saving babies' lives and saving clients from the regret of an abortion, a focus that honors God.

Answer: Yes, saving babies' lives and keeping clients from the regret of an abortion is honoring to God. When the good news of the Gospel is shared with an expectant mother who is contemplating abortion, you are speaking *more fully to sanctification of human life*—something that centers desire to preserve and defend. Rather than being mission drift, the Gospel can strengthen our mission of life, the potential resurrected life for the expectant mother and the sustained life of her child.

The medical function is highly useful for reinforcing the message of choosing life for the baby. Though this function often changes an abortion-minded client's decision, it should not replace the fuller scope of a new foundation for our client's life through Christ. By hearing and responding to the Gospel, there is greater assurance that a risky lifestyle will transform into one of healthier choices because of a personal relationship with the Lord.

2. Question by a prospective advocate in training: Many of the women who arrive at the center are already traumatized. I don't want to add pressure or make her feel more stress by cornering her with another monumental decision like following Christ.

Answer: This answer begins with three questions to the Christian, pro-life person.

- First, have you personally asked Jesus Christ to enter your life as your Lord and Savior? After (presumably) hearing a yes, then the next question follows:
- After you received Christ into your life, would you say that you have experienced certain benefits from the decision? (Such as experiencing more peace, comfort, security as well as the assurance of eternal life, etc.)
- Why would we, as believers, want to refrain from sharing all that Christ brings to our personal lives that could also benefit our client's life?

Some have implied that sharing the Gospel puts added pressure on a client. On the contrary, as opposed to legalism's "measuring up" beliefs, Christianity addresses a heart for the Gospel through a relationship with a loving God who extends grace—not *earning* His acceptance. If someone decides to receive Christ based on pressure, not a heart to do so, then it's not a true commitment. No bludgeoning with the Gospel! If someone is patently not interested in hearing the good news of the Gospel, the matter is dropped. Willingness to share our faith is to accommodate a client's interest in the spiritual aspect of life.

3. Question: Do I need to have the "gift of evangelism" to share the Gospel with clients?

Answer: No. Paul tells the entire Colossian church *with their varying spiritual gifts*, to "Walk in the wisdom of God as you live before the unbelievers and make it your duty to make him known" (Colossians 4:5 TPT).

Scripture makes it clear that the special gift of evangelism is not needed to share one's faith. Paul doesn't tell Timothy to *be* an evangelist (identify with the gift); he tells Timothy to "do the work of an evangelist" (2 Timothy 4:5 NKJV).

4. Question: What if I don't know how to respond with spiritual adequacy when answering a client's questions?

Answer: We're reminded of this Scripture: "Do not worry about how or what you should speak. For it will be given you in that hour what you should speak; for it is not you who speak, but the Spirit of your Father who speaks in you" (Matthew 10:19–20).

As an honest response, you can say, "That's a good question. Let me do a little research on that to give you the best answer I can, then get back with you." Your client will respect the humility of transparency that fosters credibility. It will also provide you with another opportunity for contact.

Refocus the conversation on your personal testimony. "Knowledge is a good thing, but the reason I personally believe isn't due to academic knowledge of the Bible. It's because I've had personal experiences of God like . . ."

5. Question: When a client has heard you present the Gospel and accepts Christ into her life, isn't it counter-productive just to "release" them back into our sinful world? Our pregnancy centers don't ordinarily disciple clients!

Answer: Acts 8:26–40 speaks of a divine appointment arranged by God—just as we consider clients our divine appointments. Philip has encountered someone who could be called a seeker of truth. In this case, the seeker is a eunuch who is reading the Scriptures but is unable to comprehend. (The "veil" still covers his mind.) Phillip begins to speak to him—more than that, he gets into the chariot, and the spiritual discussion continues as they travel. After the eunuch hears the Gospel message, he becomes a believer. Soon they come upon an area with water, and at the request of the new convert, Philip baptizes him.

Notice this is a *one-time encounter* sovereignly led by God. Rather than viewing the Ethiopian being "released into the world" as something negative, why not trust God with His new child? Before a new believer leaves the center, she receives resources for church contacts, discipleship groups, etc. Centers must cover every new believer in prayer and entrust her to God's keeping.

NOTE: Our appointments at the center are considered divine. Although a client may return for an additional spiritually oriented session, centers do not continue to disciple clients as part of our center's program. (Though we would avail the client a spiritual track for our Earn While You Learn program. We could use a basic new believer Bible study and/or videos for the purpose of discipling the new believer.) We also have follow-up material for the client—list of churches, Bible studies, etc. She could also be personally invited to church by her advocate or matched with another staff member who could meet the client at her church. Some church home groups have shared with us their willingness to have one of our clients join their home group. We have drawn up a procedure for this. Online resources for growing in her faith are also helpful.

---

6. Question: How can I share the Gospel with a client who barely speaks English?

Answer: Cell phones now have translation features. In addition, we have spiritual tracts for English language learners in multiple languages that align verbatim with English versions. For tracts in a language we don't have, tracts can be found online in many different languages. (See Resources.) PRC's can contract with interpreter service organizations to provide interpretation over the phone in various languages. There is also the ongoing option for the client to bring a friend or relative who can translate.

7. Question: What if my client says, "I don't believe in God."

Answer: There can be a myriad of different responses to this statement. For instance, (1) a conversation can begin by saying, "That's interesting. If you don't believe in God, then how do you make wise decisions—what do you use for your moral compass? She may say, "Myself!" And the response could be, "Does that always work well for you?"

(2) Another response to an atheist client is to ask, "Would you like to be *able* to believe?" If she says no, ask her how she finds encouragement when things aren't going well for her. If she responds, "I have good friends" or "I find it peaceful to spend time in nature," you could respond, "I understand why that would be peaceful. Nature is actually a gift that God has given us. However, for me. . ." (Share testimony.)

If your client replies yes to having a desire to believe, say, "I recall a time in my own life when I was searching for something more." Lead into your testimony—share your personal experience of God. You can also share Jeremiah 29:13: "And you will seek Me and find Me, when you search for Me with all your heart" (NKJV). You could add, "This Scripture reveals that God is very much aware of you and that He is a God who wants to be found by you."

- Ask if she would be willing to pray the agnostic's prayer: "God, if you really do exist, I give you permission to reveal yourself to me." Ask the client if you can pray for her before she leaves the session. Even non-believers love to receive prayer!

Appendix B: Resources

Ordering (Paper) Spiritual Tracts

Would You Like to Know God Personally?
Crustore.org
(Available in different languages by the Cru and The Bright Media Foundation.)

Have You Heard of the Four Spiritual Laws?
Crustore.org
(Available in different languages by the Cru and The Bright Media Foundation.)

Have You Made the Wonderful Discovery of the Spirit-Filled Life?
This is excellent follow-up material for the new believer and addresses the *how* to live the Christian life!
Crustore.org

Bridge to Life
navlink.org/bridge
or
www.navigators.org/resource/the-bridge-to-life

In Search of the Greatest Treasure
Crustore.org
Children welcome this cartoon version of *The Four Spiritual Laws* tract, which we freely give to a client's child or children with the parent's permission.

I Am a Catholic
1-800-662-0909
This booklet assures the Catholic believer that the way to salvation is explained, by specific verses, in their Bible as well.

Convenient Apps

GodTools

GodToolsApp.com

A review of the app: "This app is so amazing It is better organized than most so people can enjoy it while I share the good news with them. I just thank the developer so much for creating this app, and I'm so ready to share the Gospel with others now! Thank you!"

Varied Evangelism Materials

Tips for Talking with Atheists and Agnostics

www.rose-publishing.com

Christianity, Cults & Religions

www.rose-publishing.com

(Helpful, quick guide for key beliefs of comparative religions)

How to Share the Gospel

Dare2Share.org

(A crash course, four-minute video.)

Evangelism Online Resources

God's Simple Plan of Salvation

GodsSimplePlan.org

An Online Resource for sharing the Gospel in another language. (The mentor can use her own native language and give the client the printout in the language in which she is proficient.)

(Look under Tracts and Languages in Print.)

Preborn Evangelism Tool (Free training for pregnancy centers)

Evangelism Tool: The Bridge to Life

(The Navigators official Bridge illustration for Gospel sharing)

navlink.org/bridge

(Click on PDF to print)

For Multi-Cultural Clients

Dare 2 Share
Dare2Share.org
Learn backgrounds of different religions and the questions that serve as good entries for witnessing.

Ministering to Muslims
www.ministeringtomuslims.com

4 Spiritual Laws
www.4laws.com
(4 Spiritual Laws bilingual in over fifty languages)

God's Simple Plan
GodsSimplePlan.org
(God's simple plan in other languages)

Arabic Bible Outreach Ministry
www.ArabicBible.com/printed-materials.html
(Free Arabic Christian materials)

Google Translate
translate.google.com
(An online resource that gives immediate translation to English words keyed in)
This can be helpful for the office administrator answering calls from a client who doesn't speak English. Often used responses to her can be researched ahead such as: "Bring an English-speaking friend to your appointment." Days of the week or appointment times could also be looked up in order to make the appointment.

A Father's Love Letter
www.FathersLoveLetter.com
(A new believer take-home letter online, available in many languages.)
This letter can be printed in full color and makes an affirming gift for the new believer. Based entirely on Scripture, it is like a personal love letter from God to the believer. This, along with a Bible, will send the new believer on her way with encouragement.

Growth for the New Believer Free Online Resources

GotQuestions.org

JesusWalk.com

Crosswalk.com

WhatChristiansWanttoKnow.com

GospelHerald.com

DavidServant.com

GoingBeyond.com

NOTE: Regarding paper spiritual tracts versus online, we have found the small, hand-held tracts are effective when the advocate speaks personally with the client. When the client receives Christ into her life, the date of her salvation (her "spiritual birthday" in Christ) is written on the back of the tract. Online resources can also be given after a decision for Christ to provide positive reinforcement.

NOTE: Regarding Bibles, donor churches are a faithful resource to the center, often willing to provide a Bible for every newly believing client. (Tell donors providing Bibles that the print should be an easily readable size.) Depending on a center's clientele, some non-English Bibles can be kept on hand as well. (Some centers, for instance, with large Hispanic populations of clientele, keep Spanish Bibles in stock.) For other populations where English is their secondary language, a few Bibles could be kept in stock of assorted languages—either New Testaments for them in their native tongue or a full Bible, Old and New Testament.

Appendix C: Forms and Handouts

Guest Speaker's Form for Staff and Volunteer In-service

(Can be filled out by staff based on a phone conversation with the speaker. A request for outline of talk can be optional or required.)

Name of guest's ministry or employment/background:

Mission:

Guidelines for guest speaker (regarding topic, etc.):

Name of prospective in-service presenter:

Topic and date under consideration:

Presenter's background in context with the topic:

Relevance/applicability to mission: (How do you foresee this topic enhancing our client sessions to better fulfill our mission of pointing a young woman to the choice of life for her baby and/or reinforcing her spiritually in her situation?):

Length of time preferred for presentation:

How much time would you like to allot for Q and A interaction?

When could an online or hard copy of your talk be available?

Any additional comments?

Trainee's Evangelism Questionnaire

(To be filled out by trainee prior to advocate training.)

Name: ______________________________ Date____________

Email:__________________________

Cell Number__________________ Home Number_________________

Advocate Training Date: ___________________________

1. Explain how you personally view evangelism.

2. Would you be willing to share your testimony and the Gospel with our clients if you were trained to do so?

3. Have you ever led someone to Christ or led someone up to the decision of salvation, of accepting or rejecting the opportunity? (Please describe.)

4. How would you describe the Gospel to someone?

5. How would you describe how the Gospel has impacted your life?

6. How would you describe the difference between sharing the Gospel and having a spiritual discussion?

Now What?

The following are tried and true suggestions for the client who has just prayed the prayer of salvation.

- Write the date of her "spiritual birthday" on the spiritual tract she'll be taking home with her. Tell her this is your special birthday, that is, when you were born spiritually.
- Discuss the remainder of the salvation tract (after the prayer section) with your client. She is now in the family of God. She is no longer a child of wrath because God's anger (wrath) over sin has been satisfied by receiving Jesus's gift of giving His life for her sins.
- Suggest to the client that she re-read *Would You Like to Know God Personally?* tract and write her questions and comments. (Offer the opportunity to make an appointment to come in or call for a phone appointment to discuss questions.) Also suggest that she read through the material you've given her, especially the pamphlet *Have you Made the Wonderful Discovery of the Spirit-filled Life?*
- Discuss that her sins have been forgiven. (Ask, "Do you believe that all of your sins—past, present, and future—have been forgiven?") Show her the Bible verse from 1 John 2:12. "I am writing to you, dear children, because your sins have been forgiven on account of his name" (NIV). Explain to her that the verb tense of "have been forgiven" indicates that something happened at a point in time, and the results are ongoing.
- Discuss by asking her: "Why wouldn't we just go ahead and sin now that our sins are forgiven? There's an answer to that! It's because we now have new hearts to serve Him, and sinning sets up an uncomfortable inner conflict. We are new creations in Christ!"
- Discuss with her that God hears the prayers of His children. Encourage the client to pray every day. Ask her, "Do you have any special requests I can be praying for you?"
- Make sure she is given a Bible to reenforce her new commitment to Christ. If your center doesn't normally stock Bibles as a gift, speak with the director of the center about arranging a church donation of Bibles.
- Suggest she begin to read the Bible, such as the Gospel of John or the Gospel of Luke. Sometimes, a daily chapter from the book of Proverbs is a fun place to start. Thirty-one chapters correlate (mostly) with the days of the month. As she begins, suggest she ask the Lord, "What is it you want me to know today from your Word?" (Suggest that she asterisk and date the verse in the margin.)
- Give your client a new believer packet, which includes handouts and/or booklets such as, *Finding a Good Church, Have You Made the Wonderful Discovery of the Spirit Filled Life?, What on Earth am I Here For?,* a list of churches in the area, a printout of *Who I Am in Christ,* and a copy of the *Holy Bible.*
- Feel free to personally invite your client to attend your church. Offer to meet her at the entrance. (Adhere to your center's policy for transporting a client after hours.)
- Encourage your client to tell someone about her new commitment to Christ; it will reinforce her faith commitment.

- Query her interest in the parenting course for those "intending to carry" clients. Some centers offer the program called Earn While You Learn. However, a spiritual track for enrollees can be developed. Consider putting together a spiritual track if your center has none. For instance, videos could present pertinent sermons; the *Case for Christ* film would reinforce her faith, Priscilla Shirer's teaching films, pastor/teacher Gary Hamrick of Cornerstone Church has archived teaching lessons, etc.
- Distribute spiritual resources—can include Bible-believing churches nearest to her home. Some centers arrange contacts designated to meet spiritually interested clients at the church. (Be sure your center has a prepared client form to procure the signature of the client to grant assent for contact.)

Suggested Spiritual Questions on Center's Intake Form

Do you have a faith or religious background?

If so, have you found a place of worship?

At end of intake form:

Was the Gospel presented to client? _________

Outcome? Dedication/Rededication

Spiritual discussion with client? _________

Comments?

Continuing Education In-service: Client Appointment Practice

Welcome and prayer.

Introductions of attendees.

Plan for either a new or seasoned advocate to share an inspirational client story.

Divide class into pairs for the exercise and distribute a handout of fifteen client statements taken from *Appointed for His Glory*, pages 183–196.

Option One: Have each person of the pair select one client statement from the list for the practice intake form exchange. Taking alternate turns, one of the pair will choose one of the fifteen client statements to verbally insert during the practice. The person who is acting as "the advocate" will respond with follow-up questions to draw out "the client." They are instructed to also look for opportunities to offer an excerpt from their personal testimony.

Option Two: Begin this option with a review of how to present the two charts before the exercise begins. Since many clients believe they *earn* their "good, religious standing" with God or *earn* salvation based on their good works ("I should get back to church"), this presentation to a "client" explains the beauty of a relationship with Christ. It entails jotting down two brief charts to simplify the contrast between living from grace versus living from legalism. The presentation clarifies truth and disrupts distorted beliefs about faith. See pages 185–188 in *Appointed for His* Glory for background information and a discussion of the two charts: *Do, Value, Be* versus *Be, Value, Do*.

Client statement #3, on page 185 of the training handbook, initiates the advocate/client discussion: "With two abortions, I deserve hell." The advocate responds to the client: "Going to heaven is related to our relationship with Christ, not our burden of sin. As a gift to us, Christ died on the Cross to pay the penalty for our sins, then rose from the dead to give us the life of His resurrected Spirit. May I show you how God enables us to experience more freedom in our lives?" (The advocate, using the training guidelines to progressively fill in the chart, explains to the client how God's grace, when hearts are surrendered to Christ, frees us from living by a legalistic approach to faith.)

After the class has ample time to practice, lead them in class discussion to include Q and A following the exercise.

End in prayer.

Advocate In-service on Testimony Practice

Freestyle Practice for the Counseling Trainee

Welcome and prayer.

Introduce the in-service by telling a client story involving testimony sharing and salvation.

Select sections from chapter 4 regarding the personal testimony and discuss.

....

Instructions: "We will be working in twos for this portion of our training. The practice partners will alternate turns, covering each client statement on the handout. Keep in mind that if your client is single and coming to the center for a pregnancy test, this indicates she is off-track spiritually and may be open to dedicating or rededicating her life to Christ.

"If your client claims to be a Christian, ask appropriate questions to confirm she is a bona fide believer. Perhaps you would query how her beliefs, after her commitment to Christ, affected her life, perspectives, peace of mind, etc. *How was she different?* For those clients who rededicate, this is not a salvation issue but the need to restore her walk with God.

"During client sessions, the *topic testimony*, instead of the advocate's *salvation testimony*, can be powerful also. ('When I was going through a challenge in my life, God came through for me in a special way,' etc.)"

....

After the class has divided into sets of "partners," begin by each trainee partner sharing a three-minute personal testimony with the other. This will enable a better exchange of ideas during the simulated client session.

Tell the in-service attendees, "With your prepared testimony finalized, you will now be practicing how to insert your personal story into different client scenarios. Each attendee will have a copy of the intake form, (completion of the intake form during this practice is not necessary since the focus is on responding to client statements.)

Statement Handout for Practice and Discussion

1. Client: "I want to know God better but don't know how!"

2. Client: "This baby isn't planned, and everything is happening so fast."

3. Client: "With two abortions, I deserve hell."

4. Client: "I'm a Christian but haven't lived like it; the worst part is I might be pregnant!"

5. Client: "I know I've messed up! I feel so far from God and need to get back to church!"

6. Client: "I used to attend church growing up but don't go anymore."

7. Client: "I would never get an abortion!"

8. Client: "I'm a Buddhist. We believe in karma." (Their goal: Remove karmic debt.)

9. Client: "I am a Buddhist." (Client response to "We're a Christian ministry.")

10. Client: "I believe that there are many ways to reach God."

11. Client: "But I *do* believe Jesus lived and died on a cross."

12. Client: "I am a Muslim. We believe a lot like you do."

13. Client: (Was asked, "Who is Jesus?") Reply: "Jesus is the Son of God, but He is not God."

14. Client: "We all pray to the same God."

15. Client: "I believe that Jesus was a good man—I believe He was a great prophet."

16. Client: "There are many contradictions in the Bible."

17. Client: "For me, it seems like a perversion of justice that God had Jesus die."

18. Client: "Christians believe in more than one God, right?"

The in-service can close with discussion about the roleplays and questions that have come up. End with prayer.

Appendix D: Ten-Week Evangelism Workshop for Advocate Trainees

Appointed for His Glory: Study Questions for Personal or Group Study

A suggestion for a group study would be to assign one chapter (or more) weekly and discuss the questions corresponding to the designated chapter. The chapters can also be a one-on-one study with a seasoned advocate, though it's advantageous to hear input from others who are learning more about sharing their faith. It is recommended that the answers to chapter questions be written in a separate notebook.

CHAPTER ONE

1. Define *kairos.* Describe its significance in the context of Gospel sharing.
2. If you have served as (or observed) a client advocate during a client session, describe the event of a kairos moment that led to sharing one's faith with a client.
3. Look up the following Scriptures. Which one strengthens you personally to bypass fear you may have of sharing the Gospel?

   2 Timothy 1:7

   Joshua 1:9

   Psalm 34:4

   2 Corinthians 2:17
4. This chapter cites numerous real-life client scenarios. Describe one that is personally meaningful and carries a helpful message for your ability to serve clients well.
5. What is the relevance of Dr. Pasteur's story to prompt an *intentional* spiritual discourse with your client?

CHAPTER TWO

1. Why do you think that an *intentional* evangelistic approach removes the element of chance from Gospel sharing? How do you think the *spoken* Gospel exceeds the outcome of the *unspoken* Gospel?
2. According to former Harvard President Derek Bok, what was the number one struggle of the university's students?

3. Salvation records, kept at respective pregnancy centers, serve what helpful purpose(s) for staff, board, volunteers, and donors?
4. Describe how a belief system regarding evangelism directly affects its outworking.
5. Many clients believe their pregnancy is the problem, but it's their perspective *about* the pregnancy that is causing the problem. In your own life, share how your perspective enlarged when God used a problem to create something positive.

CHAPTER THREE

1. Regarding the temple of Solomon, describe the historical background of the veil.
2. According to 2 Corinthians 3:14–16 (NKJV), how could you participate in the removal of the veil over the mind of an unbeliever?
3. Define the significance of Jesus uttering the word *tetelestai* on the Cross. How might it relate to a client burdened by a guilt-ridden past?
4. If you have discerned that your unmarried, pregnant client is authentically a believer, yet has scheduled a pregnancy test, what could be said to get her back on track with the Lord? (How would you adapt your testimony to her situation?)
5. Was there a client story presented in the book that has encouraged you to share your faith?

CHAPTER FOUR

1. What are some of the benefits of testimony-sharing for both speaker and listener?
2. Describe the difference between *power* and *authority.* How do these two concepts encourage the sharing of one's faith?
3. Satan's interference with salvation has been and is being overcome: "And they overcame him by the blood of the Lamb and by the word of their testimony, and they did not love their lives to the death" (Revelation 12:11 NKJV). The testimony has been granted high significance—elevated alongside of "the blood of the Lamb." Why do you think the believer's testimony is given such relevance?
4. Which case of client advocate hindrance do you most relate to?
5. Clients often have forgiveness issues because of abandonment by the baby's father. What personal story could you share about forgiveness, and how could you transition to the Gospel message of forgiveness?

CHAPTER FIVE

1. What is a *salvation* testimony, and how does it differ from the *topic* testimony?
2. What are the three major categories in a salvation testimony? (Note: Even when a person is reared in a Christian home, a decision to follow Christ must personally be made.)

3. How would you describe the apostle Paul's progression to salvation based on the three major categories cited in the previous question?

4. Regarding the three categories, describe your own progression to a personal commitment to Christ. (If timelines are blurred, then describe in more general terms your journey as a follower of Christ.)

5. Explain what the word *transformation* means in its biblical context.

CHAPTER SIX

1. Biblically, how does one become *transformed?*

2. How did the building of the tabernacle reflect that whomever God calls, He equips.

3. The common thinking distortions mentioned can hinder spiritual outreach. Do you see any that may be true of you?

4. What do you think is meant by the statement, "The biblical mandate of the gift of evangelism is functional?"

5. How is the Gospel God's method of spiritual growth?

CHAPTER SEVEN

1. Are you willing to believe that God has brought your client to the center and that, with His help, He will guide an entry to the Gospel?

2. In the interchange between Jesus and the Samaritan woman, what stands out for you?

3. Cite an example (or examples) from the dialogue between Jesus and the woman at the well that exemplifies Jesus's transition to a spiritual topic.

4. For the client unwilling to make a commitment to Christ, the opportunity for a middle step may be agreeable to her. The agnostic's prayer is a personal invitation to God to reveal Himself to her. How would you pose the question to take this middle step with your client?

5. As a blueprint to Gospel sharing, how specifically did this chapter speak to you?

CHAPTER EIGHT

1. This practicum chapter indicates that the willingness to share our faith with a client recognizes two things. Name them.

2. Select one of the five client cases that are cited. How would you have answered the client in the situation you selected?

3. What is the value of asking good questions?

4. Using the *Do, Value, Be* chart, how would you describe the legalistic, worldly approach to finding identity through *doing*?

5. Using the *Do, Value, Be* chart, how would you describe the legalistic approach to faith? Note to facilitator: Have the class practice sharing the charts with a client.

CHAPTER NINE

1. Write down your center's procedure for client intake that includes synchronization of medical with non-medical components.

2. Recalling the story of the seasoned advocate's reliance on the Holy Spirit, what is a takeaway for you personally?

3. How could Gospel sharing be a possible antidote for the prevention of burnout?

CHAPTER TEN

1. Scripture says that there is only ONE mediator between God and man. What is the significance of the believer's calling to pray?

2. What is Dr. Henry Cloud's rationale that advocates combining truth *with* grace when mentoring others?

3. Which part of Lottie's story did you most connect with?

4. Explain what is meant by "the Christian life is impossible to live."

5. Why do you think that the pregnancy center is a battlefield? Can you cite an example you have heard about or seen?

Endnotes

Preface

1. W.E. Vine, Merrill F. Unger, William White, eds., *Vine's Complete Expository Dictionary of Old and New Testament Words* (Nashville: Thomas Nelson Publishers, 1985), *tharreo*, 72.

In the Beginning

1. Elizabeth Edson Evans, *The Abuse of Maternity* (Philadelphia: J. B. Lippincott & Co., 1875), chapter titled "I Have Lost a Child," as quoted on Feminists for Life website, accessed June 18, 2020, https://feministsforlife.org/elizabeth-edson-evans-first-wave/.

2. "On Writing Commentaries: Interview with Dr. Rod Mattoon," Logos *Word by Word* blog, August 7, 2018, accessed October 1, 2025, https://www.logos.com/grow/writing-commentaries-interview-dr-rod-mattoon/.

3. Joseph Henry Thayer, *Thayer's Greek-English Lexicon of the New Testament,* s.v. "koilia," as found in *Old & New Testament Greek Lexical Dictionary*, StudyLight.org, accessed June 18, 2020, https://www.studylight.org/lexicons/eng/greek/2836.html.

Chapter One: Seizing the *Kairos* Moment

1. *Merriam-Webster.com Dictionary,* s.v. "karios," accessed December 16, 2025, https://www.merriam-webster.com/dictionary/kairos.

2. "What is the meaning of the Greek word *kairos*?," Got Questions, accessed October 1, 2025, https://www.gotquestions.org/kairos-meaning.html.

3. Fritz Rienecker and Cleon L. Rogers (ed.), *Linguistic Key to the Greek New Testament* (Grand Rapids, MI: Zondervan Publishers, 1980), 583–584.

4. C.S. Lewis, *Mere Christianity* (United Kingdom: HarperCollins, 2001), 52.

5. Bill Bright, *Would You Like to Know God Personally?* (pamphlet) (Peachtree, GA: New Life Publication, 1968), 2–13.

6. Bright, *Would You Like to Know.*

7. Bright, *Would You Like to Know.*

8. Bright, *Would You Like to Know.*

9. Howard Markel, "Louis Pasteur's Risky Move to Save a Boy from Almost Certain Death," PBS News Hour, July 7, 2016, https://www.pbs.org/newshour/health/louis-pasteurs-risky-move-to-save-a-boy-from-almost-certain-death.

10. Chris Jackson, "Joseph Meister Lived," July 23, 2020, https://chrisjacksononline.net/joseph-meister-lived/.

Chapter Two: Intentional Gospel Sharing

1. Bill Bright, *Have You Heard of the Four Spiritual Laws?* (pamphlet) (Orlando: New Life Publications, 1965).

2. Richard E. Simmons, "Living with Emptiness," follow-up article to "Answering Life's Greatest Questions," Richard E. Simmons III (website), January 25, 2018, https://richardesimmons3.com/living-with-emptiness/.

3. Johanna Younghans, "College Stress," Harvard Medical School (website), September 10, 2018, https://hms.harvard.edu/news/college-stress.

4. "College Enrollment Rates," Condition of Education, National Center for Education Statistics, U.S. Department of Education, Institute of Education Sciences, May 2024, accessed October 1, 2025, https://www.nces.ed.gov/programs/coe/indicator/cpb.

5. Vine, Unger, and White, *Vine's Complete Expository, pisteuo,* 61.

6. Merriam-webster.com/dictionary, s.v. "inference," accessed October 1, 2025,

https://www.merriam-webster.com/dictionary/inference.

7. Neel Burton, MA, MD, "Man's Search for Meaning," *Psychology Today*, June 23, 2024, https://www.psychologytoday.com/us/blog/hide-and-seek/201205/mans-search-for-meaning.

8. Paraphrased from Viktor Frankl in *Man's Search for Meaning* (New York: Washington Square Press, 1984), 162.

9. "Storytelling Statistics and Trends," Go-Globe (blog), December 17, 2024, accessed October 1, 2025, www.go-globe.com/storytelling-statistics.

10. "G1577 - ekklēsia – Strong's Greek Lexicon (KJV)," Blue Letter Bible, accessed November 13, 2025, https://www.blueletterbible.org/lexicon/g1577/kjv/tr/0-1/.

Chapter Three: Lifting the Veil of Unbelief

1. Marcus Jastrow and Bernard Drackman, "Betrothal in Talmudic Hebrew," Jewish Encyclopedia (website), accessed October 1, 2025, http://www.jewishencyclopedia.com/articles/3229-betrothal.

2. Vine, Unger, and White, *Vine's Complete Expository, apokalupsis* (*unveiling*), 654.

3. J. Vernon McGee, "Chapter VIII: The Veil Which Was Rent: The Doctrine of the Incarnation," Blue Letter Bible, last modified December 7, 2017, accessed October 20, 2025, https://www.blueletterbible.org/Comm/mcgee_j_vernon/eBooks/tabernacle/chapter-viii-the-veil-which-was-rent.cfm.

4. Vine, Unger, and White, *Vine's Complete Expository*, *katallasso,* 514.

5. Vine, Unger, and White, *Vine's Complete Expository*, *tetelestai,* 259.

6. "Tetelestai – It Is Finished! Paid In Full!," Preceptaustin (website), April 5, 2013, https://preceptaustin.wordpress.com/2013/04/05/tetelestai-it-is-finished-paid-in-full/.

7 . "Perfect Tense: A Closer Look," Ezra Project, accessed August 25, 2025, https://ezraproject.com/perfect-tense-a-closer-look.

8. Ergun Mehmet Caner and Emir Fethi Caner, *Unveiling Islam: An Insider's Look at Muslim Life and Beliefs*, Grand Rapids, Michigan: Zondervan Publishers, 2002), 205.

9. "Glory of the New Covenant, 2 Corinthians, chapter 3," Scripture Insight, https://scriptureinsight.org/study/2corinthians/3.

10. *New Spirit-Filled Life Bible,* NKJV, "Word Wealth," see footnote Matthew 4:4, (Nashville: Thomas Nelson Publishers, 2002), 1294.

11. *New Spirit-filled Bible,* 1294.

Chapter Four: The Testimony

1. Joe Lazauskas and Shane Snow, "The Strange Thing That Happens in Your Brain When You Hear a Good Story—And How to Use It to Your Advantage," Hubspot, July 12, 2019, https://blog.hubspot.com/marketing/the-strange-thing-that-happens-in-you-brain-when-you-hear-a-good-story-and-how-to-use-it-to-your-advantage; excerpted from a book by the authors, *The Storytelling Edge: How to Transform Your Business, Stop Screaming into the Void and make People Love You* (Hoboken, NJ: Wiley, 2018).

2. Adrienne Santos-Longhurst, "Why Is Oxytocin Known as the 'Love Hormone'? And 11 Other FAQS," July 12, 2023, healthline.com/health/love-hormone.

3. Elena Renken, "How Stories Connect and Persuade Us: Unleashing the Brain Power of Narrative," NPR, *Shots*: Health News, April 11, 2020, https://www.npr.org/sections/health-shots/2020/04/11/815573198/how-stories-connect-and-persuade-us-unleashing-the-brain-power-of-narrative.

4. Terry Eckersley, "The Difference between Power and Authority," April 29, 2014, https://terryeckersley2014.wordpress.com/2014/04/29/the-difference-between-power-and-authority-there-is-a-difference-you-know-a-very-important-difference-too-i-might-add-there-are-people-well-meaning-sincere-christian-people-who-fail-to-see/.

5. Eckersley, "Power and Authority."

6. Elena Renken, "How Stories Connect and Persuade Us."

7. "Who Is the Dalai Lama?," Got Questions, accessed October 1, 2025, https://www.gotquestions.org/Dalai-Lama.html .

8. Francis Anfuso, *I'm a Catholic* (pamphlet) (United States: Christian Equippers International, 1984).

9. St. Augustine, "Our Hearts Are Restless," From Augustine's *Confessions* (1.1–5), accessed October 1, 2025, https://www.ligonier.org/learn/articles/our-hearts-are-restless.

10. Bill Bright, *Witnessing Without Fear* (San Bernadino, CA: Here's Life Publishers, 1987), 69.

11. Tim Challis, "Counterfeit Detection (Part 1)," June 27, 2006, https://www.challies.com/articles/counterfeit-detection-part-1/.

12. Grace Ministries, "True Life Advanced Training," handout materials (Manassas, VA, 1990).

13. Ellen Mady, "How the Roman Practice of Adoption Sheds Light on What St. Paul was Talking About," Aleteia (website), September 12, 2017, https://aleteia.org/2017/09/12/how-the-roman-practice-of-adoption-sheds-light-on-what-st-paul-was-talking-about/.

14. Priscilla Shirer, "Stage fright," Going Beyond Ministries, *Jewelry Box* (blog), June 1, 2014, https://www.goingbeyond.com/jewelry-box/stage-fright/.

Chapter Five: Preparing Your Three-Minute Testimony

1. J.D. Greear, "5 Crucial Truths for Following God in 'Kairos' Moments," J.D. Greear Ministries (website), October 23, 2012, https://jdgreear.com/5-crucial-truths-for-following-god-in-kairos-moments/.

2. Cru staff, "Preparing Your Personal Testimony," Cru (website), accessed October 2, 2025, https://www.cru.org/us/en/train-and-grow/share-the-gospel/evangelism-principles/preparing-your-personal-testimony.html.

3. *New Spirit-Filled Life Bible,* NKJV, "Word Wealth" footnote on Philippians 3:5 (Nashville: Thomas Nelson Publishers, 2002), 1663.

4. *New Spirit-Filled Life Bible,* footnote on Philippians 3:6, 1663.

5. "What Is the Way in the Bible?," Got Questions, accessed October 6, 2025, https://www.gotquestions.org/the-Way.html.

6. Gary Manning Jr., "Paul's Name Change," Biola University (website), *The Good Book Blog* (Talbot School of Theology Faculty blog), February 6, 2019, https://www.biola.edu/blogs/good-book-blog/2019/paul-s-name-change.

7. John Piper, "Grace Is Pardon—and Power!," Desiring God, accessed October 2, 2025, https://www.desiringgod.org/articles/grace-is-pardon-and-power.

Chapter Six: Gospel Conversations

1. Abby Johnson, *Unplanned: The Dramatic True Story of a Former Planned Parenthood Leader's Eye-Opening Journey Across the Life Line* (Carol Stream, IL: Tyndale House Publishers, 2014).

2. Rienecker and Rogers (ed.), *Linguistic Key to the Greek New Testament,* 375.

3. *The Passion Translation,* footnote on Matthew 17:2.

4. As quoted in "Encountering God," *Divinely Interrupted* (blog), October 14, 2022, https://www.divinelyinterrupted.com/blog/encountering-god.

5. Bill Bright, "Have You Made the Wonderful Discovery of the Spirit-Filled Life?," accessed October 2, 2025, https://www.cru.org/us/en/train-and-grow/spiritual-growth/the-spirit-filled-life.html.

6. James Strong, *Strongs Exhaustive Concordance: Greek Dictionary of the New Testament* (Iowa Falls: World Bible Publishers, 1986), #1754, *energeo,* 36.

7. "Age Range by Generation," Beresford Research, accessed August 26, 2025, https://beresfordresearch.com/age-range-by-generation.

8. Susanna Y. Park, Jacqlyn Yourell, Kelsey L. McAlister, and Jennifer Huberty, "Exploring Generation Z and Young Millennials' Perspectives of a Spiritual Self-Care App and Their Spiritual Identity (Skylight): Qualitative Semistructured Interview Study," *JMIR formative research* vol. 7 e54284, December 28, 2023, doi:10.2196/54284, https://pmc.ncbi.nlm.nih.gov/articles/PMC10784987/.

9. Kyle Richter and Patrick Miller, "5 Reasons Gen Z Is Primed for Spiritual Renewal," October 9, 2023, https://www.thegospelcoalition.org/article/gen-z-primed-spiritual-renewal/.

10. Park, Yourell, McAlister, and Huberty, "Exploring Gen Z."

11. Richter and Miller, "Five Reasons Gen Z."

12. Chris Hewitt, "Storytelling top tips: Use storytelling and you'll be 22 times more memorable," Berkeley Communications (website), March 29, 2022, https://www.berkeleypr.com/storytelling-top-tips-use.

13. "Matthew 4:19 'Follow me, and I will make you fishers of men,'" Christ's Words (website), accessed July 11, 2025, https://christswords.com/content/mat-419-follow-me-and-i-will-make-you-fishers-men.

14. "Matthew 4:19 'Follow me,'" Christ's Words.

15. "Matthew 4:19 'Follow me'" Christ's Words.

16. "Matthew 4:19 'Follow me'" Christ's Words.

17. Oswald Chambers, *Baffled to Fight Better: Job and the Problem of Suffering* (Oswald Chambers Publications Association, 1917), 52, accessed October 2, 2025, https://www.scribd.com/document/857038524/Baffled-to-Fight-Better.

18. *The Passion Translation*, footnote on Romans 8:9.

19. *The Passion Translation*, footnote on Romans 8:9.

20. Gary Thomas, *Holy Available* (Grand Rapids, Michigan: Zondervan Publishers, 2009), 17.

Chapter Seven: Compassion in Action: How-Tos of Gospel Sharing

1. "History of the Hope Diamond," Smithsonian, accessed October 2, 2025, https://www.si.edu/spotlight/hope-diamond/history.

2. "Hope Diamond Wrapper," Smithsonian, accessed October 2, 2025, https://www.si.edu/object/hope-diamond-wrapper:npm_1992.2002.15.

3. William Fay, *Sharing Jesus Without Fear* (Nashville: B & H Publishing Group, 1999), 12.

4. *The Word in Life Study Bible, NKJV* (Nashville: Thomas Nelson Publishers, 1982), in a sidebar commentary, 1868.

5. J. Vernon McGee, *Thru the Bible with J. Vernon McGee*, Volume IV (Nashville: Thomas Nelson Publishers, 1982), 388.

6. *The Passion Translation,* footnote on Acts 20:32.

7. Juliana Menasce Horowitz, Nikki Graff, and Gretchen Livingston, "Marriage and Cohabitation in the U.S," (page 1), Pew Research, accessed October 2, 2025, https://www.pewresearch.org/social-trends/2019/11/06/marriage-and-cohabitation-in-the-u-s/4.

8. Horowitz, Graff, and Livingston, "Marriage and Cohabitation," (page 3), https://www.pewresearch.org/social-trends/2019/11/06/public-views-of-marriage-and-cohabitation/.

9. Horowitz, Graff, and Livingston, "Marriage and Cohabitation," (page 4), https://www.pewresearch.org/social-trends/2019/11/06/why-people-get-married-or-move-in-with-a-partner/.

10. Jeff Diamant, "Half of U.S. Christians say casual sex between consenting adults is sometimes or always acceptable," Pew Research, August 31, 2020, https://www.pewresearch.org/short-reads/2020/08/31/half-of-u-s-christians-say-casual-sex-between-consenting-adults-is-sometimes-or-always-acceptable/.

11. "Sexual Integrity" Women of Faith (website), accessed September 12, 2025, https://www.womenoffaith.com/sexual-integrity.

12. Bill Bright, *Would You Like to Know God Personally?*, (pamphlet) (Peachtree, GA: New Life Publications, 1968), 3–13 (used with permission).

13. Bright, *Would You Like to Know*, 4.

14. Bright, *Would You Like to Know*, 6.

15. Bright, *Would You Like to Know*, 8.

16. Bright, *Would You Like to Know*, 13.

17. Bright, *Would You Like to Know*, 3.

18. Bright, *Would You Like to Know*, 4.

19. Bright, *Would You Like to Know*, 5.

20. Bright, *Would You Like to Know*, 6.

21. Bright, *Would You Like to Know*, 8.

22. Bright, *Would You Like to Know*, 9.

23. Bright, *Would You Like to Know*, 9.

24. Bright, *Would You Like to Know*, 10.

25. Bright, *Would You Like to Know*, 10.

26. Bright, *Would You Like to Know*, 10.

27. Bright, *Would You Like to Know*, 12.

28. "Secular, Atheist, and Agnostic," *Merriam-Webster Dictionary* (blog), accessed September 11, 2025, https://www.merriam-webster.com/grammar/what-do-secular-atheist-agnostic-mean.

29. "The Bridge to Life," Navigators Discipleship Tool, accessed September 12, 2025, https://www.navigators.org/resource/the-bridge-to-life/, or www.navigators.org/wp-content/uploads/2021/02/navigators-bridge-to-life.pdf.

30. William Fay with Linda Evans Shepherd, *Share Jesus Without Fear* (Nashville: Broadman & Holman Publishers, 1999), 42.

31. Fay and Shepherd, *Share Jesus Without Fear*, 50.

32. Fay and Shepherd, *Share Jesus Without Fear*, 45–49.

33. Dan Phillips, "Spurgeon Discussed: Expect Conversions?," April 11, 2013, *Pyr Maniacs* (blog), http://teampyro.blogspot.com/2013/04/spurgeon-discussed-expect-conversions.html.

Chapter Eight: Practicum: Client and Advocate Conversations

1. *Merriam-Webster's Collegiate Dictionary*, s.v. "practicum," accessed October 3, 2025, https://unabridged.merriam-webster.com/collegiate/practicum.

2. "What Is the Meaning of 'Legalism'?," *Oxford Dictionary* via Bab.la (website), accessed October 3, 2025, https://en.bab.la/dictionary/english/legalism.

3. Elaine Clanton Harpine, "Is Intrinsic Motivation Better than Extrinsic Motivation," (from the abstract) in: Group-Centered Prevention in Mental Health, Springer, Cham, January 1, 2015, https://doi.org/10.1007/978-3-319-19102-7_6.

4. Alison Wood Brooks and Leslie K. John, "The Surprising Power of Questions," *Harvard Business Review* (May–June 2018), 4, on Center for Evidence-Based Management (website), accessed October 3, 2025, https://cebma.org/assets/Uploads/hbr-the-surprising-power-of-questions.pdf.

5. Brooks and John, "The Surprising Power," 6.

6. Brooks and John, "The Surprising Power," 8.

7. C.S. Lewis, *Mere Christianity* (New York: HarperCollins, 2001), 76.

8. John Piper, "What Is Legalism?," *Ask Pastor John* (podcast) audio transcript, August 23, 2013, https://www.desiringgod.org/interview/what-is-legalism.

9. Grace Ministries, "True Life Advanced Training," handout materials, Manassas, VA, 1990.

10. Grace Ministries, "True Life Advanced Training."

11. Watchman Nee, *Sit, Walk, Stand* (Illinois: Tyndale House Publishers, 1977) 14.

12. Tom Nash, "We Receive the Holy Spirit at Baptism," Catholic Answers (website), accessed September 20, 2025, https://www.catholic.com/qa/we-receive-the-holy-spirit-at-baptism.

13. A.W. Tozer, *The Pursuit of God* (United States: Christian Publications, 1982), 9.

14. Cindel J.M. White and Ara Norenzayan, "Chapter One - Belief in karma: How cultural evolution, cognition, and motivations shape belief in supernatural justice," *Advances in Experimental Social Psychology*, Academic Press, 60 (2019): 1–63 (from the abstract), https://doi.org/10.1016/bs.aesp.2019.03.00.

15. Geshe Dakpa Topgyal, "Karma and Purification," South Carolina Dharma Group, accessed September 23, 2025, https://www.scdharma.org/teachings/karma-and-purification.

16. Dictionary.com, s.v. "karma," accessed October 3, 2025, https://www.dictionary.com/browse/karma.

17. The Dalai Lama, *The Good Heart: A Buddhist Perspective on the Teachings of Jesus* (Somerville, MA: Wisdom Publications, 1996), as cited in Terry C. Muck, "Jesus Through Buddhist Eyes," *Christianity Today*, Books & Culture, March/April 1999, accessed October 3, 2025, https://www.booksandculture.com/articles/1999/marapr/9b2046.html.

18. Aaron M. Little, "Kamal Saleem: A Muslim Cries Out to Jesus," Christian Broadcasting Network, accessed October 3, 2025, http://www1.cbn.com/700club/kamal-saleem-muslim-cries-out-jesus.

19. James Rochford, "Was Jesus Crucified on the Third Hour or the Sixth Hour?," Evidence Unseen (website), accessed 09-16-2025, https://evidenceunseen.com/new-testament/john/difficulties/was-jesus-crucified-on-the-third-hour-or-the-sixth-hour.

20. J. Jeffrey Smead, "Trinity/1 1 1=1," Semon Central, June 27, 2022, sermoncentral.com/sermons/trinity-1-1-1-1-j-jeffrey-smead-sermon-on.

Chapter Nine: Overview: How It All Works

1. Annie Jeschke (formerly with Sanctity of Life Ministries), "Girl at the Front Desk."

2. Vine, Unger, and White, *Vine's Complete Expository*, *charis*, 277.

Chapter Ten: Prayer: Seeking Truth, Receiving Guidance

1. The personalized, intercessory scripture is based on Job 42:8–9 (NIV): "My servant Job will pray for you, and I will accept his prayer and not deal with you according to your folly. . . . and the Lord accepted Job's prayer."

2. Dutch Sheets, *Intercessory Prayer: How God Can Use Your Prayers to Move Heaven and Earth* (Ventura, CA: Regal Books, 1996), 41.

3. Sheets, *Intercessory Prayer*, 41–42.

4. Henry Cloud, *When Your World Makes No Sense* (Nashville: Thomas Nelson Inc., 1990), 29, 31.

5. Cloud, *When Your World*, 37.

6. "Changes that Heal: Growth Takes Grace and Truth," Cloud-Townsend Resources, July 28, 1992, accessed October 3, 2025, https://www.cloudtownsend.com/growth-takes-grace-and-truth/.

7. Corrie Ten Boom, *Tramp for the Lord* (Fort Washington, PA: CLC Publications, 1974) 63.

8. Shuvi Jha, "The Purpose of the Bindi," Hindu American Foundation, June 5, 2018, https://www.hinduamerican.org/blog/the-purpose-of-the-bindi/.

9. Vine, Unger, and White, *Vine's Complete Expository, shennumi, 502.*

10. Bill Bright, "The Adventure of Evangelism," Cru, accessed October 3, 2025, https://www.cru.org/us/en/train-and-grow/transferable-concepts/be-a-fruitful-witness.

11. Charles Spurgeon, "Weeping and Reaping," Bible Hub, accessed September 18 2025, https://mail.biblehub.com/sermons/auth/spurgeon/weeping_and_reaping.htm.

12. *New Spirit-Filled Life Bible*, NKJV, "Word Wealth" footnote on 2 Corinthians 5:14 (Nashville: Thomas Nelson Publishers, 2002), 1616.

13. John MacArthur, *The MacArthur Bible Commentary* (Nashville: Thomas Nelson, Inc., 2005), 273.

14. J. Vernon McGee, *Thru the Bible, 1 Corinthians – Revelation*, Vol. V (Nashville: Thomas Nelson Publishing, 1983), 229.

15. Jim Cymbala, *Fresh Wind, Fresh Fire* (Grand Rapids, MI: Zondervan, 2018), 27.

16. Dutch Sheets, *Intercessory Prayer Study Guide: How God Can Use Your Prayers to Move Heaven and Earth* (Ventura, CA: Gospel Light Publications), 29.

17. Andrew Murray, *The Ministry of Intercessory Prayer* (Minneapolis: Bethany House Publishers, 1981), 22–23.

About the Author

Kay R. Gardner views the timeless light of the Gospel as central to a ministry's mission. When Kay received Jesus Christ in her thirties, this led to her desire for others to know the transformative love of a Savior. Through years of ministry work and decades as a pregnancy resource center director, Kay loves training others to witness new life in Christ that leads to sustaining life in the womb. Over the years, she has developed numerous training materials and shared evangelism teachings through workshops sponsored by Care Net and Heartbeat International. Particularly special was the honor of speaking at pro-life conferences held in Romania, China, and Russia. Kay also ministered at their post-abortion healing conferences—a great faith booster to watch God at work to set people free from their burden of sin!

Appointed for His Glory is a handbook that will readily equip more ministries with fresh approaches to sharing one's faith. Kay has also authored a devotional packed with real-life scenarios and ladled with hope for the unequally yoked wife: *Even So, She Smiles at the Future.*

Kay lives in Northern Virginia with her husband, Kip. They have four grown children and eleven grandchildren.

Learn more at **KayRGardner.com**.

www.ingramcontent.com/pod-product-compliance
Lightning Source LLC
LaVergne TN
LVHW081401110826
845149LV00010B/1633
* 9 7 9 8 9 9 0 7 0 6 0 2 6 *